Brand New Me

CHARLOTTE CROSBY

HEADLINE

First published in 2017
by HEADLINE PUBLISHING GROUP

First published in paperback in 2018
by HEADLINE PUBLISHING GROUP

1

Cataloguing in Publication Data is available from the British Library

PB ISBN 978 1 4722 4329 4

Illustrations © Maxwell Dorsey

Typeset in Berling by Palimpsest Book Production Limited, Falkirk, Stirlingshire

All photographs courtesy of the author except:
Page 1: top © Beretta/Sims/REX/Shutterstock; bottom © Ken McKay/ITV/REX/ Shutterstock / Page 3: top © Neil Mockford/GC Images/Getty Images; bottom © Anthony Harvey/Getty Images / Page 4: top and bottom © Mercury Press & Media Ltd / Page 6: © WENN Ltd/Alamy / Page 7: top and bottom © REX/Shutterstock / Page 8: © Xposurephotos.com / Page 11: bottom © Eamonn M. McCormack/Getty Images / Page 16: top © Graham Stone/REX/Shutterstock; bottom © David Fisher/REX/Shutterstock

The information contained in this book is not intended to replace the services of trained medical professionals or to be a substitute for medical advice. You are advised to consult a doctor on any matters relating to your health, and in particular on any matters that may require diagnosis or medical attention.

Printed and bound in the UK by Clays Ltd, St Ives plc

Headline's policy is to use papers that are natural, renewable and recyclable products and made from wood grown in sustainable forests. The logging and manufacturing processes are expected to conform to the environmental regulations of the country of origin.

Papers used b   rces..

Contents

For Baby and Rhu,
for drying a thousand tears.

Introduction: It's Me Again

Hello, you! Well, it's been a while since we last hung out (or about a year if you were one of the lovely people who bought the paperback version of my last book, *Me Me Me*) so we have loads to catch up on! I can't wait to tell you everything that's been happening. I would like to start by saying that this year has made me stonger than ever. I'm stonger than yesterday, stonger than before, stonger than I've ever been. You see, 'stonger' is a new variation on the word 'stronger' and it means 'extra-powerful and able to cope with situations'. Situations like when you get sent the cover design for your new book (aka this one) and tweet it out to all your fans telling them to pre-order it on Amazon and they quickly point out that there's a spelling mistake on the front of it!

To say this past year has been quite the emotional roller coaster would be an understatement.

There have been some seriously bad times – the worst was suffering a life-threatening ectopic pregnancy. The doctor told me I could have died, which I still can't get my head around, and I was scared that I might not be able to have kids. And my relationship with Gary was once again played out very publicly and this time the split was worse than it's ever been.

But this year has also brought me some of the most amazing times, and some genuinely incredible moments. My clothing range In The Style won an actual fashion award, I launched my own make-up range called Fliqué and promoted a new dating app called ShowReal. I got a new gig presenting *Just Tattoo of Us*, I went to a fancy party on a yacht in Cannes, I became mates with Jamie Oliver and finally I found a new man who I can totally be myself with. He makes me laugh so hard and is even madder than me!

But enough of the rollercoaster, I don't want to end up sounding like a contestant on *The X Factor* – just without the violins and dramatic close-ups of Nicole Sherzinger. Welcome to the next chapter in my life.

This is my diary of the last fourteen months. There have been tears, heartache, anxiety attacks and facial rashes. But please don't start thinking it's all going to be doom and gloom. There's been plenty of stupid behaviour, saucy bits and funny moments too – like me mam waking up at 7 a.m. on Christmas morning to find me passed out naked by my new swimming pool and a random couple shagging on the table in my home office, the time I nearly lost my toe in a freak accident and a secret sexual liaison with a reality star from another television show in the south of France . . . Je m'appelle suck my bell!

Calendar of Contents

J IS FOR JANUARY 2016 AND ALSO FOR 'JUMPING'— something I couldn't do much of this month because I had a nose job and doctors told me my nose would probably fall off if I did anything too extreme. (Well, that's what I took from their warning to 'take it easy' anyway.) It also meant I had to go a bit easy on the booze . . . not something you can really do when you're in the *Geordie Shore* house! J also stands for 'Jitters' which is what I got in my belly whenever I thought about Gary. Things were going really well with us at the start of 2016. We were getting very close and I genuinely thought this was it. That we would finally, after five years, become boyfriend and girlfriend. And maybe even get married. How wrong I was . . .

F IS FOR FEBRUARY AND 'FIT BOYS AT FESTIVALS' – I spent most of this month in Australia and went to five festivals in a row. The Good Life festivals are unreeeeal (be sure to go if you're ever down under) and that's where I first met a DJ called Will Sparks – we locked eyes and had what I like to call 'a connection'. I love doing festivals because it makes me feel like I'm a singer and in an actual band with some

3

kind of talent when really I'm just standing there getting photos with people.

M IS FOR MARCH, 'ME MAM' AND 'MENOPAUSE' – Letitia became my official employee this month. She has lots of jobs that fall under the employee bracket: she looks after the dogs, she drives me around, she cleans the house, she washes my hair in the bath (I'm proud to say I haven't grown out of this habit since my last book). If I was to advertise her position it would be that of 'Charlotte's carer'. I gave her the job working for me after she got made redundant from her last job, which was as a support worker for young mams (not to be confused with young lambs even though it sounds the same in my accent). M also stands for 'Menopause', which is something me mam is going through at the moment and uses as an excuse for literally everything. She just constantly says, 'I can't do that, remember I'm going through the menopause!' She has even tweeted about the hot and cold sweats she's got because of it. Mind you, that's not as bad as the time she tweeted about being so happy with her new table she wanted to make love to it! I just ignore her tweets now. They're too much.

A IS FOR APRIL AND 'AWFUL' – this was definitely the worst month of my year, probably my entire life so far, because April was when I nearly died from an ectopic pregnancy.

M IS FOR MAY AND 'MAKING MY MIND UP' – about what to do with my future and with Gary and basically everything.

J IS FOR JUNE AND ALSO FOR 'JOURNEY' – which, although once again makes me sound like I'm auditioning for Simon high-waisted-jeans Cowell, is something I definitely started in this month. A new journey in my life because I quit *Geordie Shore* and everything changed for me. But I know it was all for the positive and the better.

J IS FOR JULY AND 'JACKPOT!' – I started enjoying myself again and met a gorgeous new man. So I felt like I'd really hit the jackpot of life again.

A IS FOR AUGUST AND A MAN CALLED 'ASH' – this is the month I realised I was properly falling for Ash Harrison . . . at the same time as I was filming a show called *Celebs Go Dating* on E4. Oh dear.

S IS FOR SEPTEMBER AND ALSO FOR 'SUN, SEA, SAND AND SNEAKY PAPS' – I had my first holiday with Ash in Ibiza which was nearly ruined by someone taking our picture on the balcony. (While Ash was showing off his washboard abs, I looked like I'd just climbed out of a washing machine.)

O IS FOR OCTOBER AND 'HUNGOVER' which I was after Halloween when I went out dressed as a schoolgirl (Ash was a sexy pirate). O is also for 'Ostrich' because I was burying my head in the sand and pretending things were good with Ash when really they were starting to fall apart because we didn't really have anything in common. I just liked the fact he had long hair.

N IS FOR NOVEMBER AND THAT STANDS FOR 'NOT WORKING WITH ASH' – and NOOOOOO! What am I doing?!

D IS FOR DECEMBER AND 'DAMN' – I've finished with Ash and I've fallen for Stephen Bear.

J IS FOR JANUARY AGAIN (BUT THIS TIME IT'S 2017) AND 'JUMPERS' – me and Stephen were caught wearing the same jumper, aka we had been spending virtually every night together since filming *Just Tattoo Of Us*, aka we were inseparable, aka it didn't take a detective to work out our tongues had touched a bit more than once.

F IS FOR FEBRUARY AND 'FUN TIMES' – at the Brit awards and 'Full on' with Bear. F is also for 'Fuck!!' because this is when *Celebs Go Dating* came back on air and this time Stephen was in it. . .

M IS FOR MARCH AND 'MOVING ON TO EXCITING NEW THINGS' –
- A romantic holiday with my new man.
- A new show on MTV called *Just Tattoo of Us*.
- A new make-up range that's going to give Kylie Jenner's a run for its money (well, it's got a ten-piece highlighter palette for starters).
- A new set of bedding that's like a nappy and doesn't get you wet when you wee on it but doesn't crunch when you sleep on it like the ones you give to toddlers. If no one has invented a luxury version of this then I need to do it. I'll call them Charlotte's Secret Sheets and the

advert can whisper, 'Ssssh, no one needs to know your shame with this sensuous, smooth bedding. You can wee to your nunny's content and *he* will wake none the wiser and you will both be warm and dry and smelling of roses instead of urine.' (This whole last point was a joke by the way. Before you start trying to pre-order them on Amazon.)

Charlotte's Guide To Who's Who And What's What

LETITIA CROSBY

Me mam. She's funnier than me, which is annoying, but I love her and she makes a really nice chilli. I like it when she smiles because she lights up the room. Her heart is so big and kind I like to think it's made of candyfloss.

GARY CROSBY

Me dad. The great leader and finance handler (the intelligent one). I love him. He really is the best dad in the world. He is the foundation and backbone of the family. Without my dad we'd be nothing.

NATHANIEL CROSBY

Me brother. Little child with glasses. Funny, clever, my best friend. I like it when he insults our mam. I love him. If anyone was to hurt him I'm scared of what I might do.

BABY

The first born, my little puppy. The loyalist little girl I've ever seen. My dog twin! We both have blonde hair.

RHUBARB

The other dog. She's a fat little pudding. She's a bit thick BUT extremely cute. She looks a bit like a cat and has a snaggle tooth, but we can't all be perfect.

ANNA ROBINSON

My brilliant friend from home. We have the best laughs. My road-trip buddy (we always find ourselves travelling the country together).

MELISSA WHARTON

My oldest and longest best friend. With twenty-four years of friendship we are more like sisters. Friendships like these are very, very rare! I feel very lucky to have her in my life. Even though we argue like CAT AND DOG.

KATE O'SHEA

My second mam! And my agent. Without Kate I'd be lost. She's been my agent from the very beginning, so we have both been on this crazy journey together! Kate knows absolutely everything about me . . . Kate is the ORGANISER – she organises my life.

ANNA PARKIN

The *Geordie Shore* BOSS. The bearer of bad news! The strawberry-blonde MILF!

GARY BEADLE

My nemesis. The other half of my *Geordie Shore* journey. The name I will for ever be haunted by.

SOPHIE KASAEI
The first friend I made in *Geordie Shore*. We have shared memories that will last a lifetime! I truly love her with all my heart.

MARNIE SIMPSON
My little *Geordie Shore* sister. This girl has a diamond beautiful soul. We are soooo alike it's scary. We both have gluten allergies and get 'the bloat' and we have exactly the same dress sense so are always giving each other clothes advice.

SCOTTY T
My *Geordie Shore* big brother! It's rare these days to be able to have such a good friendship with a boy. I do love him.

HOLLY HAGAN
My *Geordie Shore* sister and best friend. Boy, we have been on a roller coaster! We've been there for each other through thick and thin. She's been my shoulder to cry on for years. My rock.

CHLOE FERRY
My other little *Geordie Shore* sister. Crazy little radgie pancake. I love her so much. Me and this girl have laughed so much together. She is the one to put a smile on my face no matter what!!!!!! She makes me laugh sooooo hard.

MARTY MCKENNA
Fellow *Geordie Shore*-r who always makes me laugh but who got me into serious trouble with Gary after a really stupid decision to snog him. This also upset Chloe who *really* liked

him at the time and I would never want to upset her in my entire life.

LOIS HARDING

A mate I acquired through Sophie and she's really good fun. She helped me get myself back on my feet romance-wise after Gary.

LAURA GIBSON

My oldest friend. One of my original group of mates I've grown up with. She's amazing. Her dog and my dog Baby are boyfriend and girlfriend. She's also a great cook and I could eat her meals all day and all night.

AARON CHALMERS

My *Geordie Shore* brother. I'm closest to him out of any of the *Geordie Shore* boys and tell him everything. He's a very good listener and has awesome tattoos.

ADAM FRISBY

My best, best friend and business partner. I met Adam through joining forces and taking over the fashion world with In The Style (it's true, we have an award). It's very rare you meet someone through work and create such a strong bond. We are the type of friends who just take the piss out of each other every single day and laugh so hard at it. Me and Adam are always the last people standing at the party.

JAMIE CORBETT

The other half of Adam! I met Jamie through In The Style as well. I can always trust Jamie to be BRUTALLY honest with me. He will tell me if I look like a dog bitch! He's the most caring person I have ever met. Whenever I am poorly he's my nurse and I love him.

DAVID SOUTER

My trainer, but now one of my very dearest of friends. He's the bald one who does the bit for pussies in my DVD. It's so strange how much I care about David. I feel like he became like a family member over the three years we worked together, we WhatsApp nearly every day! He's a bit like a crazy uncle.

RICHARD CALLENDER

My other personal trainer. He's the one who does all the hard bits with me in the DVD. I always get scared to go to a training session with Richard because he makes me feel like I'm dying, in a good way.

MITCH JENKINS

My ex-boyfriend . . . the serious one. The only serious thing I've had in my life since the crazy journey began.

WILL SPARKS

The Australian DJ I had a massive crush on for a month or two!

JOEY ESSEX

My good thick friend! Hahaha, me and Joey are like two peas in a pod! When we are together we have such a laugh!

CRAIG ORR

Commissioner at MTV. Me and Craig have been on a bit of a journey and I absolutely love him to bits, even when I'm ringing at 3 a.m. from McDonalds to give him abuse that I don't remember the next morning!

JAMIE LAING

That posh one off *Made In Chelsea*. We formed a friendship that I think will be everlasting now. Together we are crazy! We like to laugh, be loud and cause mayhem together. I can always rely on Jamie for a favour.

ASH HARRISON

An ex (sort of). We weren't together long enough to be able to really call it an official relationship but he was lovely and handsome and had beautiful hair. I think that's why I was so obsessed with him.

STEPHEN BEAR

That arsehole off the telly . . . Or in my world the funniest, most gorgeous, sexiest, kindest person I have ever met. My new best friend and NOW BOYFRIEND. He's the one – I can feel it. I think we're gonna get married.

January 2016

Side-profile selfies I've taken of my new nose: Approximately 500

Emojis to show how I'm feeling about Gary right now: 🖤🖤🖤🖤🖤🖤

Saturday 2nd

It's so nice knowing that Mam and Dad have finally forgiven Gary after everything that went on between us. He stayed over again tonight. Mam has started to like him and has forgiven him for his past with me, but she's not as close as she can be with my boyfriends. She's usually best friends with them to the point that she starts texting them separately to me and arranging nights out (which is actually a bit weird). But I think she's still a bit cautious with Gary. Either that or she doesn't fancy going out with him.

Even though me and Gary have known each other for five years, I don't feel like we've ever spent this sort of 'normal time' together before. Everything we've ever done has been on *Geordie Shore* and in front of the cameras so it's really nice gradually letting things happen between us without it being turned into the 'Gary and Charlotte Show'.

Sunday 3rd

Gary's agreed to go on *Ex on the Beach* in April. I believe he won't get with anyone – for the first time ever I really do – but I still wish he wasn't going on it.

Monday 4th

Started doing press for the new DVD today. Have about a million days of it. Because it's called *Charlotte's 3 Minute Bum Blitz* I'll basically be talking to everyone I see about my arse! I might as well just walk around with no pants on so they can just see it for themselves. It's definitely got a lot perter since all the exercise though and it was a pancake before I started so at least I can say the DVD works! Maybe Kim Kardashian will get jealous because I'm trying to steal her bum crown. Ha! Imagine literally having to wear a crown on your bum! What would you call it? A Bown? A Crum?

Was a guest on *This Morning*, I love Holly and Phil so much. They're always so nice and the studio has just been redone and looks amazing. I feel like I want to stay there, eat my lunch and watch telly with them whenever I'm on the show. It's not like you're on telly, more like a really well-lit lounge with a few people with headphones on.

@charlottegshore
Great time on This Morning, thanks for having me @Schofe @hollywills love the new layout of the studio too!

Just heard that my first DVD, *Charlotte's 3 Minute Belly Blitz* has sold out on Amazon! Imagine if I'm number one and two in the charts!

* * *

Am on *Big Brother's Bit on the Side* tomorrow night for the launch of the new series of *Celebrity Big Brother.* So excited! The press are saying Scotty T is going in and he will SMASH IT! I can't wait to see what he does. He makes me laugh so much and I know everyone is going to love him. There's so much more to him than you see on *Geordie Shore.* And after Vicky winning *I'm A Celebrity . . .* last year, us Geordies are on a mission to win over the world.

Tuesday 5th

I am literally SO EXCITED about getting a new nose next week. I have wanted to get the bump sorted on my bridge for so long but it's taken me ages to find the right surgeon (and to convince everyone around me that it's the right thing to do). I can tell Melissa doesn't think it's a good idea because she always says that I'm 'naturally beautiful'. She keeps saying, 'You're lovely as you are.' But I know I will be a million times happier and more confident once I have a new face. I *nose* it! (Geddit?!)

@charlottegshore
'WHERE'S MY BOYYYYYY?' 👏

Was buzzing to see Scotty T go into the *Big Brother* house. Mind you, I'm not happy he said that I stink on camera! I would go on that show again in a heartbeat if I could. It was the most amazing experience ever.

Wednesday 6th

This is turning into the best month of my life so far. Everything has been going so well. Gary has been in contact all the time and he's like a changed person. I'm going to have a beautiful new nose moving in on my face. My new fitness DVD is doing brilliantly. I feel good, my body is in good shape (give or take a few uninvited christmas puddings still lingering around my waist area) and work has started on my new house! At the moment it's just like a shell with no proper rooms in it so it seems massive. I think the guy I bought it off ran out of money and couldn't finish it because the pool area is just a dug-out hole. I know exactly how I want it to look – it's going to be so good and everyone will want to live there. I keep seeing all these things I want to put in it like giraffe wallpaper and giant playing cards. Maybe I'll have to do themed rooms?!

Dad is the project manager. I can't get over how good he is. But then his actual job *is* as an operations manager so he knows what to do at all times. I can't imagine project managing the house because there is so much stuff to do. Dad knows about buildings and painting and plumbing. I wouldn't know where to start. I mean, if the house needed to get its nails done I'd know what to do. Or if it needed its make-up done or a good blow-dry I'd easily be able to project manage the house. But this is a different kettle of fish. Me mam keeps telling me what an 'immense project' it is. Can't be that hard, can it?

@TheMimmyWoman1
Well drained off today! That however was the best bath I have ever had. Bite to eat bed and another big day. #Friday

Me mam does tweet some weird shit. Although she's right. Baths are amazing.

Thursday 7th

Been thinking about all the people I've met over the last few years through my clothing range In The Style, my fitness DVDs and my make-up Fliqué. I'm so lucky to have people like Adam and Jamie, Shane from Easilocks and my personal trainers Richard and David in my life. Although I don't feel so lucky when my PTs make me get up at stupid o'clock to train with them. Speaking of which, I'm up again tomorrow. Better get some zzz.

Friday 8th

The main builder on my house is called Alan. He's only been on the project for a few weeks but already I feel quite close to him and I think we've got a good bond. He's got a little bit of a pot belly, he wears overalls and has grey hair with a very good tan. He's a bit like the Tom Jones of the building world. I really like him. He's been showing me round the plans of the house and telling me what he's going to do. It's going to look like one of those places in California where there are loads of split levels and stairs going up and down in different directions.

Monday 11th

We're off to Australia soon!! Can't wait! Mam and Dad are coming with Nathaniel and we're going to stay in a villa with Adam and Jamie while I do promotion for In The Style and *Geordie Shore* press for MTV. It will be so good having them there with me. I miss them too much when we're on the opposite side of the world to each other.

Tuesday 12th

Spent what feels like the last 800 days going up and down the country talking into microphones about my *3 Minute Bum Blitz* DVD. I'm sure every journalist must be fed up with me going on about my arse.

Wednesday 13th

New nose tomorrow! WHAT AM I GOING TO LOOK LIKE? I'm so excited!

It's taken such a long time for me to convince everyone around me that I know what I'm doing. Mam and Kate have been trying to tell me I don't need one but, as I pointed out to Mam, I didn't enjoy having braces for two years when I was a kid but she made me have them so my teeth would look better. So what's the difference? I hate the way my nose looks in photos. If I didn't have the job I have, in the public eye, then maybe I (and hundreds of trolls) would never have noticed, but I see myself from the side angle about a million times a week and I am so self-conscious about it.

Thursday 14th

Got the train to Birmingham with Melissa. Me mam drove down to meet us there. I am getting a new nose on my face in a few hours! I CANNOT WAIT! (I'm not even that worried about the operation . . . which is very weird for me).

* * *

Got to the hospital and I started to get bit nervous. When I was in the loo Melissa began asking the doctor loads of questions and whispering to him like she didn't want me to hear. What was she asking? Maybe she was asking him out because she fancied him!

When I first woke up after the operation I felt fine. What's all the fuss about surgery? I don't even have any bruises. I had the plaster cast on my face and when I saw myself in the mirror I decided I quite liked the look of myself in the cast. I think I look quite trendy and special. I might keep it afterwards and wear it as an accessory. Just wait, everyone will be wearing them on the catwalk at London Fashion Week! Or I could even bring out a range of them for In The Style.

Maybe I'm still a bit high on the drugs . . .

* * *

Melissa and Mam came into see me afterwards and I said, 'What do you think? Can you take a picture?'

But Mel said, 'It looks a bit swollen at the minute.'

Basically she was trying to say I looked like Miss Piggy but didn't want me to panic. I know it won't look great to start with but I have every confidence the end result will all be worth it.

* * *

Have to get the plugs pulled out of my nose tomorrow. This is the bit I've been warned about by Aaron and Kyle after they had their noses done. The plugs are like two tampons shoved up your nose and the boys said when they get removed it feels the same as having your brains pulled out.

I can't afford to lose my brain.

Friday 15th

Woke up really early and couldn't breathe. The pain has started. Yesterday was clearly just a mirage of drugs and false hope that surgery was going to be like having a cup of tea because now this shit feels real!!

I texted Mam and Melissa as soon as I woke (which was about 5 a.m.), 'The plugs are coming out in one hour I need you both here! Why aren't you here??'

Mam replied, 'Me and Melissa are going to get some breakfast in the hotel first before we drive home.'

'Oh for God's sake!' I replied, 'You're meant to be my carer!'

So I had to go it alone with no friends or carer in sight. It was the most surreal and horrific brain-sucking feeling. It was quick but it felt like forever. I HAVE NEVER FELT PAIN LIKE IT!!!

When Mam and Melissa eventually arrived they looked all flustered and made out as if they'd rushed straight over. I think they were shocked because I was fine by the time they got here after making such a drama about them being here with me. The bruises have appeared in full force under my eyes. I look like a boxer with good hair.

@TheMimmyWoman1
Very proud of @charlottegshore she's been a brave Bibby girl. Love looking after her I always do

Saturday 16th

Apparently your nose keeps on changing for about a year after surgery. Maybe I'll look like loads of different people every month!

* * *

I am so addicted to *Celebrity Big Brother* I don't know how I will survive the rest of the year when it's not on. David Gest is my spirit animal. He's so FUNNY!

Sunday 17th

I've had a falling out with Alan. He wanted me to choose a worktop in the kitchen and I had to tell him I'm not really that bothered. But he keeps saying its important so I've got to go and look at them with Mam.

Monday 18th

Am officially in hiding (or recovery as it's medically referred to) which means I have to chill out at home until my cast comes off. I've agreed to talk about it exclusively in *heat* magazine. We did a really glamorous shoot (not!) with the bandage all over my face. Baby was in it too so that was good – her first celebrity-magazine shoot!

Tuesday 19th

Nathaniel says he's glad I'm not allowed to do anything in the public eye before the *heat* article comes out because it means less people will go on about it to him at school. He hates the fact that he's my brother because he's getting too much attention. All the girls tell him that they'll go out with him if it means they can get to meet me! He just tells them to piss off. His male friends try and protect him and keep people away from him. You'd think he was Justin Bieber or something. About a month ago he told me he won't be on my Snapchat any more because he says whenever I put him on it everyone talks to him about it at school. I can only put him on it if I film him on the sly and obviously I can't do that with a gigantic plaster cast on my face when I'm meant to be revealing my nose in *heat* magazine.

Wednesday 20th

Mam dragged me to the kitchen showroom today (Alan's orders). I had a long coat on and had my hand covering my nose so no one could recognise me. Not that there was anyone much about. I walked around trying to find something I could imagine cooking a chicken stir-fry in, but I hated them all. Mam kept saying, 'Do you like this one?' and I just replied, 'No, it's shit.' They were all really bad. The only thing I have actually found is a granite worktop. Alan won't be happy.

Thursday 21st

It's been five years this year since *Geordie Shore* began. How crazy is that? I can't believe how much it's changed my life. It's also really weird to think that me and Gary are still circling around the subject of being proper boyfriend and girlfriend. It just shows how strong the feelings are between us for so much to have happened, so many other relationships, and those feelings not to have gone away. I still don't know if I can trust him but it definitely feels like this is the closest we've been. And it's been so nice being away from the cameras because there's no pressure from anyone and no one else about to mess with our heads. But that will all be ruined now because we're going back in the house!

Kate has just told me MTV want to do a special series to celebrate the fact it's our birthday called *Big Birthday Battle*. What the hell? Seriously, they must have only just thought of it because why would they suddenly be putting it on us now?

None of us can be bothered and I'm not looking forward to it at all (that's the spirit, Charlotte!). It feels like we only came out of filming the last series about two weeks ago and now we've got to go back into that freezing house, which is actually an old factory, and it's like zero degrees in there! Why do you think we have to drink so much alcohol all the time? We need it to keep us warm! And it's a mess! Five people squashed into one room. Six suitcases to ONE WARDROBE! More to the point – none of us are 'camera ready'! We're all feeling like we're fat from Christmas. So this birthday series is going to look like a load of turkeys wobbling around Newcastle wondering why no one ate them over Christmas time. We're meant to act like we're excited but none of us are.

Rant over.

P.S. Alan isn't happy about me not deciding on a kitchen. Everything is a deadline with him!

Saturday 23rd

Get to see my new nose in all its glory tomorrow. THE CAST IS COMING OFF. I actually think I'm going to miss it a little bit though. We've got quite attached. I am also going to miss being waited on hand and foot while 'in recovery'. I haven't had to lift a finger. At times I've felt like I was under house arrest but it's actually been pretty sweeeeeet. Me mam said it's just given me an excuse to act even more of a spoilt child than before. She says that anyone who met me would think I'm an only child because I always demand to be looked after first and my poor brother Nathaniel doesn't get a look in, even though he's got autism. She says I always say, 'What about me?!' I think she secretly loves running around after me, it makes her feel special and needed.

Sunday 24th

When the cast was taken off I was so desperate to see my nose but Mam and Melissa obviously saw it first, before I got to look in the mirror. Mam just looked and screamed, 'What the hell?! That is amazing!'

Thank God they had a good reaction, otherwise I'd have panicked.

Spent most of the day taking side-profile pictures of my

new nose and sending them to everyone I could think of. I am SO HAPPY WITH IT!

Charlotte's Thoughts On: Nose Jobs

1. Take a lot of time to think about it. Speak to people close to you, friends and family to make sure you are making the right decision. No plastic surgery should be rushed into or be taken lightly. Any surgery has risks. Be realistic – do you ACTUALLY need one? I never had a problem with my nose until I got a job in TV and was being photographed from every angle and people started trolling me about it looking like I had a massive bump on the bridge.

2. Make sure you pick the right surgeon – you don't want to end up with a nose like a spade. Be sure you are going with a reputable and well-known surgeon. I met with three different surgeons before I actually picked the one I wanted to go with.

3. Take someone with you, you'll need their support when you wake up.

4. Stock up on magazines . . . HOSPITALS ARE SO BORINGGGG.

5. EAT LOTS . . . class it as a cheat day.

6. Embrace the surgical outfit and the plaster cast on your face – you need to own your new look as it starts from the moment you wake up from the anaesthetic.

7. Enjoy being looked after when you get out – this is your time to be really lazy and hope you'll have a sympathetic family to wait on you on hand and foot.

8.   And after the bandages come off, make sure you have your phone on you ready to take those new side-profile selfies at all times . . .

Monday 25th

We're in London to do press for *Geordie Shore*.

I am staying in the same hotel as Gary and we HAVEN'T HAD SEX.

All we did was cuddle and kiss. (But if I'm honest the real reason is because I have my period. I can't try and make out I've suddenly turned into the Virgin Mary. Bloody Mary more like!)

Tuesday 26th

Did my 'nose reveal' shoot for *heat* today. Can't wait for the whole world to see it!

The rest of the day was full of more press for *Geordie Shore*. It all gets very confusing trying to remember which series we're meant to be talking about to journalists when we're doing press, because so much has usually happened between all of us after filming that we forget what we're meant to say and not say. I can't keep up with myself! Especially where Gary is concerned.

My feelings for Mr Beadle have come back full-on. It's the first time we've both been single at the same time in ages. And at last he's not with Lillie Lexie. He was so good to her as a boyfriend and treated her differently from anyone else I've known him with. He has always said he didn't cheat on her. He did seem so into her. Maybe Lillie Lexie was his lesson in how to be serious with someone. I've started to believe him anyway, he's very persuasive. He goes out of his way for people and the more time I've been spending with him, the closer I've got to him. Now whenever I hear people talking about him cheating I just think, 'The Gary I know now wouldn't do that.' I don't want anything to put me off wanting it to work with us this time. We have to give it a go between us. He's tried other girls, he's managed to have a serious girlfriend and it didn't work. So if it's ever going to happen between us then NOW IS THE TIME.

We haven't outright said, 'Let's be together,' but whenever we talk about going back into *Geordie Shore* it ends up like this:

Me: 'So are you going to get with anyone this series?'
Him: 'Dunno are you?'
Me: 'No I don't think so'
Him: 'Me neither . . .'

Anyway, I'm sure the producers love the idea of us together because they are always asking what's going to happen. Neither of us have admitted anything to them yet.

Wednesday 27th

WHY DO I ALWAYS HAVE TO DO STUPID THINGS?!

DON'T EVER LET ME DRINK ON THE TRAIN AGAIN!

We filmed the advert for Series 12 of *Geordie Shore* all day and then got the train back to Newcastle because we're starting the *Big Birthday Battle* show tomorrow.

I had a couple of glasses of wine on the train because

everyone else was drinking and we were all joking about how fed up we were going to get of each other's faces having to be back in that house again. And wine helps the hours fly by when you're on a train from London to Newcastle! I picked up my car at the station to drive to the hotel – we were being put up in the city centre because we were filming really early. It was less than half a mile away, I didn't even think about it, I thought I was fine to drive.

I stopped at the traffic lights and was about a millimetre over the line when the police pulled me over. I thought, 'Just my luck.' I didn't panic because I wasn't drunk so I stayed really calm and polite and did everything they asked me to. They breathalysed me and told me I was over the limit. The police officer asked me if I knew how much I'd had to drink and I told him it was two large glasses of wine. He said that was too many units . . . FFS!

* * *

I've been in this police station so many times before that when I arrived it was quite normal. It wasn't a scary experience. It's a bit weird how comfortable I feel to be honest. But I have to stay in overnight and I have filming tomorrow! I'm so stressed!

* * *

Couldn't sleep because my nose is hurting so I keep having to ask for painkillers from the police officer. It's the same one from last time I was here so she knew my face.

I'm such an idiot. What if people find out about this? I have a ridiculously busy month . . . I CAN'T EVEN think about it. I just need to get this sorted.

I have filming tomorrow and instead of being tucked up in

bed in a nice hotel I'm in the police station and now it's 4 a.m.!

The bed is so hard and the pillow is like a brick. They only give you one blanket which feels like a carpet. You get one phone call. I don't dare ring me mam and dad so I call Kate instead. I've lost the will to live. It's actually nice to get my phone taken off me so no one will bother me for at least a night.

I've had so much press to do for MTV and for the DVD and my nose job, I just want a lie down.

God, I'm grumpy at the moment.

I asked Kate to tell me dad but not me mam, I can't bear to think of her reaction. She will have had to tell the producers what happened too because I'm going to be late. I can't imagine they'll be very shocked. They've seen it all before!

Thursday 28th

Rushed home to get some clothes but luckily no one was in. I can't face Mam. She will hate me for this. I'm not going to see her now for a month so hopefully she will have forgotten by the time I'm out of the *Geordie Shore* house.

Anyway, I can't think about it or her or anyone. I'm off to the house! Bye bye, diet and hello, hangover from hell. I know I'll put weight on in there, I always do. I just have to try not to eat too many kebabs when I'm mortal otherwise I won't fit back out the door. I always pile the pounds on when I'm filming in *Geordie Shore* even when I watch what I eat. I know it's nothing compared to when I was three stone heavier, but it still makes it feel like my clothes don't look very good.

Poor old me.

* * *

I haven't washed my hair! I'm not ready to go back into *Geordie Shore*! Why is it all so rushed?! What is going on!

* * *

I instantly felt better when I saw Gary's face. He arrived to pick me up and take me to the house and he looked handsome when he came to the door. This is the first time we have been single in soooo long.

We had a funny chat on the way and made a pact to stay single this series. I asked him on camera if he was going to pull and he looked sheepish and said, 'No . . . I want to see what happens with us first . . .'

He said I looked pretty and I said he looked handsome. It's exciting – what in the hell is going to happen between us?!

Everyone started arriving . . . there was Marnie who looked amazing and beautiful as ever, she came with Aaron and they seemed really happy. Chantelle's hair is so curly it looks like she's wearing super noodles on her head. Chloe has brought a trombone with her because she says she needs to practise blow jobs because she's not very good at them! She makes me laugh so much, I love her. Nathan is here too and I love him so much because he's such a brilliant person to have in the house because he's so funny. And nutcase Marty too with his floppy fringe. Chloe, Nathan, Marty, Chantelle, me and Gary are all back together again.

No sign of Holly or Scotty T. Holly doesn't have the excuse she's in *Celebrity Big Brother* – she's just late!

Somehow, even though we were only in here for the last series about two minutes ago the house has had a massive makeover. It looks mint. Me and Gary went straight to the shag pad to get cosy.

Everyone told me they loved my new nose. I still can't stop looking at it. My cheeks are still bruised but that's nothing a bit of Crosby contouring can't sort out.

We got mortal as soon as humanly possible. Marty kept spewing every time he had a shot.

Went to Bijoux and Gary told me how he felt about me. He got really deep and meaningful and for the first time in God knows how long I felt my guard come down because he sounded like he was being really honest. We didn't even shag. We just cuddled all night and then he went back to his own bed to sleep.

Wow. Things really are different this time round.

Friday 29th

Holly finally arrived while we were waiting for our boss Anna to turn up. (Anna is the one in charge who always gives us a hard time and looks like she has never managed to smile in her whole life. But we love her.) It was so good to see Holly. But where the hell had she been? She told us all she's single now and she's not with Kyle any more. But she says she doesn't want to talk about it. Her and Kyle will end up together again. I know it.

When Anna came through the front door we were expecting her to tell us we all had to spend the next thirteen days cleaning people's arses or something. That's the usual standard of the jobs she gives us! (Well sort of . . . we had to do spray tans once which was similar. Same colour and involved close contact with people's bums.) But no! She gave us the biggest treat ever and told us that after five years working for her we now have enough experience to run OUR OWN party nights! IT'S A COMPETITION!! A BATTLE BETWEEN TWO TEAMS!

This could be the first job we actually enjoy.

I am captain of one team and guess who got the other captain hat? Gary, of course! So we're now enemies fighting it out to the death. Team Charlotte has to win! I am so competitive I always have to be the best at everything.

Me and Gary played rock paper scissors to decide who could pick teams first and I won – obviously! I chose Aaron because I know he's hard-working. Then I got Nathan, Marty and, in the end, the way it worked out meant I had no choice but to have Holly. Literally no one wanted Holly, which was hilarious. She said she felt like a loser. I told Marnie I didn't want her either because she doesn't have any work ethic.

After Holly had stopped sulking about no one wanting her, we had to decide on a theme. Me mam always said I was a genius but this time around I pulled it out of the bag. Picture the scene: Crowns, corgis . . . and a throne! The name of our party night is going to be ROYAL RUMBLE! Gary's team chose Angels and Devils which is shit compared to ours.

THEN THE BEST THING EVER IN THE WORLD HAPPENED. I WAS GOBSMACKED.

We were all sitting about chatting about what was going to happen at our parties and the door rang. Guess who was at the door?

SOPHIE!!!!

I was in total shock. I thought she'd never come back, so I couldn't believe it. I have never been so happy!

I cried so much – it just felt like a dream. What the fuck is going on? Sophie literally just walked through the door. It means so, so much to have her back. She was the first friend I made in here and to have her in the house and back on *Geordie Shore*, I can't describe how much it means to me.

Until she decided to join Gary's team anyway!!

Devastated.

* * *

The party was amazing. I kept shouting on the microphone: 'Who wants to stroke my corgi?'

Holly didn't do any work at all, mind. She just kept saying she wasn't wanted on my team.

When we all got back to the house we had to wait for a phone call from Anna to say who'd won.

Gary went to answer it and when he came out of the phone booth he just stood there all, dramatically for ages. He was taking so long. It's like he thought he was Dermot on *The X Factor* or something.

But it was worth the wait because WE WON!! I can't stop screaming. In your face Gary!!!!

Sunday 31st

I only meant to give Gary a kiss last night but oops . . . I may have done a bit more than that. And it's not like I can pretend because it will all be on camera . . .

The first thing I said to him when we woke up was, 'Good morning, loser!' and he said 'I might have lost a little work thing but we had a little fumble in the sheets . . . So I feel like I won.'

Eh? Since when did Gary become such a lovely sweet person!?! He is just being so lovely to me. I can't believe it.

* * *

With Sophie back it has just made the dynamic of the house so much better. And we keep wondering if Sophie's back, does that mean other people are going to come back too? What if everyone comes back? Even Vicky?!

* * *

Gary has been finding his own jokes hilarious. He keeps quipping things like, 'We were meant to be going head to head. You didn't need to *give* head.' Then, when we were all sitting in a group, he told everyone I wanked off the enemy.

Suddenly there was a noise outside . . . it was a motorbike.

Fucking hell, it was JAMES!

First Sophie and now James. I can't believe another original has walked through the door. Feels like we've gone back in time five years.

Me and Gary did rock paper scissors again to see who got James in their team and I smashed it once again. I am on a winning streak!

But I didn't even have time to gloat because then the door went again and it was JAY!

What the actual hell is going on? It's just getting better and better.

How many more are coming back?

Me, Gary, Sophie, Holly, Jay and James sat together in the bedroom and got all nostalgic and emotional. Someone said we'd built the *Geordie Shore* house together. Well we didn't actually build it but if we had it would have really been a shithole.

It's so surreal . . .

But I didn't have time to get too carried away because it was time to get back to the task in hand – beating Gary! I told him that if we won I might have to actually have sex with him.

Our next party theme will be Trailer Trash – think hillbillies, trailer parks and incest. It's going to be amazing. But we've got a night out getting mortal first!

Me and Gary walked into the club holding hands. He is being so nice to me and can't stop telling everyone that he is really into me and this is something special. James is in shock and says he never in a million years thought he would hear those words coming out of Gary's mouth and wished he said it five years ago. They sat down and had a serious chat in the club.

Later that night Gary came over and told me that he was only interested in me and that he didn't want to be with anyone else. I told him it scares me because I don't want to go back to square one. But he's saying everything I've wanted to hear for so long! I can't believe it after everything we've been through. He even said HE WANTS ME TO BE HIS GIRLFRIEND. So we are now officially seeing each other. For the first time in five years Gary has actually shown me some commitment.

THIS IS A BIG DEAL.

I took the girls to one side and told them the news. Chloe and Marnie were buzzing for us but Holly and Sophie had faces like slapped arses. Holly said it was hard to believe it was actually going to work out this time. Thanks!

I'm not going to let them get inside my head. I know they care but I don't want to ruin this feeling. Tonight is up there with one of the best nights out I've ever had. I've got the *Geordie Shore* family back and me and Gary have started seeing each other. It feels so amazing and fills me with a sense of happiness that no one will ever be able to understand.

When we got back to the house everyone was mortal – it was carnage.

The competition is back on tomorrow. I hope that doesn't fuck everything up . . .

February 2016

Number of times I thought about Gary this month: 2,000,000,000,000,000,000 recurring

Accidental eye contact made with a boy who isn't Gary: Once (or twice!)

Pains in my nose: Some tingling but it's worth it

Public reaction to my new nose: 30% negative, 70% positive

Emojis to sum up my current mood: 😊😊😊😊😊😊

Monday 1st

Party night! Gary's team had a giant dinosaur walking about to attract punters. Our night, on the other hand, didn't go quite as planned. When Anna arrived to check out how we were doing, Nathan decided to try and swing her round like a hillbilly and she didn't like it. In fact, she looked fucking miserable.

Gary's team won.

PAH.

Tuesday 2nd

Anna is mad because she saw what Aaron and Marnie were up to on the kitchen worktops last night. She watched it afterwards on CCTV!

* * *

Gary says he wants to take me on our first proper date. After all these years of me and Gary going out on our own and pretending it's a date this is actually the real thing! He told me to be 'best dressed, glam and sexy'.

Arghhh. What the hell do I wear? Do I wear high heels? I don't know! I want to look so nice but I can't just wear something he will like . . . then it would just be high-heeled boots and a thong.

He knocked on the bedroom door and was wearing a shirt and jeans and looked really smart. He said I looked nice and I said he looked super handsome. I think we match, like a very attractive salt and pepper pot. When we got in the car to go to the restaurant I whispered in his ear that I didn't have any knickers on. He blindfolded me until we walked inside but all I kept worrying about was the fact my fanny was out and if I tripped everyone would see it.

When he took the blindfold off I couldn't believe my eyes – there were roses and candles all over the place. Petals, champagne, the works! What more could I possibly want? He even got me twenty-four red roses. I just kept thinking, 'This is amazing.'

Gary raised a glass: 'Cheers to our first proper date and I hope there are many more.'

It made me feel a bit nervous and giggly, like it was the first time I'd met him. He said that when we're together we are amazing and although he wasn't ready for commitment before – now he is.

He smiled, 'I want you to know I'm so happy to be with you.'

I've never felt this feeling before. I feel so special. And it's him that's making me feel like this. It's all I have ever wanted him to do and now it's here. I just feel so happy about it; it's making me cry.

The date went so well but when we got back to the house I told myself I had to remember we're on rival teams. I'm finding it hard to have a healthy balance between my work life and my personal life!

* * *

No sooner had we got back but DAN entered the house!

And then RICCI!

WWWWWWWHHHHHHHHAAAATTTTTTT???

This is the best feeling ever! We HAVE to go out and celebrate!!

* * *

As soon as we'd had a few drinks, Dan and Marty had a massive row about Chloe. Marty and Chloe have been getting it on lately and Dan has history with her. But it was all very bizarre because one minute Marty was warning Dan off 'his' girl and the next minute he pulled a totally different girl on the dance floor in front of everyone! That was all Dan needed to see because then he went straight to Chloe and made a move. Marty went apeshit.

Gary was being so affectionate and complimentary to me all night. He was whispering stuff in the club like, 'Tonight we're not having sex – we're making love.' I told him I didn't know what that meant but it sounded amazing. He then said, 'We will be kissing the whole time, it will be slow then fast . . .' It sounded so SEXY!

We snuck off back to the shag pad for our very first love-making session. All I kept thinking was, 'I hope I've shaved my fanny!' But Gary was a bit worse for wear. There wasn't *anything* sexy about that. The whole room was spinning . . . he puked all over the floor! What the hell? Gary is never sick and it stunk. If this is what making love is all about then rule me out . . . I'm alright with a quick shag.

Because of the smell in the shag pad we went back to my bed in the girl's bedroom to sleep. I had a Brucey Bonus because we woke up a few hours after we'd passed out and started to get frisky. Making love to Gary was like the first time I tried a cheeseburger. Sexy, sensual and satisfying. Only problem was . . . Sophie was in the room. I heard her shouting, 'Charlotte, get the fuck out!' She'd woken up to the sound of my moans!

Thursday 4th

Everyone was laughing about it this morning though and Marnie asked me how good it was because it sounded like I was enjoying myself. I said it was a ten. I am the happiest girl in the world. Gary is my lobster and I've finally got him.

Marty and Dan were still having a massive row over Chloe, which was annoying because they are on my team! I've decided I need to sort my fucked-up team out – nothing is going to get in the way of Team Charlotte winning this battle. I called a team meeting and, in the end, Marty and Dan had a cuddle. Hell, they even had a kiss! I told everyone I am officially changing my strategy now. I need to not be horrible to anyone any more and instead I will send out positive, empowering vibes. I don't think telling everyone they're lazy and shit was working.

Tonight's party theme is Under the Sea (my idea again!). James said he was glad it wasn't Under the Tyne because we'd be going out as toilet roll, lumps of shit and shopping trolleys. I feel good about tonight. I can smell the winning!

* * *

When the party was in full swing I was on the mic, the guests were jumping about and downing shots, the atmosphere was great and everyone was loving it. But we knew it was Anna we had to impress so when she walked in I shit a brick. She seemed to have a smile on her face by the time she left though. So I think she liked it . . . unless she'd just had a shag.

* * *

Got back to the house and was waiting for the phone to ring when the door opened and Anna was actually here. In person! She looked around the place and it was carnage because Marty and Aaron had been smashing stuff about last night (Marty was mad because of Dan). Anna was fuming: 'The damage in here is absolutely disgusting!' She looked at the door and the phone box and saw what a wreck everything was. But how the hell did she know what had happened?

Turns out Sophie and Chantelle had grassed!!

Anna said our team was going to win but because of Marty and Aaron we couldn't be the winners . . .

Sophie!! WHAT THE FUCK??

Friday 5th

We were royally screwed over last night so I tried to call another team power chat. Except Aaron has ditched us and gone out with Marnie . . . I am furious. We need to think of the best theme ever for this next party so Team Gary doesn't stand a chance. I've got it – a zoo theme! That's decided – our party is going to be called Party Animals.

* * *

We hardly had chance to practise our lion noises when there was the sound of another car outside. Who the hell was it? Ricci kept whispering, 'I hope it's not Vicky!' I think he would have packed his bags and got on the next flight straight back to Australia if it had been. Those two in the same house together again after all this time would not be pretty.

It's KYLE!

Oh my God. Ever since we arrived, Holly has been dreaming for him to be here. They're not together but Holly still wants him in *Geordie Shore* because she says it feels like a part of her is missing otherwise. He left on bad terms with some people in Greece because there was just so much fallout and so many arguments. So when he got in the house you could tell he was really nervous. He thought he wouldn't ever get the opportunity to come back.

Holly was still out shopping for fancy dress for the party

45

when Kyle got here so we decided to hide him in the last place she would expect to look . . . in her own bed. As soon as she saw him she burst into tears. She always felt to blame that everyone chose her over him so it was really moving to see her reaction. Her face was an absolute picture; I wish I could bottle that emotion she's feeling and have a sip of it every morning when I wake up.

We're going to celebrate Kyle's return by going out – again!!!

* * *

I still have doubts about whether Gary's serious about us two and every time we get pissed I always tell him. He keeps saying he couldn't be more serious but I just find it so hard to trust him. What happens when we leave? He says we will be officially boyfriend and girlfriend properly in the outside world but I just can't believe it.

When we got back after our night out Gary started doing an attempt at sexy dancing in the bedroom. I told him if he thought that was going to get my juices flowing he was having a laugh. Holly came and joined us in the bed because she didn't want to get in with Kyle and fuck things up. So that was the end of that sexiness anyway!

Saturday 6th

I had to go to the doctor's because my nose was hurting. I think I've got an infection because of all the germs in this house – it's filthy now we've been living in it for a week.

Charlotte's Guide To: Living With Messy People

In *Geordie Shore* we live in a big house and everything is dirty and I mean EVERYTHING. Even the dirt is dirty. So here are my tips to surviving living with messy people or living in a messy house:

1. Keep your own plastic knives, forks and plates. This is for one very important reason: you don't have to wash them, you can just throw them straight away! (Trust me, you don't want to go anywhere near the sink.) If your house is as dirty as the *Geordie Shore* house the last place you want to be is at the sink. That's the hotspot for the mould that grows on the week-old dishes that just lay there doomed to be unwashed and unloved. The sink is a sad place.

2. Purchase a sturdy pair of slippers, preferably with hard soles. You don't want to get what we call a '*Geordie Shore* brown foot'. That is a bare unsocked foot that has collected dust, scraps of food, spilt liquids and hair on its sole. Disgusting, I know. Oh yeah, and you know how I mentioned the hard sole on the slipper? That's to protect you from the smashed glass remains from the night before!

3. Never lend your things out. The messy people will either lose or ruin your things. For example, Chloe borrowed an expensive dress of Holly's. It wasn't actually returned. We found it outside the Jacuzzi, soaked, with poo on it. NEED I SAY MORE?

4. Last but not least – DO NOT ROOM SHARE!!!!!!!! One messy person is bad enough but mix four or five together and you have utter messy carnage. I'm talking

false tan all over the floor, clumps of hair, dirty knickers littering the place. Tampons just EVERYWHERE. If you room share you will find yourself living in worse conditions than a PIG!!!

We had to put Kyle on Gary's team because otherwise it would distract Holly. But secretly I think it's a good thing because when Scotty T finally decides to get here (when he's out of *Celebrity Big Brother* – hopefully with the crown!) that means he will have to be on my team – and everyone knows Scott is the best one to have on your side.

We need to win this! We need Party Animals to be out of this world.

But that's not the only thing on my mind. There are bigger things brewing. After losing to those grasses I am not letting it lie. It's time for some SABOTAGE! I have decided I am going to play dirty and try to get Gary out of his venue so when Anna arrives he's not even at his own party!

* * *

Just before we all went out we sat round the table to do our usual 'cheers' to a good night out. But this time it was a much more enthusiastic secret cheers because the producers told us off camera that Scotty T has WON *CELEBRITY BIG BROTHER*! We're all so buzzing for him. How amazing is that?!

* * *

Got to the club and the place looked unreal! I knew instantly in my bones that tonight we were going to be WINNERS. We had a booth and the guests could take a photo and put animal faces on themselves. How genius is that? The whole

place was buzzing with people and there was animal para-
phernalia everywhere. You felt like you were literally in the
middle of the jungle – Queen Charlotte's jungle! I just kept
thinking, 'When Anna walks in and realises she can transform
herself into a monkey in a matter of seconds, she is going to
be over the moon!'

* * *

But let's not get carried away, because it's time for REVENGE.
And it's going to be sweet.

* * *

The others distracted Anna and I snuck into Gary's party
for a snog . . . I was all over him, trying to tempt him to
leave his party and come back to the house with me. I had
Gary right where I wanted him – by the balls. Back at Party
Animals, Anna took Aaron for a walk on his lead (he was
dressed as a Dalmatian) AND SHE WAS LOVING IT! She
even dragged Holly to one side and said, 'You guys have
done absolutely amazing.' Our plan was working.

But my snogs clearly weren't juicy enough because despite
my tongue being everywhere and doing my best to be all sexy
and seductive, Gary wasn't budging. He said, 'I can't leave my
team.' So I stropped off.

* * *

WHO CARES ABOUT TONGUES ANYWAY. WE GOT
BACK TO THE HOUSE AND ANNA CALLED . . . WE
WON!!!

YES! Anna, you beautiful monkey-faced bitch!

Sunday 7th

Me and Gary slept in the same bed again last night. I kept thinking, 'We're in the best place we've ever been, the sex is great, he's giving me affection. . . I think it could be love.' I whispered, 'I care about you a lot you know.' But he was asleep . . .

* * *

Sophie has just taken me aside in the bedroom and told me that Gary was flirting with a girl in the club last night at their party and rubbing her back. Why would she say that? Why now when everything is going so well between us? Chloe was there too and she kept asking if I could really trust him. I told them I completely trust him and didn't care what they said.

But it's messed with my head and now I can't stop crying.

I understand why Sophie is worried. She's one of my best friends and has been here so many times before when Gary has broken my heart but she's only ever seen bad things with me and Gary. And he's changed, he honestly has. I just wish she hadn't said it because it has made me worry.

* * *

I don't want to get out of bed. I wish everyone would just leave me alone.

I can't stop thinking about what Sophie said and it's distracting me from the serious matter of the competition. I need to try and put all that chat out of my head and focus on Team Charlotte.

* * *

I decided we needed to have our brainstorm meeting at the pub. James said he thought we should do our next theme on the services – like firemen and policemen – but Holly suggested S&M which has lots of dirty options so obviously that's the best. It has all the ingredients for a winning party – shock and surprise!

I can't wait for Scotty T to come back. He is so competitive. And he will love an S&M theme!

* * *

Suddenly, as we were getting ready to go out, we heard a van beeping outside with a big delivery marked 'Fragile'. I thought it must be a new washing machine or something – our undies could go through it three times and they'd still have skiddies on them!

We opened it and there was no sign of a washing machine . . .

. . . it was SCOTTY T!

At LAST!

Scotty's back and there was no work tonight. I can feel my jägerbombs tingling!

* * *

We went to Bijoux and it was so good for everyone to be back together.

For about an hour anyway. Scotty T's return didn't last long because the boys were playing volleyball with the lampshade in the club and Ricci pushed it really hard and hit him in the eye with it by mistake . . . so he stormed outside and went home! He said afterwards it was so he could calm down and not make a scene. It would definitely have kicked off between them otherwise. Scotty had a massive cut in his eye!

While we were in the club Kyle told Gary what Sophie had told me. Gary took me aside to explain. He said, 'Don't let anyone fuck us up or turn your head around.' I told him I'm still wary after everything that has happened in the past but he has reassured me. He said I was not to listen to anyone but I admitted it still made me scared. Gary told me he was scared just as much as me. Which maybe he is.

Monday 8th

Scotty and Ricci made up this morning. We've only got a couple of days left in here so we can't afford any bad feeling.

* * *

Got to the venue for our S&M party and for some reason there was hardly anyone there. And it just never filled up after that. We were working our arses off and the place looked amazing with dildos and black tape and bondage gear. We decided that maybe the theme scared people off.
DAMN IT.
But then something strange occurred. It was like the theme started having a really weird effect on me, I was tipsy and horny and felt like anything could happen . . .
Marty was really pissed too and he began cuddling me and saying he loved me. We were having banter and messing about. I don't know what the hell was going through my brain but we started snogging.
A few seconds later I sat down with the others and said, 'What the fuck have I just done?'
GARY IS GOING TO KICK OFF.
Marty told Aaron and he went absolutely nuts. Aaron was

so angry with me and he's my best friend out of the boys. I was in tears.

What have I done?

* * *

We all got back to the house before Gary and the others. When they came in they were so happy. Gary was on cloud nine because his party had gone really well. But he looked at us and could see the atmosphere was awful. Instantly he knew something was wrong. I just kept thinking, 'What I'm about to tell him is going to break his heart.' I was shaking. I was so scared.

I just wanted to run a million miles away and not have to face it. I had to get it over and done with so I asked him to come outside. I wanted to say, 'Don't worry, it was a drunken mistake,' and for him to say, 'Don't worry, I forgive you,' but I knew that wasn't going to happen.

I couldn't look at him and I couldn't get my words out.

In my head I just knew I could lose him for good and I've only just got him back.

After I told him he said, 'Wow,' and walked off. He said he needed to get out of the house and calm down. And that was it.

* * *

He's gone. I am heartbroken. What have I done?

* * *

In all this mess I'd forgotten about Chloe! She REALLY likes Marty! She went nuts and came outside and in tears.

She kept saying to me, 'This has got to be a joke . . . I will never ever forgive you for this!'

* * *

I had never seen Chloe like this. She says she's never been so hurt in her whole life.

I feel so awful. I have never done this to a friend. I can't believe how much I fucked up.

Marty has just started throwing things around the house.

* * *

Gary's face was so upset. What was I thinking, snogging Marty?

Aaron's been outside to see him but Gary says he wants to leave and go back to his house for the night. He says he can't bear to be in the house.

* * *

The phone rang. Obviously Gary's team won. But he wasn't even there to accept it

Tuesday 9th

All I can think about is how desperate I am to tell Gary how sorry I am. I just need to talk to him. I need him to forgive me. We only have one more day in the *Geordie Shore* house before we have to go back home to reality. And I can't go home not being Gary's girlfriend. Not again.

* * *

In the bedroom this morning everyone was talking about it and Nathan said, 'It's such a shame because everyone was getting on so well and now this has ruined it.'

I really have fucked up big style. Marty was trying to defend my actions, saying, 'Gary has fucked you about for five years so for you to kiss someone for two minutes . . .' I know he has a point but Gary won't see it like that. But maybe part of me wanted to give him a taste of his own medicine . . .

I told everyone I can't be team leader any more so I've passed my captainship on to Holly. I'm in no fit state to lead this team to victory, I don't deserve to be up against Gary.

Everyone decided on Circus as the theme which is a good one. Holly has been great and seems excited that she's been put in charge but I just can't get in the mood today.

Jay rang Gary to see how he was and he's agreed to meet him and Kyle at the club. They need him because he's their team captain! I hope he comes back but I haven't spoken to him, I don't have a clue what he's feeling, what he wants to do or if he even likes me any more. Normally it's Gary who fucks up and hurts me but this time the tables have turned and it's all me. I never in a million years thought it would turn out like this.

* * *

Gary arrived back at the house and was with the others when I came downstairs. I asked him if he would talk to me but he refused. He said, 'It would be easier for you to just stay out of my way.' So I walked off. I suddenly feel really angry. He owes me that much at least. I don't know how he fucking dares. The amount of stuff he has done to me in the past and I always hear him out and he won't even listen to me.

* * *

I can't stop crying. The atmosphere is fucked.

I'm so frustrated, Gary hasn't give me a chance to explain and I am just stuck in limbo. I'm not having this. He HAS to listen to me.

* * *

In the end I went down to the garden and found Gary with Aaron and Dan and said, 'I need to talk to you and if you want to have this conversation in front of your friends then fair enough.'

So he followed me to the room.

He said he was so annoyed with me: 'You fucked up. You did it. You're the one that goes and does it! Do you know how embarrassed that makes me feel? I'm the one trying to impress your friends while you're necking on with fucking Marty! Is that a joke?'

I looked at him sadly. 'It was one stupid kiss!'

He replied, 'Yes and it's not going to work, Char, this is closure. I am gutted because I gave it 110%. I gave you everything you wanted and you just threw it back in my face.'

I was begging him: 'If I could go back and undo it I would. I would never do anything like that again.' I tried so hard to reason with him, 'I've given you so many other chances.'

Gary just looked at the floor and shrugged. He wasn't budging. 'You still hurt me.' He just kept repeating, 'We're done. I'm gutted but that's it, Charlotte. We're over now. There's no chance. Me and you, we're done.'

I was begging him, 'I don't want you to say that's it! Please, Gary!'

This had been the perfect opportunity for me and Gary to finally give it a chance. I don't know why I did it! Maybe deep down I wanted to push him to the limit and see just how he really felt about me? Perhaps it was my way of trying to fight what was going on? Wondering what he would do, testing him . . . Pushing and pushing to see whether he would stick around or not. To see if, deep down, he really cared.

Everyone always thinks there will be some big fairy-tale ending with me and Gary but maybe they're wrong and we're not meant to be together. And it kills me to think that.

* * *

I haven't cried this much in so long. I've just been sitting on the bed in Holly's arms shaking and wailing. I feel so, so, so sad.

* * *

But the party still had to happen. I had to carry on. I don't know how but I got dressed, put on some make-up and somehow managed to hold myself together.

I looked in the mirror and gave myself a pep talk: 'I'm not going down without a fight. I won't be defeated . . . This is now Operation Get Gary Back!'

Our party was going really well and the circus theme was amazing. They didn't need me there to help them win this one. I went to Gary's party to begin implementing OGGB.

I had to apologise to Chloe first. I can't believe I didn't even think of her in all this. I was so desperate for her to forgive me. She was dead upset and kept saying I was her best friend in the house and that she would never do something like that to a friend – to get with a boy they had feelings for. I was in tears too (there wasn't much point putting on make-up tonight) and I told her I'd made a massive mistake and I would do anything to get our friendship back. She said we can be friends again but I think it's going to take a while for her to forget this.

Before I got a chance to even speak to Gary, Anna arrived and said she wasn't going to ring us with the results, instead she had organised a big party for us back at the house.

* * *

I have a plan. I'm going to confess how much I care about Gary – I need a grand gesture to get him back and if it doesn't work I don't know what I'm going to do. We're going home tomorrow and I need to fix this.

* * *

The party was well underway when I decided it was time. This was now the peak of Operation Get Gary Back. I jumped on the kitchen table and shouted at everyone in the room to listen. My heart was pounding and I thought, 'Right this is it. It's me last chance to win Gary back. Here goes. . .'

I started talking but I couldn't hear myself. Everyone was so pissed. Gary was in the corner looking at me mouthing, 'What are you doing?' and looking embarrassed.

'Shut the fuck up please, everyone,' I shouted, 'this is already hard enough!'

Then I said, 'I just want to say that this boy here [I pointed at Gary] literally isn't just only my best friend but he's my rock. Day one I came in this house and we've been through so many ups and downs, we've had other boyfriends and girl-friends but we've always managed to get back together and I don't know why that is. I can't explain it. But I don't know a life in this house without Gary [I was laying it all out on the line now]. If I was to ever lose him I don't think I would be able to live here any more. It's only ever been Gary and it only ever will be Gary . . . that's all.'

I got down. Everyone cheered. I slumped onto a chair and poured myself a drink. Then Gary came over. He smiled. 'That was emotional and amazing and I agree with everything you said.'

He told me he still feels hurt and he can't be in the house and look at Marty and know he's necked on me. I told him I knew I had done something stupid but I just wanted him to please forgive me . . . I pleaded, 'Can't we just get back together?'

Eventually he said, 'OK. I'm not writing off us OK?' And I broke into the biggest, fattest smile ever.

'When? Tomorrow?!'

He laughed. 'No not tomorrow.' He said we're just going to have to start back at the beginning again so let's take it from there. I can't wipe the smile off my face.

As if the night couldn't get any better, Anna got on the mic to say who had won the whole competition.

'The winner is . . . TEAM CHARLOTTE!!'

Wednesday 10th

It's our last day.

The moment I woke up I felt really emotional. It feels awful. None of us want this time to end. Everyone's packing their bags and crying. Well, the girls are.

Anna is coming to bring us a present for winning the competition before we leave. We've all been getting excited about what it's going to be. A massive holiday? A car each?! Unlimited clothes in Top Shop?!

* * *

Anna arrived with a big gold box. We all ripped it open thinking there would be some special keys in there, or tickets, or a clue about the prize. Inside were just loads of trophies! Everyone was moaning and Gary's team was laughing. Holly was fuming, 'A plastic fucking trophy! We were expecting a five-star holiday. All that work for THAT!'

Do you know what? I didn't even mind. I'd got my prize when Gary said he would forgive me. I told them I thought they were all being really ungrateful. I fucking love my trophy! (It's the biggest one anyway because I'm team captain.)

* * *

Whenever we leave the *Geordie Shore* house packing to go is the saddest, worst bit. But this time is so much worse because it's a reunion and none of the originals who left like Jay, James, Sophie, Dan and Ricci will be back next series which means we'll never all be together again. Sophie has been in bits all day.

I gathered everyone around the table so we could all take it all in one last time. I did a bit of a speech (I'm getting good at these).

'Everyone being here and back together has been unreal. This time around has been absolutely crazy hasn't it? I can't believe I'm sitting . . . Well I'm standing . . . [everyone laughed at this point] looking at all of these faces. It's been amazing having everyone back!'

We all did a cheers to the best time in the fucking world. Then Kyle decided he wanted to do a speech and it was really heartfelt. 'I just want to say that when I left everyone in Greece I thought I'd lost my family but I hadn't. And I want to thank you all.' Holly was blubbing again. I wish those two would get back together. When he said goodbye to Holly he told her she was the only girl he's ever loved and he will always love her. Isn't that amazing?

Everyone left, one by one, and in the end it was just me, Gary and Holly in the house. It felt so empty. And quiet. Gary hugged us both so hard I had to say, 'Be careful of me nose!'

Then Holly said goodbye and it was just me and Gary on our own which was a little bit awkward. I needed to find out if it was possible to start afresh. Before all the stuff that happened with Marty I thought he didn't care and now I know he does.

I said to him, 'In five years' time when we're happily married we'll say, "Why were we so stupid?" and we'll laugh about it all.'

He smiled. 'Maybe we will . . .'

I said, 'Even if we can't be boyfriend and girlfriend right now can I at least have a lift home?'

'No,' he laughed and started walking to the door with his bags, 'There are buses.'

'Are you KIDDING?!' I screamed.

He was joking. He did drive me home. And after everything that's happened I actually think that me and Gary are going to be OK. It's not a knock-back, it's a move forward.

@charlottegshore
'GOT SERIOUS FOMO about missing out on the wrap party tonight 😣 WAHHH! But Australia in the morning ✈️🌍

Gary and the others are out partying with the crew to celebrate the end of the show and he's been texting me all night saying, 'I wish you were here,' so I reckon he's properly forgiven me. I can't believe I'm not with them all but there's no way I could do it with the flight to Australia tomorrow.

Mam and Dad are coming with Nathaniel and we're going to stay in a villa with Jamie and Adam while I do promotion for In The Style and *Geordie Shore* press for MTV. It will be so good having them there with me. I miss them too much when we're on the opposite side of the world to each other.

Me and Gary have said we're definitely going to meet when we're out in Australia – he's flying out there in a couple of days. We're both doing PAs but we'll be in different cities (and Australia isn't exactly small so we can't just meet in the middle for a burger!). I think there's one night when our paths cross in New Zealand. That sounds so weird, doesn't it?! He's only down the road at the moment and I'm arranging to meet up with him God knows how many million miles away! I just want to get all the stuff that happened in *Geordie Shore* out of the way now so we can move on.

* * *

While I was in the house the pictures of my new nose came out in *heat*. Catching up on Twitter and some people are saying I've 'gone too far' but haters will always have a go. Most of my fans understand why I did it, and anyway I love it! I feel so much more confident and happy in myself now the bump has gone. I don't care what anyone says.

Thursday 11th

Off to Australia today, not back until 8th March! Whoo!

Saw the magazines at the airport and the front cover of *New* magazine says that my nose is about to fall off and that doctors warn it's 'in danger of collapsing'! Where the hell do they get their stories from?!

* * *

I keep thinking about being in the house and I can honestly say it's been the best time of my life EVER.

Friday 12th

I love it when I land in Australia. As soon as I got off the plane I felt the heat of the sun on me and the amazing aroma of Australia . . . the essence of kangaroo. The show is so big out here that whenever I arrive I feel like I'm Lady Gaga! There are always loads of paps outside shouting my name and it makes me feel dead important.

Saturday 13th

> @charlottegshore
> It's Valentines tomorrow and it's the third year I've spent it in Australia with no plans. 👎

Thankfully Bree is tour managing me for most of the time I'm out here. Bree works for Stage Addiction and it's so good to see her again. She's lovely and beautiful – I've known her for about four years now. It doesn't feel like we're working because we're mates. I've been filling her in on what's been going on with Gary. She knows him because she used to do all his PAs but now he's with another company. She's always cautious of him because of the way he has behaved in the past but she likes him and says as long as he's serious this time then she's happy for me.

We're in the villa with Adam and Jamie this week. Mam's dead chuffed because Adam said she and Dad could have the best room. I hope she doesn't start thinking they're on a second honeymoon. I do not want to hear any noises coming from that direction.

I'm feeling a bit rubbish. Not sure if its jet lag or something worse, but I need to go to bed. Adam and Jamie have got some friends round tonight for a party and I can hear me mam shrieking excitedly downstairs. She's on the wine already I can tell.

Sunday 14th

@TheMimmyWoman1
Well our night in the beautiful villa destroyed me LOL! A full day in bed with a hangover. Back to normal tomorrow. Weather amazing.

Mam is suffering today. I could hear noises coming from her and Dad's room last night but it definitely wasn't anything saucy going on in there, it was the sound of her throwing up. She is moaning that she's never felt so bad in her whole life. I'm still not feeling great either and now I haven't got me mam to make me sandwiches and wash my hair. She's no use to anyone in her state.

Been messaging Gary loads. Can't wait to see him. Just one more day.

He sent me a bunch of flowers and a green heart balloon because green is my favourite colour. They both arrived at the villa and are beautiful.

Monday 15th

Seeing Gary tomorrow!!! I can't wait to snog his beautiful bronzed face! I honestly don't think I've missed him as much as this ever. I feel like we're getting to the point where we can really make a go of things and even though I know he will have gone ridiculously overboard with his sunbathing and will look more like a raisin than a human being, I just love him. And I can't wait to gobble that little wrinkly raisin head right up.

Mam still hasn't come out of her room. She says she's never drinking wine again.

Tuesday 16th

AAARGH! I missed my flight from Wagga Wagga to go to Melbourne!!!!!!

The man in the hotel we were staying in told us we'd have plenty of time to get here because the airport was only small. He said, 'You don't have to get there that early,' so I had a lie-in and MISSED IT!

He was right, the airport is no bigger than a one-bedroom flat. They don't even have a conveyor belt for the luggage. You have to put your luggage on a truck that gets driven to the tiniest plane, which only has about eight seats on it. When we arrived at the airport it was like we could see tumbleweed – it's so quiet!

I'm so gutted. Gary has been really lovely, texting things saying how much he wants to see me. I am desperate to snog him and start getting back on track. But it's like forces are coming between us. It just makes me want to see him even more. We've worked out that we can meet in Sydney but that's a whole week away.

Wednesday 17th

Mam, Dad and Nathaniel are travelling around a different part of Australia while I have to work. Mam's also taken it upon herself to give me some 'homework' of my own in the form of three huge brochures of taps, fixtures and fittings because she says I need to make some decisions on what I want in the house so the builders can get on with the work. I have to pick everything in this house! I didn't realise how much work it was going to be. Got a message from Mam: 'The builders can't move forward until you know what taps you want.' It's only a tap! What sort of decision do I need to make?

Thursday 18th

Ferne McCann off TOWIE has sent me a WhatsApp asking for advice because she wants to get her nose done and people keep telling her not to. We've chatted loads about it and she says she isn't sure. She keeps asking how I feel now about mine. Am I happier? I told her I'm so much more confident now, it's not a worry at all. My nose used to bother me and now it's fixed and I don't have to think about it any more!

Friday 19th

I'm doing appearances at all five of the Good Life festivals – the first one is in Brisbane. All I have to do is a few meet-and-greets and the fans in Oz are always so lovely and funny. Holly, Kyle, Nathan and Chloe are going to be at Good Life doing them too but they get to hang out together and I have to do my appearances on my own. I got a bit distracted during mine today because my eyes kept getting obsessed with a man in the backstage area (and he wasn't Gary!). It started to rain while I was doing my meet-and-greet and I had to go and stand under a gazebo behind the main stage. That's when I saw him. I thought, 'Our eyes have just locked for too long there . . . that means something.' It's my eyes' fault! I can't stop them! Chloe told me afterwards he's really famous out here so I was going to ask him for a photo but then bottled it. He's called Will Sparks. He's got long blonde beachy hair and is really tall. He's quite pale considering he's Australian but there's just something about him. HE IS HOT.

I have sparks for Will SPARKS.

* * *

Turns out Will Sparks is a DJ! A massively popular and talented one! I went to watch the main DJ set at the festival and it was him. He looked AMAZING. He does this high jump like he's in *The Matrix* or something, it's like he has this weird superpower. He jumps from the soundboxes back on to the floor and up again like a superhero.

* * *

I'm back in my hotel and I keep thinking about Will Sparks. Oh no! I've got a massive crush on him! It feels like when you fancy a movie star and you have a poster in your bedroom.

* * *

I just tweeted Will saying I was too scared to come and ask for a selfie and he DMed me! He said, 'You should have just come over and asked. When are you about next?'

I didn't message him back. I fancy him so much but things are next level with Gary at the moment. We've never ever been this close, I can't let him slip through my fingers again. It's so different to how it's ever been between us and I can't do anything more that might ruin it. I can't pursue the spark with Mr Sparks.

@charlottegshore
Alot on maaaa miiiiind.

Saturday 20th

Got a really bad chest infection and can hardly talk. That's going to be great fun for my next meet-and-greet when I croak in their faces. Had to see a doctor because it's so sore. I just want someone to give me a cuddle in bed. Got to get myself perked up though because it's the Good Life Festival in Sydney today. Hope I get to lock eyes with Will Sparks again.

* * *

Didn't see Will, but it's a good job because I couldn't even speak! The poor people I was meeting thought I was some Mutant Ninja Geordie. I was just croaking every time I tried to open my mouth.

Sunday 21st

@charlottegshore
I'm hungover hurt and needy 😞😞😞 someone wrap me up in a quilt like a burrito and give me love.

Gary's on the Gold Coast doing PAs tonight. He just sent me a message saying, 'Can't wait to see you tomorrow.' He said he's going to have a nap so I'll speak later.

Went to dinner with Ricci Guarnaccio. How perfect is it that he lives in Sydney now and I'm here too!? Usually it takes us months before we can see each other and this time it's only been a couple of weeks! We were reminiscing about how much fun it was in the house for the *Big Birthday Battle*. When I got back to the hotel I tried to ring Gary but he wasn't answering his phone. I texted him loads and they're not delivering. Weird. It's like he's turned his phone off. Maybe he slept through the whole day . . .

Monday 22nd

Got a text from Gary as soon as I woke up: 'I'm getting on my flight to Sydney, can't wait to see you! See you soon xxx.'

We're meeting at MTV because we're both doing a day of press. I can't wait to see his sexy hedgehog head. It feels like it's been about a million years.

* * *

Just got back from MTV. Saw Gary and it was all amazing, we were hugging and he was being really affectionate. I asked him why he hadn't picked up his phone last night and he said he'd been so tired that he'd slept right through.

Then, while I was sitting doing interviews, I got a message from Bree on WhatsApp asking, 'Are you free to talk?'

I knew instantly it was urgent because she never usually has anything serious to tell me. She sent another one: 'Are you with Gary?'

Fuck. I knew straight away this was bad. But I wasn't going to reply and say I was with Gary because I wanted to know right away what she had to say. So I lied.

'No . . . what is it?'

'Word around the Gold Coast is that Gary was out with a girl last night.'

My heart went funny. I felt sick. Was that why he didn't answer the phone last night?

'How do you know that, Bree?'

'Because the girl he was with works at the club I used to work at, she's a hostess. Blonde, exactly his type, walks around in her bra and knickers . . . he's known her for a while now, since he first started coming to the Gold Coast. They were seen at a restaurant I know. And everyone has been talking about it.'

What the fuck, man?!!

I was dying to say something to him but I couldn't because we were in the middle of an interview. I was sat there trying to smile and answer questions about an old series of *Geordie Shore* because they're so far behind us and my head was all over the place.

What is he playing at? We've been desperate to see each other this whole time! We've been texting and trying to meet up and then HE WENT OUT WITH A GIRL LAST NIGHT!!!

I was finished doing press earlier than him so I left and texted him straight away while he was still there.

'Gary, what did you do last night?'

'I told you! I went to sleep.'

'No what did you REALLY do last night?'

'What are you trying to say?'

It sounded to me from the way he was replying and the

pauses in between that he was starting to get nervous and was trying to squirm out of it.

'What are you talking about, Charlotte? I don't know what you mean.'

'Don't bother coming back to stay with me tonight, Gary.'

* * *

I'm so mad and upset. I can't stop crying. Why does this always happen?! We've booked the same hotel room while he's in Sydney but there's no way he's coming back here. I'm in bed, I've just locked the doors. He can't come in.

* * *

He keeps texting. He's on his way back . . .

'I'm coming to the room no matter what you say. You either let me in or I'll break my way in. I'll get another key from reception.'

I'm not getting out of bed. I'm not letting him in.

* * *

The man from reception let him in! I was lying in bed asleep and he had the cheek to get into bed and just start cuddling me! I was screaming at him, 'Gary! I know you took someone else out. It's you! Why would I not believe that?'

He kept saying, 'I didn't! I didn't!' but all the time he was saying it with this smug grin on his face as if he had done it and he knows that I know he's done it but I'm just going to get over it because there's nothing I can do about it anyway because he knows I've fallen for him again and I will forgive him. He knows how much I feel for him and he knows that I'll just let him get away with it because the alternative of not being with him is worse.

Tuesday 23rd

> @charlottegshore
> The last few days have been pretty shit so tonight I'm gonna get shit faced.

Wednesday 24th

Gary has convinced me he didn't do anything that night in the Gold Coast and that it's all been made up by shit-stirrers. I've started to believe him . . . He keeps denying it so much that I haven't got any choice but to think he's telling me the truth. But now I'm just paranoid all the time because it's been in my head that things aren't perfect between us and all my old emotions have come back and I feel like shit.

* * *

I'm just not enjoying myself any more. I feel rubbish and no matter how many times he tells me he only wants to be with me, I don't feel like I can trust him. We were only together in Sydney for a couple of days and now I'm obsessed with looking on Gary's Snapchat every second to see what he's doing. . . there are girls on there and I keep thinking, 'Has he taken you on a date?'

I miss my little pup, Baby, so much I could cry. Her cuddles make everything better.

Brand New Me

Saturday 27th

> @charlottegshore
> very excited for tonight, me and @hollygshore are at liquid in Rockingham.

Had a PA with Holly tonight and even though whenever we're getting ready to go out we always moan that we're tired and not in the mood, by the time we've been in the club about ten minutes and the tequilas have been downed we're lifting up our tops and jumping on tables! Sometimes I have to pinch myself that 'work' for me can mean having a great night out with one of my best mates, and meeting fans – I have the best fans!

Sunday 28th

> @charlottegshore
> I am sick of eating bad food when I'm drunk.

Holly, Chloe, Nathan and Kyle have gone to Bali and I still have to work because I've got stuff to do for In the Style. Not fair.

March 2016

Number of times I've had to think about house fixtures and fittings: I might as well have a tap tattooed on my forehead I've looked at that many different varieties! And as for tiles, maybe I could get a couple as earrings?

Suntan rating: Pretty tan good

Emojis to sum up the month: 🎉 🕺 💗 🌞 🏚 ⛏

Tuesday 1st

@TheMimmyWoman1
Came back to amazing changes in @charlottegshore house great team working on it. Plus @thediddyman1 doing fab job making me proud.

Mam and Dad are back home now while I finish the rest of my promotional work. Mam says the house is looking amazing but already she's on my case about making more decisions. Who knew there were so many different varieties of sinks? You would think a sink was normal but oh no. I'm being

75

pressured to pick a sink from one of my house-building bibles and it's giving me a headache. I can't believe how many variations of sink bowls there are – there are square ones, rectangle, circle, oblong, hexagon sinks, there are sinks that look like pebbles, sinks that look like baths. There are so many different shapes of sinks it's ridiculous!

Wednesday 2nd

@charlottegshore
I have had two hangovers today. How is that even possible?

Thursday 3rd

@TheMimmyWoman1
So I am now going through the change of life! It's friggin awful, retiring to bed in a right mood. Wearing just a top in minus temp.

Me mam's Twitter is ridiculous! She always talks about going through the menopause. It's her excuse for everything. She has the air con on in the car and I tell her I feel like I'm sitting in the North Pole. She just moans, 'You don't understand these hot flushes!'

Saturday 5th

Not long now 'til I get to see my little girlie pants. Baby, I miss you so much! I hope she hasn't forgotten me. I'm back home in a couple of days. Can't wait.

@charlottegshore
Packing my suitcase for the 116,767th time. STORY OF
MY LIFE

Sunday 6th

@charlottegshore
Anyone still awake? I'm bored on my flight . . . wanna follow
some people 💃

@charlottegshore
I'm nearly home. First thing I'm gonna do is get all my gym kit
ready for tomorrow and start the day with #3minuteBumBlitz

@charlottegshore
BANG I'M BACK..

Wednesday 9th

Gary came over and he's staying at mine for the next few
days. Mam is currently making us both eggs and bacon in
bed. He's being so lovely again. I feel really comfortable with
him here and he's getting on with Mam and Dad really well.
I think they might actually accept him as one of the family.

Mam's been made redundant from her job. She's been very
emotional about it. As usual, that means she's decided to tell
the world on Twitter.

@TheMimmyWoman1
Big day today closing the chapter on a job that brought me
amazing opportunities! Time to move to a new chapter new job!

@TheMimmyWoman1
Trying to look at my redundancy as a positive thing time for
a change but god it's going to be weird mind!

Thursday 10th

It's my court date for the drink-driving incident tomorrow.
I've been putting it out of my head. I didn't really take it in
when I got pulled over because I was so busy thinking about
having to go in to *Geordie Shore* for the birthday show the
next day. Gary's telling me not to worry but I can't help it,
I'm absolutely terrified.

What the hell do I wear to court?!

This is really serious. I've bought a long black skirt and
pointy shoes so I look sensible.

* * *

Gary's trying his hardest to make me feel better but I just
can't sleep. At all. Now I'm going to have mega bags under
my eyes. Maybe that's why some people wear shades when
they go to court?

Friday 11th

Thank God today is over. I just need a long bath now.

I had to have security with me. Kate organised it because she
said it would be a busy court and there would be paps about
so it would be chaos. It was Dave Duncan who normally does
security for *Geordie Shore*. I love Dave, he's seen me through
all the bad times, he's carried me in when I've been sick on
myself . . . so this was probably just a walk in the park for him.

When I saw him I told him I was really nervous and he said, 'Don't worry, just keep near me and I'll grab you.'

'Is it really going to be that bad?' I asked.

'Yeah, it is.'

'What the hell??'

I didn't know what to expect. I was really worried and full of dread. Why did I EVER do something like this? That's why it's good that these sort of punishments are about because it makes you realise that you really have done something bad and I never want to do anything like it again, or have to go to court. Dad was with me and was dead quiet all the way there, which made me feel even worse. I feel ashamed like I've really let him down and am an awful bad person. There were about fifteen paps outside – like something you see on the telly.

In the end I didn't wear the outfit I bought because I thought, 'Why am I dressing up? That's only going to draw more attention to myself.' I shouldn't have been so worried because when I got to court there were people in neon tracksuits! I walked in and there were proper charvas shouting, 'Charlotte! Charlotte! Can I have a picture?!' – like they thought we were at a PA or something! It was soul-destroying. There were loads of really sad people in there. I saw the skinniest man who looked like he hadn't had a meal in two years; he had a Fila tracksuit on and a cap and was standing in the corner bobbing up and down like he was listening to some kind of music (except there wasn't any music playing). It was creepy. I walked past him and he shouted, 'Charlotte, can I get a selfie?' I looked at the ground wishing it would swallow me up and walked on. I couldn't start getting selfies in court! But as I passed him I kept thinking, 'What's he going to do if I ignore him? What if he makes even more of a scene?' As I was walking further in, more and more people started coming up to me, recognising me. After a few minutes I'd formed this whole brigade of petty criminals! Luckily a kind woman saw what was happening – me looking like the Pied Piper of the courtroom – and said, 'Come on, Charlotte, come with me. We'll put you in a separate room.' She took my hand, 'We shouldn't really be doing this but we think it's necessary.' She was small and had chubby cheeks and a nice smile. She looked like she would be good at giving cuddles. She took me into a different room and I looked behind me and everyone had their phones out, shoving them in my direction snapping away. I wanted to cry!

After that I just waited and waited to go in. The court was a big white, cold and empty room. There were three people sitting in front of me, a few at the side but not many more. The public weren't allowed in, thank God. It all seems a bit of a blur now. I sat in this box thing and just started to cry and a woman had to come over and give me some tissues. . . I kept looking at me dad and I was so embarrassed. There was one person reading something about what had happened during 'the incident' and I felt really ashamed while they were talking. Why did I do it? What an idiot. It felt like it went on for ages but I think it was only about forty-five minutes. I got a fine, a ban for three years and told I had to do a course. I always knew it was going to be a minimum of three years but at one point I was warned it could be five . . . so I got the best outcome I could. My solicitor was really good and because I do a lot of work for charity, and get involved in different things like that, the court could see that I was more good than bad.

I kept looking at the magistrates wondering whether they knew who I was but they weren't giving anything away. I was thinking, 'I'm sure they don't watch *Geordie Shore*,' but then you'd be surprised who does watch it! Maybe they did!

Thank God it's all over. I never want to go through that again.

Saturday 12th

Didn't feel like doing anything tonight even though it's Saturday. After yesterday I don't want to have a drink again! Went to the gym and for a swim with Sophie, which was perfect. Now I'm tucked up in bed with wet hair. Rock 'n' roll.

Feel helpless without being able to drive my car. I actually am. How am I going to work? I think I might need to get a driver. Spoke to dad and he thinks I should employ Mam because she's lost her job. This could either be a very very brilliant idea or the worst one EVER.

Sunday 13th

Gary's been here at mine staying virtually every night. I feel so happy with him but at the same time I'm so scared about him going on *Ex on The Beach* next month. He says he has no choice but to go on the show. I'm so worried about it. I keep telling Kate that it's getting me so worked up. She's going to speak to MTV about it. There's a bigger picture here, surely they want us two to be together and make this relationship work.

Monday 14th

I have decided to officially give me mam a job as my PA and driver. Here's what me dad's got to say about it as it was his idea for me to give her the job. . .

A Few Words From Gary Crosby: Charlotte Appointing Her Mam As A PA

Charlotte has a habit of making life harder for herself, such as getting banned from driving (twice), getting removed from taxis by the police, waking up in a police cell, losing her phone, losing her credit card (ten times), amassing a clothing collection that twenty women could use, losing shoes and bags on nights out etc. The one person she has to support her in any recovery is her mam Letitia (apart from the credit card which falls on me). This has always been based on a mother-and-daughter bond, that special relationship based on loyalty and love. However, Charlotte has well and truly abused this over the years . . . 'Poor Letitia' is a common term used by Charlotte's friends when talking about her mother.

Supporting Charlotte comes naturally to Letitia, she is a wonderful mother. She is also a qualified support worker who has assisted young persons in her career. This came to an abrupt end in early 2016 due to redundancy, which coincided with Charlotte losing her driving licence. Not wanting to pre-empt any decisions Charlotte would make, there definitely seemed an opportunity to get Letitia more involved in her business.

Charlotte has become a very successful business woman, she has her own limited company and has many collaborations and income streams. I help out with the financial side – accounting, VAT, tax etc. – and she also has her accountants and management team to deal with the business side, but she is the final decision maker. It's hugely time-consuming as she needs to go to many meetings at various UK locations on top of all the travel she does for work – TV, PAs, promotions, etc.

Dad: So, your mam is not working with the support agency now. She is free to help out?

Charlotte: Well . . . I need a driver now [sad face and apologetic expression]

Dad: She can do that, but also assist you much more. Your business is growing each month and it's a lot to manage for you?

Charlotte: Well she did OK on eBay, selling my old clothes. She is a good packer! She is good at putting things in parcels and posting them.

Dad: Erm . . . I think she did a bit more than that??

Charlotte: [thinking long and hard] Yeah . . . she wrote the labels out too! Let me have a think . . .

Later that day, she sends her mam a WhatsApp message, not a single one, but split over six different messages delivered within seconds of each other. (That's how Charlotte likes to message you, so you pick up your phone and get really excited when you have nine messages, only to find its all of the same conversation!)

Charlotte: Mam, I've decided to employ you as my personal assistant. You will work for me. And be ready to serve my needs. Whenever I need. I will pay you a salary. And I will be your boss.

Letitia: [really excited, and only glad to help] Fantastic x x x So excited! I will be the best personal assistant ever. Can't wait to get started.

Charlotte: [in typical laidback style]: But me and Dad will monitor your performance for the first few months. See if your are up to the job. Me and Dad will have a board meeting about it.

So it became. Charlotte has appointed her mam as her PA.

The typical 'mother' duties remain: cleaning, washing clothes, ironing and, of course, tidying up the bedroom after a night of getting ready. Now she's also supporting her in making business appointments, arranging hotels, planning travel, coordinating her diary with Kate . . . and of course driving and packing parcels!

@TheMimmyWoman1
After today I go into a four-day countdown, exciting times ahead different but I hope exciting! God @charlottegshore gonna sack me every week!

Tuesday 15th

Gary's gone to Mexico for MTV to film *Spring Break with Grandad*. Spring break is basically a shagfest for Americans who go to a beach when they're on holiday from school or college and just get mortal and get off with everyone in sight. In the show each person who goes takes one of their grandparents, which is going to be mental. Gary is taking his grandad, Raymond. Not sure how I feel about him being out there but I have to trust him. And what can he really get up to with his grandad there?!

I just wish he wasn't going into *Ex on the Beach*. That's the thing that's making me most anxious.

There's a party for In The Style tomorrow so I've come down to London early to see Adam and Jamie before I go to Cape Verde for a detox with the girls. Was so excited when I saw them at their hotel that I got really pissed. They kept telling me they had an early start in the morning because there's so much to organise but I wouldn't listen when they tried to get me to leave and just got into bed with them. Must've fallen asleep because I can't remember much else.

Wednesday 16th

Adam was laughing so hard this morning because he said I fell asleep in the middle of him and Jamie then they both woke up at 2 a.m. soaking wet because I'd had an accident in the bed. Apparently I started putting pillows in the middle and lay back on top of them and carried on sleeping while they had to try and change the sheets around me!

Went to Boots to get the morning-after pill. I'd run out of my pill since Australia and me and Gary had sex just before he went to Mexico. I think I've left it a bit late but am within the 72-hour time frame you're meant to take it.

* * *

The In the Style party was fun and I didn't wet myself this time.

Thursday 17th

Off to Cape Verde with Sophie, Holly and Chloe and David, my trainer. I've lost count of the amount of times we've been out here. We always stay at the Melia Dunas Hotel in Sal, they always take fantastic care of us, they're a contact of Kate's. We come to create workouts or rehearse for the DVDs or just when we need a boost – that's why David comes with us. It's lovely out here but it's not like a holiday – it still feels like I'm working because David is constantly making me do squats! It's like a fitness excursion or a beach-shaped prison that keeps me away from all the boozy temptations of Newcastle. And stops me having late-night-hungover kebabs. Thank God my prison officer is someone I genuinely like! David and I are such good friends now.

Can't wait to get some SUNSHINE!

Friday 18th

Only been here a day and already I feel properly relaxed.

Here's a typical day. We've got all the beds into one room because we're used to sleeping in one room in *Geordie Shore* and don't like being apart. Both rooms have two single beds so we've got the two mattresses from the other room and now in this room there's a single bed, a mattress, a single bed and another mattress at the bottom. And all we do is scroll . . . you know when you scroll your phone? We love scrolling every hour of the day!

We'll be sunbathing and one of us will get too hot so we'll say, 'Shall we go inside for a scroll?'

We scroll every app: Snapchat, Instagram, Twitter and the *Daily Mail*. We all talk about the things we scroll past: 'Have you seen this?'

'No! Whereabouts? Oh there, OK I'll scroll.'

Chloe never goes on the *Daily Mail* because she's not interested so we have to tell her who's on there.

We'll scroll in the evening too. Everyone else is out in the bars and we're just lying in bed scrolling, no telly, we just scroll! We might get some crisps as a treat and we'll end up scrolling till 1 a.m. The problem is you always see more things to scroll so you can end up there for hours. There's always someone new to scroll and you end up stalking people . . . you'll see that your ex is dating someone so you'll go on to her and then her friends. . . it's like a family tree of scroll.

Charlotte's Guide To: Scrolling

1. Make a fake account, it's so much easier to stalk all the people who may have blocked you. Always make your fake account's name utterly ridiculous! My last fake account was called: SARAH BANJO CLIT (trust me, they will never suspect).

2. NEVER like their photos. Now this tip is a hard one to follow and, believe me, there has been many a time I have accidentally liked a photo or sent a friend request. The sheer panic afterwards is just not worth it! Make sure you keep those wandering fingers very, very steady.

3. REMEMBER TO ALWAYS SCROLL THROUGH ALL
APPS. My daily scroll involves: Instagram, Facebook,
Twitter, Snapchat, *Daily Mail*. This is a warning to
you forgetful scrollers: if you do miss an app you will
have a strange feeling that you have forgotten something all day. You know like that feeling you get when
you think you have forgotten to lock the door? Or
when you think you might have left your phone in
the house? Well it's exactly like that, when in actual
fact you just forgot to go on Instagram and check what
your ex's new girlfriend 'Jade' has had for breakfast!
Be WARNED.

Saturday 19th

We've made up a song about scrolling. We changed the words
from the song. 'They See Me Rollin'' to 'they see me scrollin''.
Once we got going the lyrics started getting really good . . .
'I'm on tagged photos from 24 weeks ago.' There's a bit about
how you've liked someone's Instagram by accident: 'We're
gonna get a notification! We're gonna get a notification!'
We performed the song to David – he was dead impressed.
I think we should release it.

* * *

We were in a scrolling session just after our lunch and I found
out Mitch has got a new girlfriend! This is the first time he's
had one. I am gutted.
I've scrolled him pretty much every day for about six
months and there's never been any evidence of other girls,
no tweets, no tags in photos, no mentions, nothing. I was so

close to Mitch and haven't been like that with a boy in a long time – we were like best friends. I've scrolled him casually ever since and because I haven't seen anything I've felt secure in the fact that I've never had to see anything that could hurt me.

AND NOW IT'S HAPPENED.

He put a picture up of him and this girl and I can tell it's his girlfriend by the comments. Then I saw another one of them out for a meal and I started looking at hers and I saw LOADS of pictures of Mitch on there. She's very orange though. She looks like a Wotsit with hair. But she's not ugly, and I think that's what hurts the most.

I didn't cry straight away, I just said to the others, 'I think Mitch has got a new girlfriend.' Then I started getting teary-eyed. David turned to me and said, 'Charlotte, are you getting upset? Are you going to cry?' He'd never seen me cry before. He gave me a hug and that was it.

* * *

I've been crying ever since.

It's just hard to see that he's finally met someone and I know that she must mean a lot to him for him to post about her because he doesn't do that lightly. For the last six months he's kept quiet and now it must be serious. The girls said it was bound to happen and also that I've got Gary so why am I bothered about it? I don't know. But it's so weird that it's the end of an era. Mitch has got someone else now. It makes me feel really flat.

@charlottegshore
Everything is pissing me off 😠

89

Monday 21st

We usually organise to get some pictures done while we're here – it's far better doing it that way, when you have control over the ones they're taking, than getting caught out! No matter how secluded and private you think a holiday is there's always a sneaky pap hidden under a flip-flop somewhere. And it's really annoying because, no matter how good shape you're in, the photographer's not trying to get you at your best angle. He's always trying to take the picture when you're bent over or you're sat down and have a couple of rolls of flab showing. Who doesn't have rolls when they're sat down?!

Tuesday 22nd

It's Gary's birthday today. Wonder what he's getting up to? He's with his grandad so he can't be doing that much . . . can he? I miss him so much.

I spoke to the girls about how it's been going and how we're going to make a go of it. He's convinced them he's serious about me which is good because it's so hard being with him when no one else is on our side or thinks it's going to work.

@charlottegshore
So it's Derby day tomorrow 😔 sadly Gary is filming and hasn't got his phone so I'm not going to be able to torture him when we WIN again!

Derby Day is a famous day in Sunderland and Newcastle where the two football teams play each other and we always wind each other up saying Newcastle will win but they never ever do – it's always Sunderland.

Wednesday 23rd

The sun's not out and I've got a lot of energy to vent. I haven't been on the booze so there's no excuse not to go to the gym. We've only got pissed on one evening. We've been quad-biking and horse riding. Anyone who watches us on *Geordie Shore* would be shocked – and ridiculously bored – if they could see what we get up to here! There's only two bars in the resort and it's pretty chilled, which is why I like it. I haven't been on a proper piss-up holiday since Dubai with Mitch. I want my next holiday to be in Barbados. I've never been before but it looks so good, there're loads of nice hotels and Simon Cowell always seems to be on a jet ski with his hairy chest flying about the sea.

Thursday 24th

I miss Gary. I want kisses. I wonder what he's up to? And how's poor Raymond coping?!

Friday 25th

So excited about the release of my fitness book *Live Fast, Lose Weight*. I've had to keep it such a secret but we're announcing it in a couple of days. I hope it does as well as the last book. I've loved doing all the recipes for it. Made me feel like Jamie Oliver. Or Jools Oliver. I'll be doing another two-week book tour around the UK, which will be brilliant because I get to meet the people who've bought it and I have such funny fans.

Saturday 26th

Gary got his phone back for one day and has been messaging saying how much he misses me. I am buzzing.

Sunday 27th

Home from Cape Verde. Baby got so many cuddles she nearly couldn't breathe. I have missed her sooo much!! I can't even imagine life without that girl. I only got her last year and she has completed my life.

Mam told me she went on a date night with Dad the other day and in the middle of dinner he announced that he thought they should get back home to the dog! Even he's fallen in love with Baby. Everyone has. I think we need to get a little sister for her. It's only fair so she doesn't get lonely when people go out on dates.

@charlottegshore
It's Easter weekend and I haven't been out or had a drop of alcohol. WHO EVEN AM I ANYMORE??!

All I've done all day is do loads of washing, was in bed by 9.30 p.m. and now I've just woken up at 4.30 a.m. with jet lag so I'm hanging it all out to dry. I've got to pack my cases again for London tomorrow.

Charlotte's Guide To: Living Out Of A Suitcase

This one is a crucial one for me as I'm ALWAYS living out of a suitcase. I'm usually on the train on my way to London, spending three weeks away from home, with two cases and one holdall! Train-hopping and flying with all of these bags can be a nightmare – this is why my first tip is to master the art of NOT TRAVELLING LIGHT (LOL). Make sure you always have the cases with four wheels – the modern ones that can move in any direction when you push them. This is the key to travelling with two cases. By having the four wheels you can just push each case either side of you in each hand, balancing the holdall on top of one of the cases.

It's actually got to the point where I have learnt not to wear underwear. Living out of cases and in and out of hotels means there's never a chance to wash all those extra garments. So I just go au naturel now and it frees up more case space.

Monday 28th

Got the train down to London and Mam had packed those three brochures in my bag so I could look at taps and tiles! Everyone else was on the train reading something fun like *heat!* or *OK!* or even *Fifty Shades of Grey*. And I had to sit there with *Tile of the Year* magazine.

* * *

Gary's back in the UK.

I've just seen a story about him and there's a picture of him squeezing Miss Nottingham's bum. I don't know what went on but I'm so angry and upset. I can't speak to him.

Spoke to Kate, she's trying to get hold of his agent to find out what happened. I feel so upset. What's he doing? What the hell is he going to be like in *Ex on the Beach*? I can't have him going on that show. It's driving me mad thinking about it.

I've messaged Gary all day and he's just being really dismissive and almost angry. He's saying nothing went on and

94

I need to calm down and that it was a party back at his after a PA and loads of people were there. It's making me feel like shit.

Tuesday 29th

I've seen on Snapchat that he's been making a dig about it. He's been trying to explain himself because of the stories, and having a go at me, but he hasn't had the decency to call me and explain to my face! How can this be happening all over again?

> @charlottegshore
> All I want is to be in my new house with little Baby and the new doggie addition and my life will be complete.

Wednesday 30th

Was a guest on *Celebrity Juice*. I love being on that show, but this time I got really emotional when Keith asked me about Gary. Melissa had come with me and was in the audience and she said after she could tell I was about to cry because she knows me so well. I didn't expect to get upset but I just can't handle it at the moment. I laughed at first and then I started blubbing and Keith thought I was joking and said, 'Oh shit, is that real?' It was OK in the end and we managed to have a laugh about it afterwards. I said I didn't mind if they kept it in because that would at least show people I don't want to talk about it any more and that I'm genuinely upset about Gary.

Thursday 31st

Kate sent me a message to say she's been in touch with Gary's agent Kay, to try to get this whole thing resolved. He says he hasn't been able to get hold of Gary at all but that 100 per cent he wasn't trying to get with the girl, it was just a party back at the hotel because a load of the old *Ex on the Beach* cast were at a PA beforehand. Kay said that, apparently, 'Gary's head is wrecked with the mixed messages from Charlotte.' They are trying to get a summit meeting in for the four of us. I need to know what's going on before he goes away for *Ex on The Beach*. Kate also told me she spoke to MTV about it and they told her they aren't forcing Gary to do anything.

It's his decision whether he goes on the show. Why is he doing this to me??

April 2016

Number of nights spent lying in pain next to me mam: Too many (but I'm so glad she was there)

Number of times I cried over Gary: I have literally lost count

Number of times Michael Jackson kept me awake: Five

Emojis that sum up this month: 😭 😭 😭

Friday 1st

> @TheMimmyWoman1
> I woke up to the most amazing voice message from my daughter @charlottegshore it brought tears to my eyes.

I told me mam how much I loved her, she deserves it and I like doing that sometimes.

I've written a draft in the notes of my phone of what I want to say to Gary before he goes on *Ex on the Beach*. We have to shoot the advert for the *Big Birthday Battle* series of *Geordie Shore* in a few days and I haven't even spoken to him yet. I'm so worried about everything. I just want a chance to tell him how I feel before he goes.

The problem that I have is I'm trying to move forward and I feel like you are moving backwards.

I spoke to you once while you were in Mexico, once that was it! It was an absolute joke! And then when I did go out of my way to text you after I tried to WhatsApp and DM you on Twitter I got no reply. I honestly feel like you're not really even that arsed if I'm honest.

When I go into something I go into it 100%. I make that person my priority and I love them unconditionally. They come first in everything I do! That's why I have held back with you, because I don't think you would do the same for me! While you were in Mexico and weren't allowed to use your phone you could have told any amount of people to get in touch with my and let me know the situation but NO. You could have told Andy, Becca, Eddie, Joe Deen, Josh! They all have my number, they could have passed a message on!!!!!!

Now you expect me to sit around and wait for you while you go on *Ex on the Beach*. I DO NOT THINK SO. I will flip a lid! It's not like any normal relationship, Gary! I'm twenty-six years old! And I am about to move into my own house and I won't be sat around worrying about the boy who says he wants to see how things are going with me but is going on a dating show! I'm older now, Gary. I'm not wasting precious time in my life on something which is some big JOKE.

Five years we have been going around in these circles. I won't have it go on any longer. It's fucking pathetic.

Saturday 2nd

Still haven't spoken to Gary and it's killing me. I just want it to go back to how it was and for us to be properly boyfriend and girlfriend. If it can't work this time, when can it work?

Sunday 3rd

We're filming the the *Big Birthday Battle* advert tomorrow. I haven't even seen Gary or spoken to him! I called Kate and begged her to come to the shoot because I'm scared of how he will be. She's getting on a 6 a.m. train.

Monday 4th

As soon as Gary walked into the studio for the shoot we instantly forgot about the rows and any hurt. It was like it all melted away because it didn't mean anything. I felt so relieved. He's going to Thailand to film *Ex on the Beach* tomorrow and all day I kept thinking about it. I want us to be together. I wanted to take him to one side and talk to him to see where we were at because he's now going on a dating show and I want to know if he's going to get with anyone! But there were people around all day and I couldn't speak to him privately. He was so lovely to me though, it felt like nothing else mattered. We were all over each other and it was on our Snapchat too so there's no hiding things now! We were kissing and kissing and I think everyone else got a bit 'Leave it out, you pair!' but I don't care.

Kate left at about 2 p.m. because she could see everything was OK between us. I told her I was so grateful she'd come. She is the best.

Before she left I asked her if she could get me some paracetamol. All through the filming of the advert I've had the worst period pains of my entire life. (Can't believe I've got my period when I have one final night with Gary before he goes to Oz – great!) It's like a stomach cramp I've never experienced, I think it's because I took the morning-after pill when I got back from Australia . . . but it's *really* killing me. No one on set seemed to be listening though – I think everyone thought I was hungover.

As the day got near the end, I started to panic about Gary. I kept thinking, 'If I want to make a go of this then I've got to say something now because he's going away and I don't want him to do anything bad!' I'm willing to put all the rumours about other girls in the past and just try and start again. It's just about us and it's now or never.

* * *

I can't even describe the pain, it's awful. It's going down my leg to the point that I can't walk at times. Luckily most of the advert has been based around us in a bed so I haven't had to move!

* * *

Gary came to stay at mine and tonight I made my first sandwich for a boy! It only took me twenty-six years! It was ham and cheese with some little cherry tomatoes – I was under strict instructions to lather the butter thickly on the bread. I don't like butter on my sandwiches, but I was pretty impressed by it.

I took my time – about twenty minutes – and I was generous with the ham. I'm very proud of my little sandwich. And Gary loved it.

In bed I tried to broach the conversation about him going on *Ex on the Beach*. At first when I tried to talk to him he seemed a bit off and dismissive: 'I don't know what's going to happen, Charlotte.'

I said, 'Gary I will be so hurt if you get with anyone else, I thought we were going to give this a go. We've spent so much time together, it's nothing like before, we've been sleeping at each other's houses and going for meals. We've never been this close, ever. I've never been this close to you, I thought we were going to give it a go?'

But he still wouldn't commit to anything and wouldn't say he definitely *wouldn't* get with anyone. He just shrugged. 'I'm probably not.' That's not what he said last time!

I felt so awful and started crying, 'But it would really hurt me.' I thought perhaps if he knew how I felt and how much I cared then he might not do anything. Then my tears turned to anger. I said, 'OK then, if you're going to get with someone out there, just tell me now because I'm not going to sit at home and wait for you like a mug.'

Suddenly he looked at me and his facial expression changed, like he was a whole different person. He seemed almost surprised. 'Why? *Would* you wait for us then?'

'Well of course I'll wait for you!!' I said and gave him a massive kiss.

It was such a wonderful, amazing moment. He told me he isn't going to get with anyone.

As we were lying in bed just about to go to sleep, he gave me a kiss and held my hand, then we drifted off to sleep.

Tuesday 5th

Got up early to get the train together to London. I had to do an In The Style press day and Gary flew off to Thailand. We had a massive kiss and cuddle goodbye and were papped and it went in the *Daily Mail*. So now it's no secret, everyone can see that we're together! I love him so much and I know, deep down, I always have. It's only ever been him. Even when I was with Mitch. Deep down, it's always been about Gary. God, I hope it works this time. I can't bear the thought of him on *Ex on the Beach* with all those other girls but I have to trust him, otherwise what's the point?

The pains didn't seem too bad this morning but this afternoon they got bad again. They just keep coming and going, I think I need to just go to bed and sleep them off.

* * *

I miss Gary already, can't believe he's now on the other side of the world. I just have to trust him though.

* * *

Wednesday 6th

So much work to do this week! I have to do the launch of my new Easilocks Miracle Makeover hair range and YouTube tutorials, and I've got a shoot coming up with the *Sun* for my fitness book. The pains came back even worse today and I feel like I've done nothing but moan and complain to people all day. But they're so, so bad.

* * *

Looked in my knickers when I went to the loo and noticed my bleeding wasn't the same as a normal period where you get clots and it's thick; it was almost like cranberry juice – really thin and light red. Kate keeps saying I should go to the doctor but there's no time. I'm too busy. The paracetamol helps anyway. It must just be REALLY BAD period pains. I'm never taking the morning-after pill again if this is what it does. Gary has been messaging me in between flights saying he wishes he was here with me. I miss him.

Thursday 7th

I had a personal training session this morning with Richard but the pain is still there. We've been doing kettlebell swings and it's never hurt so much down the side of my belly.

* * *

Gary's got a day before he has to go into filming so we've been able to message each other. It's all much stronger between us now, we feel closer than we've ever been before. We've been talking about everything we're going to do when he gets out, we're going on holiday together somewhere remote and amazing where no one can bother us and I can't wait. One of his texts says, 'I will not get with anyone,' and I totally believe him. We're going to have a proper relationship. I am going to give it my whole heart . . .

* * *

Tonight the pains were horrendous. I was having my nails and hair done because I've got a big shoot with the *Sun* tomorrow and I was on the phone to Kate crying. Kate kept saying, 'If it's that bad then you need to go to A&E!' But how can I go to A& E when I've got a photo shoot tomorrow? Who's going to do that photo shoot for me? I need to be there.

I know it sounds a dream to have your nails and hair done but it's not, it's a task and I am in pain. I don't want to sit for four hours getting my hair and nails done! I want to be in bed! If it was up to me I would walk around looking a mess every single day but I've got to look nice to be on camera. It's not always a pleasure in life!

Kate is insistent that if it's that bad I really do need to go to hospital. I feel like maybe even she thinks I'm lying now. She told me to ask Shane from Easilocks where the nearest A&E is and she will meet me there. But the fact of the matter is I can't turn up to a shoot with no hair on my head. I've been taking four paracetamol and four ibuprofen at a time. You're not allowed to take that much but it's the only thing that seems to be helping.

Got back to the hotel and rang Kate again. The painkillers have kicked in. 'I'm not going to the hospital, it's died down. I'll have a sleep. That means I can get through tomorrow's shoot and I'll sort it out afterwards,' I said.

'Well as long as you're sure.'

In bed and started Googling 'pains' 'period' 'stomach' 'bloating' 'bleeding'. . . and some stuff has come up about pregnancy. I keep seeing words like 'miscarriage' and 'ectopic'.

CAN'T.
DEAL.
WITH.
THIS.

Friday 8th

When I woke up the pains were back again, only a trillion times worse.
    WHY DO I HAVE TO DO THIS PHOTO SHOOT?

* * *

I feel so bloated. I had to wear these swimsuits and they all felt like they were cutting into me; I was so tender everywhere. All I was doing was moaning and moaning – the photographer must have hated me. I just kept saying, 'Can we get these pictures done as quickly as possible?' We were trying to get a doctor to come to the shoot, but we were over in Kingston-on-Thames, so we cut back on the number of shots so we could finish earlier and Kate booked a doctor to meet me at my hotel in London.

I had to wear a panty pad because the Tampax was hurting too much to stay in. And I kept thinking, 'This is the worst period EVER.' I was having to smile for the photos while inside I was just wincing and crying.

We finished the shoot and got in the car to head back to the hotel. As we were driving along I was thinking about what I'd seen on Google. 'No doctor who comes to the hotel is going to be able to see what the real issue is here.' The pains were so bad. I was crying and crying in the car and I just couldn't move.

Kate saw how much pain I was in. She knew that there was a private A&E walk-in department at the St John and St Elizabeth hospital, which wasn't too far away, so we headed straight there.

I went in and was seen by a doctor straight away. I explained what had been happening over the last week, that I'd been getting pains that were much worse than my usual period pains and that the bleeding looked different too. I also told her that I'd taken the morning-after pill but that it was one I'd never taken before, a 72-hour one.

She immediately made me do a pregnancy test then said, 'You're pregnant. It's either ectopic or a miscarriage.' Then she put a drip in my arm and said, 'We can't get you onto a ward until there's a bed free.'

It doesn't feel real. This can't be happening.

I know the baby was Gary's; he's the only person I've slept with since I came out of the *Geordie Shore* house in January.

I just remember the doctor's face looking so tense which started stressing me out. She said, 'If it's ectopic you might need to have an operation, it's so so serious . . . how long have the pain's been going on?'

I said, 'It's been a week.' She looked shocked.

'We need to get you seen straight away.' She couldn't believe it. 'How on earth have you dealt with it?'

Then Kate walked into the room and I said, 'I'm pregnant.'

Her first reaction was to put her arms out and say, 'Wow! Congratulations!'

'I'm either miscarrying or it's ectopic.'

'Oh my God, no.'

* * *

When I finally got onto a ward I met the gynaecologist who said, 'I'm going to walk you over for a scan so we can see exactly what's happened inside.'

But I just felt so weak . . . 'I don't think I can walk.' I was in so much pain.

He looked at me like I was stupid. 'We'll get you a wheel-chair then.'

So he put me in a wheelchair and as he was pushing me along I felt myself going really faint. Apparently I slid out of the wheel-chair on to the floor and was fitting. I just remember feeling like I was underwater. My ears felt weird and I had this cold sweat, then I went heavy and felt like I was falling. I was getting carried . . . I could hear voices . . . then I fell onto the floor again and onto the bed. It was so scary, I was petrified. I didn't know what the hell was going on and I was in so much pain.

Kate told me afterwards that when that happened she was the most frightened she's ever been. She said she couldn't believe that I'd got through the whole of the last week while this was going on inside me.

* * *

The scan showed my fallopian tube had ruptured. That's what all the pain was and it revealed how much damage it had caused. Because I'd left it a week before coming to the hospital it had actually torn open the tube so the bleeding I was seeing was internal bleeding. The gynaecologist said, 'It's so dangerous. If you'd have left it any longer there's a chance that you could actually have died.'

It was when he told me the next bit that I just burst into tears. He said, 'We're going to have to remove your fallopian tube.'

I was so scared that I wasn't going to be able to have babies. I was crying and crying. I was just so frightened and overwhelmed . . . I want to have children so much. He reassured me that I will still be able to have children but I'll just have to try a little bit harder. And he said I have to keep an eye on it because if it was to recur then I'll have to get my other fallopian tube removed and I've only got that one now . . .

I couldn't even lift my head off the pillow. I got taken to the surgery and I wanted it to be over. I was just so scared. When I was put on the operating table I felt so relieved. I wanted to be put to sleep because I wanted it all to be over.

Saturday 9th

When I woke up it was the worst pain of my whole life – I was screaming – because they apparently pump your belly full of air so they can see inside you during the surgery. Obviously the air has nowhere to go so it travels up into your shoulders and gets trapped! It feels like I've woken up and someone has stabbed two daggers in my shoulder blades.

* * *

Me mam is here with me now, she rushed down on the train. I'm still in so much pain I had to have one of the injections you have when you're in labour, something called pethidine. It zonks you out . . .

* * *

I'm convinced the ectopic pregnancy was partly to do with the morning-after pill. You have a 72-hour gap to take it and I took it quite late into that time. It didn't work and that's why it got trapped in the fallopian tube. I didn't realise it could be such a serious thing.

* * *

I want to tell Gary, but he's just gone into filming. He doesn't have his mobile phone because they get taken away from you. I can't even talk to him about it. I don't know what to do. He's the only person I want to speak to. I'm going through this massive thing and I can't even ring him to tell him. And the pains are still really bad.

Kate rang Craig Orr – who's high up at MTV – when I was in surgery. She was crying on the phone to him telling him Gary needed to know, that he needed to come home. Craig said he would get in touch with Gary but because of the time difference I can't speak to him until the morning.

I've lost so much blood from the surgery that they were going to give me a transfusion but in the end they put me on iron tablets. It meant I get really dizzy all the time. The doctor said it takes about a month to regenerate the blood you've lost.

* * *

I'm feeling really down, I'm in pain and I feel awful. I look a mess and feel rank.

Sunday 10th

The pain in my shoulders is still there. The doctor says it takes a few days to go because you need to walk it off in order to get the air travelling back through your body and I can't walk because of the surgery. I can't move!

Mam and I are going to stay with Kate, at her partner's, for a couple of days while I rest. I'm not allowed to go home.

The doctor said we were crazy to think I could sit in a car for six hours after the delicate surgery I've had, so I'm stuck in London. Mam has to help me to the toilet because I can't even get out of bed. I feel really weird and embarrassed that Mam has to see me go through all this. It's bad enough that I got pregnant by Gary but for her to have to look after me makes me feel awful.

* * *

I finally got to speak to Gary. I told him everything and was crying down the phone and he was being so lovely. He kept saying the kindest things to me and it made me feel so, so much better. He said, 'I don't care how many fallopian tubes you've got, I will always stick by you.' And he was saying stupid things to make me laugh like, 'I'll make sure I have sex with you as much as I can to get you pregnant!' He's talking like we're in a proper relationship and I feel so much happier.

* * *

All I've been doing is lying in bed with my laptop while Mam has been flopped beside me constantly scrolling on Booking. com for apartments. We can't stay here the whole time, it's not fair. But Mam has been driving me insane, she's been on the computer for hours! At one point I shouted, 'Why does it take you that long to find an apartment, Mam?'

She said, 'I just want to get us a good one. We're going to be there a while so I want to make sure it's nice for you.'

'Mam – that's all you've been doing for the last nine hours – it can't take you that long!'

In the end I grabbed the computer off her and said, 'I'll do it! Let's see how long it takes me!'

I found one in Leicester Square, central – 'There – looks fine! What do you think?'

'Well, yeah, I guess it looks alright.'

'Just book it then.'

'OK . . . it's done. We're going tomorrow.'

Monday 11th

Moved to the 'apartment' we'd booked in Leicester Square. I could hardly walk because of the pain I was in, the doctor says I'm anaemic and although I'm on iron tablets, I get really faint and can't stand for very long. As we arrived, I saw this really run-down building. There were three homeless people sat outside on the floor asking for money and I nearly collapsed on them. I didn't know what we were heading into. I stood waiting in the corridor while Kate and me mam tried to get in. I looked around and thought, 'Oh God, I can't look at Mam because I know she's going to say, "I told you so." We opened the door and it was just AWFUL.

There is just one double bed and you can see the springs through the mattress. There's a little round table and a tiny kitchen and a telly that's the size of a plate.

AND WE'RE STUCK IN HERE FOR A WEEK.

Kate's face just dropped and as she and Mam put our bags down, everyone just went silent. Kate whispered, 'Right, OK, where's the toilet then?' We searched around for the toilet and finally found a door that opened to what can only be described as a small cupboard. The shower cubicle is like half a shower – you have to stand sideways to get in – and there's some sort of loo in there. I don't know what the hell I've done.

* * *

MTV have let me speak to Gary at 2 p.m. every day. His phone call is the only thing I care about. It's the only thing I can muster up any energy for. It's the only thing I look forward to. Gary just tells me about his day and what's been going on and I sit and listen to him and tell him I miss him and wish he was here. He asked if I wanted him to come home but I told him he should stay there because I knew the cast and crew would all need an explanation if he left, and I wasn't ready for everyone to know.

I've had lot of time to lie and think about things this last few days and all I can think is, 'What if I can't ever have kids?'

* * *

Scotty T keeps texting me asking if I want to go for dinner and I can't because I'm bedbound. In the end, I had to tell him why. I think he struggled to know what to say. He just replied, 'Shit . . . hope you're OK.'

* * *

It's fair to say our apartment is in the heart and soul of the city because you can hear the heart and soul screaming at you everywhere you move. Oh, and there's a Michael Jackson musical on and it's RIGHT OUTSIDE THE WINDOW.

We got into bed and Kate texted, 'Why don't you come back here?'

But I was adamant. 'No, it's perfectly fine, I've got a bed and a toilet, that's all I need.' I couldn't admit defeat.

Mam keeps trying to get little digs in about the size of the apartment by saying stuff like, 'Oh right, I'll just try and fit into this shower then, shall I?'

* * *

I'm in so much pain from the surgery and every time I close my eyes I can either hear Michael Jackson or I think a car is about to drive on top of me. The beeps are so loud! The men on the rickshaws outside might as well be living in this place with us too we can hear every bit of conversation they're having with their drunk customers.

At one point Mam and I were lying in bed and it went silent. Then she turned to me and said, 'You know what, love, sometimes I just feel like Michael Jackson is in this bed with us,' and we both just burst out laughing! It's the first time we've laughed for ages. We laughed and laughed and laughed. We couldn't stop. We laughed so hard that it hurt. I felt like when I was at school and someone would say something under their breath and you wouldn't be able to control the giggles. Every time we tried to close our eyes and go to sleep one of us would start again and we'd just be in fits. At that moment I thought, 'I'm so glad I booked such a shit apartment because that's what's made this whole thing funny and we will remember it forever now. Out of all the bad that's happened we can still find the fun. It's a real moment I'll never forget. Like sunshine through dark clouds.

@charlottegshore

I ate a huge Cadbury's chocolate bar. I watched every housewives on TV. I browsed Women's Health then ate pringles. G'night.

Tuesday 12th

Woke up and it's like a massive cloud has lifted. We've actually started to have the best time in this apartment now. We still can't stop laughing. This morning we were drinking our cups of tea in the rickety bed and every time we moved the bed squeaked. It sounds like there's a budgie in the room. So now we just look at each other and say, 'Oh, there's that budgie again!'

The doctor told me I need to get on the move to get rid of all the air inside me. It's still sooooo painful . . . It feels like I have two knives stabbing down inside me. But the doctors say the only way to get rid of it is to start walking about so the air can start travelling back down and come out of me. (I presume it will emerge in farts or maybe squeeze out of my fairy hole.) I have been trying to walk to the smoothie shop down the road from the apartment. It's next to the big screens in Piccadilly Circus. It's not far but it's so hard just to make it there. Mam has to hold me up on the way back because I get so dizzy and out of breath.

Showering hasn't been easy either – especially with the half shower!

* * *

Gary's been asking me if I want him to come back but I told him he's in there for a reason and it's work, he should get the show out of the way.

I said, 'Try and come back a bit earlier, don't do it all . . . maybe come back halfway through, just leave.'

And he said, 'Yeah I will.'

I wish he'd leave now though. I need him here with me. I don't want to go through this on my own. Marnie and Sophie are in London tomorrow and want to meet up. I'll try and go out for a meal if I can. Don't know how I'm going to physically do it but I have to get out of bed! All I'll have to do is sit there on a comfy chair.

* * *

Aaron messaged me asking where I was and if I was OK as he had texted the other day and I hadn't replied so he thought something must be wrong. He knows I'm worried about Gary being on *Ex on the Beach*. I told him what had happened but made him promise not to tell anyone. It was so good to chat

115

with him and after I'd explained it all he said there was no way Gary would get with anyone now. And he would chin him if he did! He reckons there's going to be little mini Charlottes and Garys running wild ten years from now.

David Gest has died. I'm gutted. I'm glad he's not been on telly while it happened though. It would be worse to be watching him and then for him to suddenly get torn out of my life.

Wednesday 13th

I'm slowly starting to feel like I have more energy now and like I can move about a bit more. Mam went out to the shops to get some food and I was sat on the bed bored so I decided to message Mitch and ask if he wanted a catch-up. I told him I wasn't very well and I'd been in hospital. I think about him a lot and I feel like I want to see him even though I know he's got a girlfriend. He said, 'I can't come for food, it's not fair on my girlfriend. We can't speak, we can't see each other, you can't message me any more.'

I got really upset. 'Why can't we just catch up? Just as friends? We don't have feelings for each other any more so what's the big deal?'

Then he said, 'Look why can't you just fuck off with Gary, you're seeing him now, aren't you?' He sounded really jealous to me.

I replied, 'Why are you even saying that if you're not bothered?'

'Look, he's only going to fuck you over.'

I got really defensive. 'Gary would never do that to me. He knows I'm poorly at the minute but he's working so as soon as he's back he will come and see me. He would never do that to me, he loves me and cares about me, we've known each other for five years. He would never hurt me like that.'

'Look, Charlotte – he shags all the time. I know loads of girls he's shagged.'

'You're lying, let's just stop speaking. Block me from WhatsApp. It's too hard for me knowing that now you're so happy you don't want to speak to me or even be friends any more.'

We had a massive argument and I deleted all his messages. I never want to see him again. I was really upset afterwards though; I couldn't stop crying. When Mam came back from the shops it must've looked like I'd been attacked by the ghost of Michael Jackson.

I feel like such an idiot.

Wish I had stayed in bed and never, ever moved.

* * *

THEN THINGS GOT A MILLION TIMES WORSE.

I felt like I could cope with having some food so we went to Gilgamesh. It was me, me mam, Marnie, Sophie and Marnie's agent who also looks after a girl who was in *Ex on the Beach*. We all ordered our food and I said to Marnie, 'So do you know anything about what's happened out there with the filming? Have you heard anything?'

She looked at me, stony-faced, 'Please don't do this to me, Charlotte.'

My heart dropped. I felt sick. Like I was going to faint. As if I'd been run over by a train. I actually thought: 'I know what's coming.'

How? When? Why? He's been on the phone to me every day!

I looked at Marnie and begged, 'You can't do that now, you've got to tell me.'

She said, 'I just don't want to upset you when you're not very well.'

'Please just tell me, Marnie!!' I pleaded. I felt wobbly and thought I was going to faint.

In the end she said, 'Well, he slept with someone on the first night.'

On the first night? Why? It hurt so much. He'd told me he wasn't going to go with anyone else. We'd planned to go away together. So why do it on THE FIRST NIGHT??!

I couldn't eat.

Mam was so, so angry. She's let that boy back into our house, she'd been so lovely to him and she'd accepted him again.' She was absolutely furious, everyone was.

WHY??

HOW??

I can't stop crying. What the hell?

* * *

Can't sleep. Can't stop thinking about him with another girl. . . Marnie told me who it was that he slept with and it makes it even worse. Not only has he slept with someone when he told me he wouldn't, but it's someone I HATE.

I know he didn't know but I can't stop thinking how the night that I was in surgery getting my fallopian tube taken out, he was sleeping with HER.

I rang Aaron. He couldn't believe it. 'He wouldn't dare; you can't be right!?' he said. He was adamant it had to be a lie. 'Gary would never do that.'

'Aaron, believe me, it's true'

Thursday 14th

I've got my 2 p.m. phone call with Gary. I don't know whether to tell him on the phone or to just hold it back so I can keep speaking to him every day . . . I can't bear this to be true and for it to all be over. These phone calls are all that's been keeping me going, I cling to them. They're part of my daily routine. The painkillers make me really drowsy so I wait till I've spoken to Gary and then take them. I can sleep better once I've spoken to him.

If I tell him then we're going to have a huge argument and he's going to go off and start sleeping with more girls. I feel so poorly and so sick, I can't even stand up. He is the only person I want to speak to because it's our thing . . . this baby was about us. I'm having to go through it all alone and I just don't want to be hurt any more. Maybe if I don't tell him then hopefully he won't do anything else?

* * *

As soon as he answered the phone, I had to know. I couldn't hold it in. He started telling me what he'd been doing that day like he normally does and then I said, 'So, Gary, what's been happening then?'

And he went, 'What do you mean, I've just told you!'

I said, 'No, what's really been happening?'

He paused before replying, 'I don't know what you mean, Charlotte?'

I burst into tears. 'Gary, what happened on the first night that you were there?'

Then the phone went dead silent . . . you could have heard

a pin drop and it was like that for about twenty seconds. I just cried and cried. 'Why have you done that to me? Why? We were pictured together before you left, everyone thinks we're together. I've been saying to people I want to be with you and you've done *that* on the first night? You've just mugged us off massively.'

He said, 'I'm so sorry, it was just that one night, I was so drunk . . . nothing's happened since then. I've not even been near another girl . . .'

Is that another lie?

I said, 'I don't even think I can ever speak to you again, Gary. I've been through this all on my own. You could be here with me now but you're not. Why didn't you come home?'

He said, 'I'm going to come home, I'm not staying here. I'm going to come home in the next two days. I'm going to be there for you.'

'I don't believe it. I just don't believe anything you say anymore, Gary . . .'

Then he had to get off the phone because they wanted him for filming.

* * *

I am so sad, I can't do anything to take my mind off it, I can't get out of bed. I can't get it out of my head. He was trying to say it was my fault because he didn't know where he stood with me. And I was like, don't you fucking dare use that as an excuse.

Aaron messaged me – he says Gary doesn't know what he's playing at.

Friday 15th

The phone calls have been stopped, Kate's been told they are
'interrupting filming'. I just wish he'd come back. Why is he
even still out there?

@TheMimmyWoman1
It's ridiculous how many cakes I had in London. Damn the
Italian cake shop on the corner of the apartment. I am huge!

A Few Words From Letitia Crosby:
Looking Back on Charlotte's Ectopic Pregnancy
and our Time in the Apartment in Leicester Square.

When Kate called me that evening I was not expecting what
I was told: Charlotte was going to need surgery because she
was having an ectopic pregnancy. This was awful. My imme-
diate thoughts were, 'Is she going to be OK to have children?'
I wanted to get on a train down as soon as possible. I knew
Kate would look after her until I got there but I never slept
a wink worrying and hoping she would be OK.

Charlotte has worked incredibly hard the last five years.
She's achieved so much and sacrificed so much to do it. She
is not around as much we would like and we rarely have
much family time at all. This has always been her choice and,
like most reality TV stars, the work and travelling is immense.
This is why me and her dad will do anything to ease the load.

When I arrived at the hospital I was so upset seeing her
there. She was so helpless, so lost, and on top of everything
she was worried about her future. Obviously we knew she

was seeing Gary again, which me and her dad were not really that enthusiastic about, and that he was away filming *Ex on the Beach*. I have never held any hope he would make her happy. It's so hard when you don't really like someone's choice but you feel you have to just go along with it. It's so much easier when you approve and see your kids happy.

The plan was that we go to Kate's for a few days till Charlotte was strong enough to be moved into a hotel or apartment. So we were sharing a double bed. 'Great,' I thought. 'We will end up killing each other being this close.' I had the laptop as she wanted me to find us somewhere to stay for a week. I just love being on the laptop looking for hotels and apartments, so I was taking my time to find the right place – a bedroom each, nice views, close to shops. I felt like I had been all round London.

Then Charlotte snatched it off me saying I was taking too long and just took over and booked something. I was fuming! I was so angry as I had a few nice ones in mind.

The day came to leave Kate's and off we go and end up in a bloody apartment which is more like a shoebox. Right opposite the theatres, with blaring music coming out.

I went to enter the building and the doorknob flew straight off in my hand!

The room was tiny and had a tin shower, a bed that was practically on the floor and a kitchen all in the same bloody room. I wanted to kill her. The curtains didn't even fully fit the window. I set the fire alarm off every day when I was cooking. But I wouldn't change that week or the apartment or the shit TV because we laughed together and cried together.

When Charlotte found out Gary had slept with someone I wasn't shocked. I don't believe he ever told the whole truth to Charlotte. But she went mental. She was crying and distraught and it was so painful to watch my daughter go through that. Charlotte's became a stronger person because of all of this. She had true feelings for someone and had her heart shattered to a million pieces. But me and her dad will always be there to put it all back together again.

Charlotte made a good recovery and I hope will go onto have a family one day. My saying in life, which all Charlotte's friends now know, is 'YOU HAVE ONE LIFE, LIVE IT'. Both me and Diddyman (her dad) truly believe this.

Saturday 16th

Back in Newcastle

I just hope . . . even though he's done what he's done . . . I hope I get a text off him saying he's been given his phone back and he's in the airport back in the UK.

I can't stop looking at my phone. I'm checking it all day.

@TheMimmyWoman1
My daughter @charlottegshore is the sweetest daughter anyone could wish for I literally love her being home.

* * *

Is there ever going to be a text?

* * *

I had to go to hospital and get my stitches out. Mam came with me and it really hurt. But none of the physical pain is as bad as how I feel knowing Gary isn't here. I can't tell him how the check-up went or anything. I'm still hoping he's

demanded his phone back and has got on the next flight home
. . . but I don't think he's done either of those things.

TWEET
@charlottegshore
Oh I just hit 1 million on snapchat – HOLLLLLAARRRR.

At least that's something positive in the midst of all this pain.

Monday 18th

People keep tweeting asking what's happened to my book sign-
ings. Obviously I had to cancel them but I don't want to tell
anyone what's really happened. I can't sit in a van for fifteen
hours a day driving from one end of the country to another
while I'm still recovering from this op, but at least I can sit on
the sofa at *This Morning*, the doctor said I'm OK to do that.

@charlottegshore
Feels so lovely to be back in bed. On @itvthismorning
tomorrow so nice early start. Promoting my new book #live-
fastloseweight

Tuesday 19th

First day back at work and I was on *This Morning* to talk about
Live Fast, Lose Weight. Was still in a lot of pain from the
surgery but I felt really glad to be doing something productive
again. And Philip and Holly were really lovely as usual. Melissa
was with me and kept checking I wasn't going to start crying
but I held it together. No one would ever have known; Melissa

does my make-up and I look like nothing happened – but nothing will ever be the same again . . .

Wednesday 20th

All the magazines have been writing about me and Gary falling out – everyone is saying it's because of what happened on *Ex on the Beach* but they don't know the half of it. Gary keeps saying that we were never in a relationship. It makes me look like such a psycho, as if I'm getting so angry only because he slept with someone, when really it's so much worse. If only people actually knew the whole story. I don't want to do any interviews in case people ask me about Gary because I just don't know what I'm going to say or how to deal with the questions about our relationship.

> @charlottegshore
> I would just like to stop the confusion. I am single I have been for a while. Mrs SINGLE Crosby being all single and stuff.

Friday 22nd

There have been other girls.

There was a story on the *Daily Mail* website.

The first night wasn't the only time Gary slept with someone on *Ex on The Beach*.

Gary's hurt me a lot in the past but this is a whole different type of hurt. I felt like we'd had such a stronger connection this time around and we'd planned to go on holiday together! I've never felt like this with Gary before. He's slept with a lot of people, I used to live in a house where he had to bring a lot of people back all the time, but it never made me feel sick like this. Now the idea of him being with anyone else gives me an empty horrible pain in the pit of my belly . . .

My head is flooding . . . I thought I'd have a family with Gary . . .

I am in love with him and I feel so so so hurt. Why would he talk to me like he did on the phone and then go and do that? How could he even do that as a friend? We've known each other for five years. I respected him as a friend and I would have thought that even if he had no feelings for me he wouldn't have done something that could hurt me like this. I had just had an ectopic pregnancy, I was still in recovery, I couldn't even get out of bed . . .! He supposedly cares about me 'so much'? He says it a million times on *Geordie Shore*. So why did he get with someone else?

I am heartbroken.

Before he went away he literally slept at mine nearly every single night. Me mam and dad let him back in the house and he didn't just betray my trust he betrayed theirs.

@charlottegshore
I wish the moon wasn't so far away . . . I'd like to climb to the top and take in the views.

Sunday 24th

@charlottegshore
Seen some lovely comments from you all over the past few days. Just want to acknowledge that I do see them and I'm so grateful.

Ever since the pregnancy I've been speaking to a psychiatrist about what I've had to go through. There's been so much pressure because I've had to promote the new book and all every journalist wants to do is ask about Gary and I haven't known how to deal with it. I've said I never ever want to see him again but I don't think they can understand what's so bad this time, as they know I've forgiven him before. But I can't tell them what really happened. It's still so raw. I've known the psychiatrist a while because he worked with us on *Geordie Shore* and I had to speak to him before I went into *Celebrity Big Brother* too. Kate said I need to talk everything through because it's a lot to have to deal with. I keep going through waves of depression.

Sometimes I just feel like everything's getting on top of me and it's hard not feeling able to tell the truth. It's difficult enough anyway, but if any normal person went through this they would have loads of people to talk to about it and they wouldn't feel they had to hide it from the world. Everyone would be more sympathetic because they would know what had happened. And a normal person wouldn't have to watch the man who was the father of their baby having sex with someone else on TV. . .

I've felt sad before and I've been heartbroken and I've been stressed and I've thought I was a little bit depressed at times but this is all of those feelings jumbled together times a hundred. It's the most intense feeling I've ever had. I've never experienced anything that compares to the thoughts and emotions I'm having now. I don't know how to deal with it. I have so many scenarios going on in my head: the fact that I just lost a child, the fact that Gary isn't there for us to help me cope with losing a child, the fact that I am still in love with him but he's been doing stuff with other girls. How am I going to feel when he gets out? What if he texts me and tries to bring it all back up again? All these scenarios playing out in my brain. Every day I have been crying.

Monday 25th

There was an article in a magazine about celebrity transformations – in other words, stars who look like they've had loads of plastic surgery – and I was one of them. Now loads of people are saying I look like Michael Jackson. I decided to do a Snapchat and sing 'Thriller' to tell them I take all comparisons to the King of Pop as a compliment.

I am not going to show the world how I'm really feeling inside.

Tuesday 28th

I'm number one in the pre-order chart for my book *Live Fast, Lose Weight*! WHOOOO! This has beaten Harry Potter's new one. This is an amazing day.

Friday 29th

Gary is back from *Ex on The Beach* and he's messaged me on WhatsApp. The first message said, 'Can we talk tomorrow, just talk, no shouting, no arguments'. I didn't message back. The next one must have been when he landed off the next plane . . . he said, 'I'll take that as a no then.'

May 2016

Number of tears I've cried: I think I've run my tear ducts dry

One word to describe how I feel about Janet Street-Porter: Rude

One word to describe how I feel about Jamie Oliver: Amazing

Emojis to describe how overwhelmed I've felt by the public reaction to my interview: 😄😳💕💋

Sunday 1st

The girls have set up a WhatsApp group just to talk about Gary and what has happened. The profile picture is half Gary and half Russell Kane the comedian (an old picture of him when he had a blonde streak in his hair). That's who Gary looks like now because he's got a stupid blonde bit in his hair. He looks like a pigeon has pooed on the front of his head and he hasn't wiped it out.

Monday 2nd

Speaking to the psychiatrist has made me realise I am depressed. He made me feel so much better. It's the first time I understood why people have to go through therapy. Most of the time we speak on the phone. He talks so much sense and makes me feel it's going to be OK. I keep wondering how am I going to cope and he helps me understand it all and makes everything seem so much more logical.

Tuesday 3rd

I keep thinking the ectopic pregnancy is going to come out somehow. I know none of the *Geordie Shore* lot will say anything but all it would take was one of them to say it to one other person when they were drunk or something and the whole world would know.

* * *

Maybe that would be for the best. Everyone just thinks I'm making a massive deal out of nothing by not ever wanting to speak to Gary again but they don't know what really happened.

Saw a picture of Zayn Malik with Gigi Hadid at this big party in America called the Met Ball. He had a weird robot arm on for some reason. I don't know why, but looking at the picture of them all over each other made me quite upset because I love Perrie. I met Little Mix at Radio 1's Teen Awards a few years ago and they were so lovely. Perrie is my number-one girl crush. She is beautiful! Her and Zayn seemed so happy when they were together and it made me sad to see it all fall apart. It must have been hideous having it all played out in public like that with some leggy super-model holding onto his robot arm.

Wednesday 4th

I'm so worried Gary will start talking on his Snapchat about us. I don't know why but I am terrified of him doing it, it will upset me so much because I still don't want to say anything about what really happened.

The psychiatrist thinks it would be best if I do make contact with Gary because I need closure. He told me to think about what I'd write in a text. If it was up to me I'd have said, 'You broke my heart, you hurt me so much, this has killed me.'

But he said that putting everything out there like that just opens up your emotions even more and allows you to get rejected and hurt again. He said, 'Remain shut off, don't show any emotion.' That's such good advice, I wish I'd known that soooo many other times before. He told me I should just send Gary one simple text, very emotionless, so I don't get dragged into letting him know how I'm feeling and that way I'm in control. So I did. He wrote it all out for me and I copied it into the text.

Hi Gary, while you've been in Thailand I've gone through quite a lot, as you can imagine. I'd really respect it if you had any shred of respect for our relationship or friendship or whatever you call it to not take to Twitter or Snapchat and start kicking off. I don't know if I'll ever be ready to speak to you but if I am I'll let you know.

As soon as I sent it he replied saying, 'Is this you?' He could tell it wasn't anything I would usually say. So I had to then send a voice note to prove it. I said, 'Yes it's me,' and that was it.

I had really needed him and he hadn't been there for me. Deep down I had wished that he would get on a plane and fly home. Even now he could drive to my house and refuse to take no for an answer.

* * *

I won't ever speak to him again.

> @charlottegshore
> What a buzz I think I might have my appetite back. Nom nom.

Gary's tweeted: 'There are two sides to every story.' What the hell can he possibly mean by that FFS?

Thursday 5th

I'm getting it in the neck again because I need to make some more choices on the house and I'm being too slow. I feel like I'm holding everyone up because I haven't picked a skirting board! Who even knows about skirting boards? Why are they even called skirting boards? I wouldn't wear them as a skirt!

Friday 6th

> @charlottegshore I couldn't sleep last night thinking about my new house . . . all sorts were running through my head . . . not long now!

Aside from Alan and his crew, there are two other key parts of the building process for my house and they are called Kev and Phil. They have been our painters for twenty years and have always painted every house we've been in so me mam and dad know them really well. They're so cute, Kev looks like a meerkat and Phil looks like a wildebeest. They think I've got these out-there crazy ideas of how I want the rooms to look and so they keep trying to shoot me down saying it won't work and I can't have it (they've been hanging out with me mam a bit too long). They think they know everything. I told them I want them to paint the sitting room grey and they keep saying it will close the room in and make it look small and dark. I will prove them wrong. I'm having the sitting room grey and that's that. They are going to eat their words. Or their paintbrushes.

Monday 9th

Back at work finally! I feel so happy and alive! Rylan Clarke has got a new show on Channel 5 called *Up Late with Rylan* and I was asked to be the very first barmaid. I'm on the show every night for a week. I was so glad to be there, just being out and doing stuff makes me feel human again. There's a barman on the show who's so good-looking too which is helping! He's called Paul and I'm obsessed with him. He has really long hair all tied back. He looks nothing like Gary. He is so cute and handsome. We kept making eye contact.

* * *

Am on *Loose Women* tomorrow but I don't want to do it. Have just found out that Janet Street-Porter is one of the presenters and I know she will give me a hard time. I just feel like certain older women don't like me. I told Melissa I didn't want to do it but she kept saying, 'What's the worst they can do? They can't be horrible to you, they are on national television, they have to be professional!' Katie Price is also going to be on the panel and I'm mates with her so Mel told me to message her. Katie said, 'Don't worry, I've got your back. If anything makes you feel uncomfortable I'll butt in.'

Tuesday 10th

Kate has told the producer they can't ask any questions about Gary but they are insisting they need to ask. Obviously they don't know the full story. Kate has put her foot down; they think I don't want to talk about the fact he's been with other girls (I mean that's bad enough). I knew it was going to be awful before I even got on the show and when I was sat with Melissa and Kate in the green room I was really nervous and burst out crying! They told me I was overthinking it all, but I was completely overwrought . . .

I was on there to promote my book, *Live Fast, Lose Weight*, and Janet Street-Porter just started laying into me about my nose job. I was honest and said I had insecurities and that 'I couldn't bear to watch myself on TV'. Then bag lady Janet started saying she didn't think I was setting the right example for my young fans. She said, 'I want to say good luck to you but what message does that say to young girls who might follow you on Twitter and Facebook and Instagram who think, 'My nose has a lump in it but I don't have £4,000 to spend on it?' I told her I understood her point and maybe it wasn't the best message to put across but it was my choice at the end of the day. 'I could have tried to hide it but people might notice.'

Then she carried on! 'Why couldn't you – just to be contro-versial, when you imagined you had a lump in your nose and no one would talk to you and you'd be a social cripple – why couldn't you have counselling? Why didn't you seek some kind of therapy to live with the face you had rather than just moving it all around five inches?'

I had to just pick up my cup of tea and shrug it off and try and laugh, 'There's too much to think about there, Janet. You lost me in the first sentence.'

I told her I did talk it through, I had that counsel off me mam every day before I went to do it. It's not like I hadn't thought about it!!

I felt like I was being properly bullied on television!

@xmellinsx
So So unbelievably proud of my @charlottegshore you did amazing on @loosewomen despite the old hag trying to go in.

There have been loads of tweets supporting me so that's made me feel loads better.

Me mam was so angry. She doesn't understand why everyone is so obsessed with my nose. Although she didn't originally want me to get it done she totally understands now why I chose to. She says, 'Two of my friends have had nose jobs and no one would ever be rude to them about it!'

When a person is self-conscious about something to the point that they need to get it changed, surely it's a personal decision to do something? How can anyone think its OK to be rude to someone? Out of 1.5 million people in the world who have had surgery why are they deciding to have a go at me? I know a crew member from MTV who had her nose done because she hated her old one. No one would ever question why she was having it done to her face. It's not like I didn't have anything wrong with my nose before. It had a horrible bump in it. I would understand if my nose was straight and perfect but it wasn't! You wouldn't know there was a bump when you looked at me from the front but on the side it was very noticeable. If I hadn't been on TV and didn't have to see pictures and videos of me every day from all angles I might not have even noticed it but hundreds of photoshoots and side profiles – not to mention comments from TROLLS – will give anyone a complex!

Celebrating my platinum-selling DVD '3 Minute Belly Blitz'!

Not the best of days.

Mam and Anna painting my fence.

Me and the boys after rehearsals.

Sisters for life.

With my *Geordie Shore* family, old and new.

Me, Sophie and Holly love our Cape Verde trips.

Our first day in Oz.

My mam and dad take a good selfie.

Me and Ash coming out of Neighbourhood.

Love my girls like they came
from my womb.

Mark actually has better hair than us.

Celebs Go Dating
on the move.

My date with Brad. I took my own gravy.

* * *

Geordie Shore: Big Birthday Battle is on telly at the moment and I just know that when the episode airs where I snog Marty everyone will be watching thinking it's all my fault that Gary and me are over. Gary seems to be loving the attention he's getting on Twitter because people can see in the show he likes me (or claims to) and now they know we're not together any more it looks like it's all down to me. But that's not the whole story.

But I'm not bothered about what happened five months ago, I'm bothered about what's happened since then . . . Just because it's on telly now don't try and use that as an excuse because you know fine well what we were like since then and what our plans were.

Wednesday 11th

Paul the barman was looking so hot again tonight on *Up Late With Rylan*. Mel kept taking the piss saying it's really obvious I fancy him. I decided to ask for his number! I never do things like that but, after everything that's happened, I need some male attention to cheer me up!

* * *

Got back to the apartment we were all staying in and Mel decided we should ring Paul's number. HE GAVE ME A FAKE NUMBER!! It said: 'This mobile number is currently out of use.'

I am mortified.

137

Thursday 12th

Mel kept teasing Paul and saying, 'You fake-numbered Charlotte!' and it was so embarrassing. Even Rylan was getting involved so everyone on set knew. Paul took me aside in the end and said, 'I'm so sorry but I have a girlfriend.' I felt so awkward!
GREAT.

Friday 13th

There are so many stories in the magazines about me and Gary but no one knows the whole story. IF ONLY THEY KNEW!! They're all saying we've split up and it's looking like I'm the bad person here and that I've just started kicking off for no reason. No one knows. I want to tell people. People know he's been on *Ex on the Beach* and people think it's just to do with that. I do a regular thing on heat Radio and they asked me about it. I said, 'I don't want to ever speak or associate with Gary again.' But without the background of what's happened it just makes me look like I'm being some dramatic overreacting diva. All Gary keeps saying in interviews is that we were never really a couple or properly back together but THAT'S NOT THE FULL STORY! Even though there's only a handful of people who know about the ectopic pregnancy, I'm worried, I feel like it's only a matter of time before it comes out.

We're due to go into *Geordie Shore* filming again soon and everyone is just waiting to find out what happens. I don't know if I can go back, I can't be in that house again with him. Gary keeps telling the press that it's going to be 'make or break this time' and one of us will have to leave *Geordie Shore* if it doesn't get resolved.

RESOLVED?

HOW CAN YOU RESOLVE LOSING A BABY?!

I'm fed up of not being able to say what's happened.

The worst thing is that the ectopic pregnancy's not a secret any more. More and more people are starting to find out. Kate messaged me saying, 'Someone else from MTV has told me they know.'

What if it gets out?

I'm worried it's going to be in one of the papers and I'll have no control over what's said. People are starting to ask questions. I spoke to Kate and said, 'Wouldn't it be best if we just say it all in my own words?'

We're going to do it with Lucie Cave at *heat* magazine because that way it can all be controlled and we trust her. I'm worried though. The thought of bringing it all up again makes me scared. It's still so raw.

Saturday 14th

Got my new dog today! She is a Pomeranian like Baby, except she's black, and I'm calling her Rhubarb. She is sooo funny. I can already tell what her personality is like. I found her on Pets4Homes. I'm not sure Baby likes her but they'll learn to love each other. I always wanted Baby to have a companion because when she's in the house alone I can tell she's so sad.

Charlotte's Guide To: Getting A Pet

1. See the pet.
2. Imagine the pet is yours.
3. Think of all the reasons the pet is going to make your life a better place filled with rainbows, unicorns and fluffy clouds of candy floss.
4. Decide you're getting the pet.
5. TELL EVERYONE YOU KNOW ABOUT THE PET (apart from your parents or people who may stop you getting the pet).
6. Make sure the pet is looking extra cute for the big surprise introduction.
7. Usher the disapproving unaware ones (Mam and Dad) into the room where the pet is hidden.
8. Ask them how they can ever be angry with something that look soooooooooo cute.
9. Take great care of the pet for two or three days.
10. Go on holiday (this a great chance for the once-angry ones to form the real bond).

Sunday 15th

I've been filming a thing called *Show Us Ur Phone* for MTV as part of their Snapchat channel. If it does well it will be turned into a whole TV show. It's the first time I've been a presenter and I've got a full camera crew with me while I run about the streets of London.

Monday 16th

People have got wind of the fact I'm filming and I got accosted by someone from *Reveal* magazine on Carnaby Street. I was there with a megaphone so it's not like I was disguised! Different journalists have been coming over to me saying things like, 'Can we just have a few words?!' because they want to know what's been going on with Gary. I was literally on the street and they came and approached me! I just said, 'No, sorry.'

The show is really fun. I hope it does get commissioned for a proper series. The main part consists of me running around and finding couples on the street, then I tell them it's a phone-based game show about how much they trust each other. If they agree to go on it then we take their phones off them and the production team look through the phones to see if they have anything to hide from one another. After we've looked through the phones then I have five questions about the other person's phone so I say something like:

Question One. This is for you, Sarah. We went through Dave's phone and on a group WhatsApp chat with the lads did he say:
a) "Let's book a lads' holiday so I can get my end away."
or b) "I've been looking at engagement rings, what do you think the most is I can spend on one?"

There's always a bad answer in there and you always get the girl in panic mode because there's a 50 per cent chance it's the truth. And they're both panicking because they're not allowed to look at each other. For each question they win money – they can win £50 – and at the end they have a chance to double their money. Some of the couples are lovely and the answers have been dead fun and funny, some of them were just clearly not suited and there have been walk-outs because one of them has been cheating!

Tuesday 17th

One couple I met today were quite young and the girl was so in love. She didn't have a clue that her boyfriend was full-on having an affair – literally having phone sex with this other girl! She had no idea. To be a girl who thinks you're so in love and for that to be exposed is so awkward.

When I got told about the concept of the game show I was worried at first. I didn't want to be roaming round the streets of London making people unhappy and breaking couples up! But since doing it, I've met some lovely couples who are so happy and looking through their phones I've seen they haven't done anything wrong or got anything to hide and it's so nice. It's actually restored my faith in relationships.

Then, when I meet the cheating ones, I don't feel bad because I think, 'You're an arsehole, how dare you be treating this person like this? You don't deserve them.' At the end of the day, if you're a cheater it serves you right if you get found out about it I need to save people from bad boyfriends and girlfriends. I'm the relationship superhero!

I'm a bit like an evil cupid. I'm saving their hearts: Stupid Cupid!

Wednesday 18th

@charlottegshore
My birthday today! Whoop! (Well I've been in better places on my birthday but I need to stay positive!)

Gary tweeted happy birthday with a green heart, which I think was him trying to put on a mild display of affection in public. I don't understand why he wouldn't just text it to me otherwise?

@charlottegshore
Start ignoring people who threaten your joy. Literally, ignore them. Say nothing. Don't invite any parts of it into your space.

Thursday 19th

Got the *heat* interview tomorrow. I'm nervous but I'm looking forward to getting it out in the open and out of the way at the same time.

I'm nervous but I know it's important. I just want everyone to know the truth and for it to be a warning to other people. I didn't even know about ectopic pregnancies before it happened to me and they're so so dangerous.

I'm working with Jamie Oliver in the morning which should take my mind off it. I've never met him before. I reckon we'll get on like a house on fire (as long as it's not a kitchen on fire we'll be OK).

* * *

I feel really anxious. Like I have a massive knot in my belly. I hate the thought of having to talk about everything.

Friday 20th

Jamie Oliver is so fun!

I was filming for his *Food Revolution* where he's trying to get people on the healthy-eating bandwagon. It was such a laugh and everything went out on Facebook Live. He had loads of different celebs coming and helping him. I was on with Alfie Deyes and Cheryl Cole was on after us. Jamie's even filthier than me! He kept saying we should do a show together; like a really rude late-night one where we get drunk and can say what we want. He says we should call it *Meat and Two Veg*! He's so funny. I really enjoyed it. He told me I was too good for Gary, him and Jools are fans of the show AND he said he has a single mate called Andy who's an electrician. He said I should go out with him and he will cater our wedding if we hit it off! How amazing is that?

* * *

The *heat* interview was emotional and I am SO HAPPY IT'S OVER. It actually felt therapeutic to be able to say everything that had happened and get it all in the open. I couldn't stop crying though. A photographer was taking pictures while we were chatting and I had to keep stopping to blow my nose because everything was running. I am going to look like a puffy-faced weirdo. But I don't care. It's done.

After the *heat* team left it felt like a weight had been lifted off my shoulders, like the stress has gone in some way. It feels good to know that it's going to come out in my own words. That's what I've been worrying about for so long: what if someone else had gone to the press with it?

The knot in my belly has totally disappeared. I feel so glad I've done the interview.

Monday 23rd

Met David Walliams in the flesh at last!

I was on the *Britain's Got More Talent* panel and Stephen Mulhern went on the stage at the end just before the main show finished and announces the guests going on his show. When he said my name David Walliams actually shouted, 'Oh, Charlotte Crosby! I want to meet her!' right in front of everyone!

I was buzzing! Oh my God.

We met up afterwards and I had a selfie with him. We've tweeted each other so much before and now we've finally come face to face. He's so funny. He is a handsome man . . . but not my type in that way.

Wednesday 25th

Am going to donate the money for my *heat* interview equally between the Hospice of St John and St Elizabeth and the Ectopic Pregnancy Trust. Kate got in touch with them both to tell them and they were really chuffed. It's quite a bit of money so I hope it helps people like me.

Thursday 26th

I can't wait for the *heat* article to come out so everyone stops speculating about stuff between me and Gary. It's worse because of everything that's airing on the TV in *Geordie Shore* at the moment. People think I'm the bad one in the relationship because of Marty. There was an article online today all about how I wasn't sure about being Gary's girlfriend outside of the show. Apparently Gary said, 'Outside of *Geordie Shore*, I'd ask Charlotte, "Can we just go to the cinema instead of an event?" I'd take her on dates and not put a foot wrong. She was a bit scared, I think.'

YES I WAS SCARED AND DO YOU BLAME ME?

He keeps saying that he can't have cheated on me because we weren't officially together.

And then in the *Mirror* a 'source' has apparently told them that David Hawley turned up on *Ex on the Beach* and told Gary he and I were texting the day before Gary went on the show. It's such a load of rubbish. I have every single text that I sent to David and they are completely harmless! How the paper can make out I was trying it on with him behind Gary's back I will never know.

Anyway, it wasn't the day before, it was when I was in Australia, but that's not the point. If anyone saw the texts they would just realise. He was asking where his friend could get a vitamin drip and I told him my doctor did them and then I told him he was still logged into my Netflix account! That was it! How is that flirting?

Friday 27th

The sitting room has been painted and me mam says Kev and Phil are in shock because it looks really good. When I saw it I was blown away. I knew I was right! They are going to have to get used to that taste of paint now they've got to eat their brushes.

Saturday 28th

I can't stand to be in the same room as Gary. I've got to a stage of my life where I don't want to go back around in circles, I want to move on now. Before I wanted to be stuck in a house with Gary because I really liked him, now I can't think of anything worse. I don't even want to speak to him. I don't want to go back on the show because there are so many big opportunities out there I could be getting on with. I've told Kate I'm not making any decisions yet though. They're all going back into filming next week and I can't anyway because I still need to get my twelve-week scan from the doctor. So I couldn't even if I wanted to.

In other news, I've decided I want the walls in my bedroom painted black. Me mam thinks it's going to look horrendous and keeps telling me it's too depressing to have a black bedroom. I told her she has no vision or sense of style and she needs to listen to me. Look at what happened with the sitting room! I've picked the colour and it's a like a chalky black colour – she will love it when she sees it.

Sunday 29th

The interview is out tomorrow in *heat*. I feel a bit nervous but have no regrets.

I'm sick of everyone thinking Gary's such an angel just because of what he's been saying on TV. I just want this weight to be lifted off my shoulders and for people to know that this is it with me and Gary. It's totally and completely over now and hopefully people will stop asking me about him, because it's not something I want to talk about any more. I've told everyone everything now, there're no more questions to be asked, it's over.

* * *

Can't sleep.

Kate told Gary's agent about the *heat* article coming out tomorrow. Gary just texted and said, 'WOW.'

I haven't texted him back.

Monday 30th

Somehow I managed to get a bit of sleep. When I woke up and looked at my phone I couldn't believe the amount of messages I had. I was so overwhelmed, I cried. Everyone was so amazing and lovely. There were thousands of tweets of support. I feel so relieved. I can't believe how nice everyone is being.

@charlottegshore
Thankyou everyone. Your support means a lot.

I posted a message on Facebook and Instagram to say thank you to everyone.

I'm overwhelmed with all the supportive messages from everyone . . . I want to explain that I did this for my own peace of mind and sanity! And mostly closure. My life is so public I was scared it would come out from someone else. I wanted to explain it all in my own words. It's been really really hard and painful physically and emotionally carrying this on my shoulders and having to see Gary blame alot of things on me and see hurtful things written about me. These past two months I've had a lot to deal with and now I do feel a weight lifted off my shoulders. I really hope by doing this people respect the fact that I don't want to be asked any more questions about Gary. This will be the last time I talk about him or the situation and I hope everyone respects that.

I deserve better, I realise that now. I have alot of really exciting things going on and some amazing opportunities coming up. I'm gonna fling myself into work and focus on everything great. Love you all alot.

Oh my God, the messages just haven't stopped coming. The story has been picked up by all the papers and has gone everywhere. I can't quite take in how many comments and messages of support I've had. It's just incredible. There are over 45,000 comments on my Facebook post – I've checked. There are just so many inspirational women out there. I feel so supported, so overwhelmed, so touched. Kate says the reaction the story has got has been 'phenomenal'. It puts everything I've been through into perspective. Reading them all has made me feel so much better.

One girl wrote that it had happened to her and she now has three little girls. Another said she thought the reason mother nature gave us two of everything (kidneys, lungs, fallopian tubes) was 'just in case' anything happened, which is a nice way of looking at it. Loads of people told me they thought they had no chance of having kids after having their fallopian tube removed but, I think they all went on to have healthy, amazing babies. And there were so many women saying they had experienced 'Garys' in their lives (aka, bad relationships) and they came out of it stronger and happier.

@TheMimmyWoman1
My daughter @charlottegshore has been incredibly strong to do this interview. I have no doubt in my mind its still a raw subject #proud

* * *

The *Sun* contacted Kate tonight saying that Gary is trying to suggest I didn't give him a right to reply. He's saying it should have been a private matter but I think that's only because he doesn't want everyone to know what an absolute fucking arsehole he is! It's ridiculous.

June 2016

Number of 'in the heat of the moment' tweets I've done: Too many (including announcing that I'm leaving *Geordie Shore* . . .)

Anger count at Gary's selfishness: 1,000,000,000 x ANGRY!

Therapy sessions: Loads, and they've helped me so much

Surprise holiday fling which came right out of the blue but was JUST what I needed after a shit last few weeks: One

Wednesday 1st

I've been sitting in the US Embassy all day because I've got to try and sort my visa out. I want to go on holiday with the girls but can't get to America because of the driving ban so had the appointment booked for today – of all days!

Was waiting in a queue reading messages from people about the *heat* article when I found that Gary has 'written' an article in the *Daily Star* called 'The other side of the story'. He wanted to 'break his silence'.

He's saying me snogging Marty back in February (which is going to be on TV next week) is proof that it was him who wanted to make a go of things and that it was me who was too scared, and that's why I did it.

He says how great everything was in Australia and how we were planning things so we could spend more time together. No mention of the row in Sydney after Bree told me she'd heard he'd been seen out with another girl . . . Instead he says that when we were interviewed he wanted to say we were seeing each other but I always said we weren't, like I was the one that was scared to commit. I can't believe it.

His take on what happened on *Ex on the Beach* is that he thinks that the night before he went to Thailand one of us should have said 'let's get in a relationship' but neither of us did. He says he doesn't know why, but that he *did* say he wouldn't do anything while he was abroad and that we'd speak when he returned to the UK.

So why did he?

He's says he was all confused on his way out to Thailand, and then got smashed and ended up in bed with HER on the first night. Before he knew about the ectopic pregnancy. He didn't think he could tell me after he got the phone call.

And then, when I found out about that first night, apparently he said, 'I am single, so are you. We should have made it official.' He said that after that call he was told he couldn't speak to me and that I made it clear it was the total end of us. According to the interview he was really worried about me, but didn't really know what was going on back home because he didn't have a phone and couldn't see any press. So it was all a shock when he got back.

He also says it was a shock to see it everywhere yesterday, and that 'some things need to remain private'. He claims to be 'devastated' for both of us about the ectopic pregnancy, and that it's all ended the way it has. He even says he wishes me all the best.

This is how he finishes, so you can see how ridiculous the whole thing is:

Sorry this is so long-winded and confusing, but imagine all of this going on in your life and everybody having an opinion. Not always the right opinion. There are two sides to every story.

I know I'm no saint, but I hope this clears a few things up.

I can't believe what I'm reading.

I can't stand him. I can't ever EVER be in the same room as him again.

I know I should be silent but I can't not say anything in response. I can't bear any more of his crap. All this shit and backlash. I HATE HIM SO MUCH! This is the absolute final straw. I know I can never go back to filming with him ever again.

@charlottegshore
Sadly because a certain some1 can't admit to being in the wrong and have to write a short story full of excuses. I have made the . . .

@charlottegshore
very hard decision to Leave the show. it's something I have went back and forth with for a while now. But I am willing to sacrifice that part of my career.

153

On and on I tweeted. MTV called: 'Put your phone down and get off Twitter.'

I didn't, obviously.

* * *

I couldn't stop crying all day. It wasn't so much that I was upset, I just felt so frustrated and agitated. I didn't really know how Gary would react, I thought he might ignore it and not say anything. Why couldn't he for once in his whole life just do the decent thing?

After my tweets the *Geordie Shore* girls kept messaging me: 'You can't leave! What are you saying?' No one believes me but I mean it this time. In fact, it's like a weight off my shoulders. A horrible, wrinkle-faced parsnip of a weight off my shoulders.

The girls keep sending me things like: 'You'll come back!' But I won't. This is it.

I think Kate is over the moon, if I'm honest. I think she's secretly relieved. She's always had reservations about *Geordie Shore* being bad for my health and that I was being put into so many stressful situations. She also thinks my liver was suffering from drinking so much! She didn't say much when I spoke to her. She just said, 'Let's talk about it when you're feeling stronger.' Literally nothing fazes her!

@charlottegshore
I am hugely sad and it kills me to write this, I will miss *Geordie Shore* with all my heart, it was my life and I 🖤 you all so much 😔

Woah. What have I done?

@charlottegshore
I'm embarrassed about having that ridiculous outburst. I still stand by my decision but I shouldn't have let my temper get the better of me.

@charlottegshore
My head feels as though it's going to explode at the moment . . . it's a difficult time. But anything that needs to be said now will be said in private.

Friday 3rd

I can't believe I'm not going back into the show. I wish I hadn't been so hasty now but I have to stick with my decision. I know deep down it's the right one.

Kate told me she thought it would help if I spoke to the *Geordie Shore* psychiatrist again about everything that's been going on. He asked me how I was feeling since the *heat* interview came out and what's happened since Gary's article. I told him I feel relieved because the stress of it all is off my shoulders.

Saturday 4th

Rhubarb is just hilarious and I laugh at her all the time. I never laugh at Baby in the same way. Baby is very intelligent, clever and loyal; Rhubarb has an attitude problem and she is thick. She doesn't how to do any tricks. Baby is dancing and doing backflips and she just sits there! These dogs have really made me feel better about life though. All I need is a cuddle from them and they make everything disappear for a bit. I think I'm more like Baby, I'm not as thick as Rhubarb. And Baby is more independent.

Sunday 5th

I've messaged Will Sparks a few times. I've been looking at videos of him DJing online and he is so hot when he does that jumping thing in the air. I still really fancy him and I need to take my mind off Gary. Anyway, I'm booked to go to Australia again in a few days so maybe I'll get to meet him for more than just an 'eye-locking session' this time. He's really shit at messaging back though and it's frustrating me. I need someone to fancy and talk to and he takes about a week to reply!

> @charlottegshore
> When you realise you've made what seems like the worst decision of your entire life. . . I've lost my family my life. . . Cast and crew 😭😭😭

Monday 6th

Gary has tweeted saying he wants me to come back to *Geordie Shore*. Hmm. Funny how everything he does is always in public.

> @gazgshore
> It's not to late. . . Get a bag packed and get your arse here. . .

I should be heading off with everyone into *Geordie Shore* but I'm not and it feels so weird and sad. I feel quite emotional about it.

Was looking on Chloe's Snapchat and Marnie was on there saying they're at Barcelona airport. Then Marty said they were going to 'Maga' which must be Magaluf. I've found out Sophie is going back into the show as my replacement which made me feel a bit weird. Oh my God they are going to have so much fun! ARGH! I'm not going to be able to help but want to check up on what they're doing.

But I have to remind myself there's no way I could be near Gary.

I am actually glad I'm not going. I thought it would feel harder than it does.

* * *

Every time I think about my future I get really upset. I'm not needy, I just want to meet someone nice and settle down and maybe have a sensible relationship.

Tuesday 7th

Will is the absolute worst person ever with his phone. It's so shit. It's not even flirty. What's the point? This is the first person I have fancied in ages other than Gary and I'm texting him and getting nothing back!

I am so excited about having a whole massive amazing garden to myself in my new house. I've got a landscape gardener called Paul and he's really good-looking but a bit hippyish because he likes all that eco-friendly stuff. He's got so many ideas about what to do and I get the impression I'm not going to be able to have much to do with it because it's a very complicated project. I know I want it to be *Lord of the Rings* themed so I said I don't care what he does as long as it looks

good. It's going to take the rest of the year to finish! We're
going to get a sunken pond and a firepit and walls built into
the walls that you can fill with flames. And we're going to
have this shelter in the middle with heaters and a table. It's
all white with fairy lights and there are little rounded hills
like in *Lord of the Rings* (and also *Tellytubbies*). So it will basically be like Lord of the Tellytubbies when people come over.

Wednesday 8th

Me mam – aka my number-one employee – said to me today
she feels loads happier because she can see I'm more myself
again now. Saying goodbye to *Geordie Shore* has opened up
so many other exciting things and opportunities. Even when
I get down I need to remember this is a life-changing experience for the good.

And having Rhubarb and Baby always makes me feel a lot
better. How did I ever have an existence without dogs in it?
Even Dad has fallen in love with them and I never thought
I'd hear him say that . . .

A Few Words From Gary Crosby: Becoming An Accidental Dog Lover

Charlotte's history with pets has been, shall we say, not
particularly successful. Her first pet was a hamster/gerbil
thing. She liked to walk around the house with it on her
head and come up to us saying, 'Do you like my hat?' Poor
thing must have been stiff with fear. She has had rabbits,
guinea pigs and goldfish over the years but the pattern is
always the same:

1. Bring home pet, be hugely enthusiastic about the new arrival.
2. Two weeks later, lose enthusiasm for the new arrival.
3. Another two weeks, pass on all responsibility for pet care to her dad.
4. Generally forget that she even has a pet.
5. Become hugely saddened and grieve when finding out pet has died, for a couple of days.

We once had to video a burial in the garden for one of her goldfish which was quite bizarre as she hadn't fed the thing for six months (see #3 above).

So, then she starts sending us pictures of small dogs she likes. Which in 2015 became pictures of the same small dog, a puppy called Baby. Comments like, 'Isn't she cute . . . this is the dog I will get when I'm older . . . I much prefer small dogs like this, do you?' Which became, 'Do you think it will like us?' and within twelve hours had developed into, 'Right . . . this is my new dog and I'll get her in four weeks.'

Dad: Charlotte, what do you mean get her in four weeks?
Charlotte: Yes, I've spoken to the breeder and she says I'd be a perfect dog owner.
Dad: You didn't tell her about your previous pet experience, then?
Charlotte: She interviewed me and I passed with flying colours!
Dad: But your mother is allergic to dogs?

This is what Letitia had been telling me for the last twenty years whenever I suggested getting a dog. I had grown up with dogs but had become accustomed to never having one, in fact becoming pretty anti-dog over the years.

Charlotte: Well she will just have to manage. If she gives it plenty of walks it will be good for her fitness!
Dad: Your brother doesn't like dogs.
Charlotte: He will get used to it quickly enough.
Dad: But you work in London 50 per cent of the time, spend a month in Australia, holiday in Ibiza? Who will look after them?
Charlotte: I think you will look cute walking her around the block.

I'm six foot four and a former nightclub doorman! I'd be better out walking a Great Dane or a St Bernard.

Dad: I think you should think about it . . .
Charlotte: I've paid the deposit . . . see you later!!!

So that's it. The dog is paid for; when it reaches twelve weeks she'll collect it. A tiny, tiny little Pomeranian/Chihuahua. Called Baby! The whole thing is repeated again about eight months later when she gets another one . . . 'to keep Baby company'. It's called Rhu.

The pet process starts again and we are still at #3, but they have had an astounding impact on all of us. They are loved to bits. This time, I can't see it ever getting to #4. Whenever she is away, we need to send her videos and pictures and when she comes home she is all over the dogs for days. We have become the official dog walkers to add to all our other duties for the grandmaster Charlotte. The official dog feeders, groomers, washers, vet couriers and all the other duties of dog care. They have become a huge part of our lives, and I don't care what anyone thinks when a six foot four well-built man is out walking two little midget dogs!!

  Dad: So your mam is not really allergic to dogs?
  Charlotte: It seems that way. Bet you're glad I got those dogs.
  Dad: Suppose so, they have become part of the family.
  Charlotte: Yes, what do you think of this one. . .? [Sends picture of another puppy . . . Aaarrrggghhhhhhhh!!!!!]

Thursday 9th

I'm back in Oz to promote In The Style! I can't tell you how good it feels to escape to the other side of the world after the last couple of months. I bloody LOVE Australia!

* * *

There's going to be a new dating show on E4 called *Celebs Go Dating* and the producers want me to go on it. Kate has been speaking to them but I don't want to do it. I'm not ready for everyone to watch me be messed about by boys on telly again.

Friday 10th

I messaged Will on Twitter to tell him I was here. I can see he's on tour in America – typical!

Saturday 11th

It's the Queen's official ninetieth birthday today. I'm so happy for her because I think she looks amazing for her age and seems to be really getting about fine. She's walking around happily with no one having to prop her up and she still does the queen's wave with ease. She's not exactly in an old people's home, is she? Give me what the queen's got when I get old please! The queen gets two birthdays so this isn't even her real one, she just gets to party on this date. I wonder if she got to pick the date of the official one? If I could pick a second birthday I'd have it on 26th December so just when you get all depressed because Christmas is over – bang – it's your birthday!

Monday 13th

Will's back in Australia and he called me ON THE PHONE! He's here in Melbourne and this is the only night I'm here before I have to go off again. We're going on a date tonight.

What am I GOING TO WEAR!?

What am I going to SAY TO HIM?

* * *

We went to a Japanese restaurant. I wore jeans and a little off-the-shoulder top. I've never been so nervous. This is the first proper date I think I've ever been on!

We had the best night ever though. We went to the strippers!

Will said, 'All the boys on a Wednesday go to the strippers.'

I replied, 'Oh my God, that sounds amazing! Can we go to the strippers?'

And he looked so shocked. 'What the hell?' I think he thought I was joking.

All night he kept saying, 'I can't believe you want to go to a strip club! This is so amazing!' I don't know what the big deal is, I always end the night in Newcastle in a strip club because it's open the longest!

We had a really, REALLY good night. I stayed over afterwards at his – nothing happened though. I got so drunk I passed out. Thankfully I didn't wee myself.

Tuesday 14th

Woke up really early and we were laughing about everything from the night before. We snogged loads. Then I got in a taxi and had to go to the airport. I don't meet boys very often because I'm so busy all the time – it's hard to meet anyone you like so I just want to cling onto Will! I really like him.

It was the final episode of *Geordie Shore* tonight back home – the one where I stand up on the table and do my speech to try and get Gary back. People were tweeting me about it. At least I gave it my all. God, how much has happened since then though?

@charlottegshore
I'm proud that even though it's my last ep I gave it my all! And went out on a high! Hope you all enjoyed it as much as I did experiencing it 🖤

Wednesday 15th

I really like Will but maybe it's just because of Gary and I'm fixating on him for no reason.

Have been checking in on house progress and Mam says that despite their reservations the builders (and me mam included!) love the bedroom now they've painted it. I knew it! Can't wait to see it.

Thursday 16th

Me and Will been texting a bit but he's just as shit as before so I don't think I can be arsed with it. The spark with Will Sparks has gone.

I've found a bath and I need it in my life NOW. Sent Mam a picture of it and she replied, 'Yes it's nice but how much?'

'£20,000.'

'Are you HAVING A LAUGH, CHARLOTTE?! Nobody pays £20,000 for a bath! You are bonkers.'

I know its ridiculous. I don't want to pay £20,000 for a bath. But it's the only one I can find that's so perfect.

Friday 17th

I said in a couple of interviews recently that I was going to quit Newcastle for Hollywood and become the next Bridget Jones, but it was only a joke and now it's all over the internet!

I need to learn to keep my mouth shut sometimes.

Mam is in a panic and keeps messaging me saying: 'You can't afford a £20,000 bath. Where are you getting the idea that you can??' So I've set her on a mission to find one just like it but much cheaper.

Saturday 18th

The dating show producers have been in touch again. What have I got to lose? And I might actually meet someone.

Monday 20th

Back from Oz and hardly had any time to unpack before I'm off to Cannes tomorrow! Been invited to be on a panel at this thing called the Cannes Lions Festival for advertising people. The *Daily Mail* is hosting some sort of yacht thing. Should be a laugh.

Mam and Dad took me to the house to see the latest work that's been done. Saw my new black bedroom and I've decided I don't like it any more so I think I'm going to change it all. Mam had her head in her hands. 'You're giving those poor men such a headache. Kev and Phil are going to cry!' Mam kept asking me why I didn't like it any more and what had made me change my mind. To be honest, I don't know why I wanted it black, it was a very bad decision. I blame the fact that I'm getting bored of this whole process. It's too many things to think about. I told her to tell them not to be upset but it's just not what I'd envisioned. Ultimately it comes down to the fact that I can't imagine myself straightening my hair in a black bedroom.

Mam and Dad will have to break it to Kev and Phil. I never tell anyone anything.

Sent Kate a message:

Me: I've been thinking quite a bit recently that I'd want to go back into *Geordie Shore* for the last two nights. Do you think that's a bad idea?

Kate: I think it's a terrible idea. This is me at the thought of it 😭😭😭😭😭😭😭😭😭

Take that as a no then.

Tuesday 21st

I told Kate I feel ready to start dating again. Maybe *Celebs Go Dating* is not such a bad idea after all. I need to try and go on another date in private before I get out there on TV again though.

* * *

I've recruited some of my mates to help with my dating needs. I told them I need to put myself out there. Lois says there's a boy she knows who's a footballer at Newcastle and he wants to meet me. I've never been one of those girls who dates footballers. I'm not someone who hangs around tables in clubs trying to look nice and get bought drinks. I usually fall over the tables!

She's been messaging me about him all day! In the end I replied, 'Go on just give him my number then.'

He's called Kev. And he's French. A French fella called . . . KEVIN!? LOL.

* * *

Vicky has WhatsApped me. It's been so long since we last spoke it took me out of the blue a bit. It had been a bit awkward last time I saw her – at *The X Factor* final – because I was there with Gary and she was with HER. She's messaged me to say she hopes I'm OK and hopes I will never be going near Gary again . . . We chatted a bit about the *X Factor* thing and then she messaged, 'You dare quit *Geordie Shore* over him mind.'

Wednesday 22nd

It's the EU referendum and I've voted out. Me mam and dad think that we could be a better country on our own and the way they said it seemed to make sense to me. Brexit sounds a bit like a biscuit too so I like it.

Even though I've voted out it doesn't mean I can't date French Kev. We've exchanged a few texts. We're going on a double date tonight with his mate and Lois. He's dead handsome, quite tall. He has dreadlocks and he's been leaving me voice notes on WhatsApp because I said I wanted to hear his accent. He has a lovely voice. Doesn't sound at all like a Kevin.

* * *

Verdict: It was a GOOD DATE! But the thing is – and I don't know if this is because he's French – but Kev didn't give off many 'signals'. So I can't really tell if he likes me. Usually if I'm with someone and they like me they're a bit touchy-feely but he wasn't flirty at all and I didn't get that vibe.

We did snog at the end of the night but we were pissed so I don't think that counts?

Thursday 23rd

The people who voted Brexit have won. We're leaving the EU.

And now everyone seems so upset! Everyone is going on about what a shock it is and it's all over Facebook and the news.

I don't know if I made the right decision. Oh dear. Who knows?

Kev's been messaging all day saying he had a good night. He sounds keen so maybe it's OK after all. He wants to go out again so I'm going to meet him when I'm back from my trip to his home country.

Sunday 26th

Turns out quite A LOT can happen in Cannes. It's been a pretty eventful few days!

Adam and Jamie were out there to shoot Binky Felstead for her In The Style range because *Made In Chelsea* were filming in Cannes. What a stroke of luck!

The panel thing with the *Daily Mail* was really fun and was basically just a conversation on stage with Jonathan Cheban, Gemma Collins and Katie Hopkins. I've met Katie before because we were on *Xtra Factor* together a while ago (when she said one of the boybands on the show had an STI!). We have quite a good bond – even though she's never followed me on Twitter. I told her she needs to because I've unfollowed her now.

The *Made In Chelsea* cast were staying in these incredible villas. The *Daily Mail* threw a massive yacht party and literally EVERYONE was there – every Tom, Dick and Harry who was someone – it was really wild and amazing. Jamie Laing messaged me before. We've always got on really well so I knew it was going to be fun with him out here. Alex Mytton was DJing and at one point Jamie took me to one side and shouted in my ear, 'Alex fancies you!' I was a bit taken aback (and pissed) and just replied, 'Oh right, OK,' and carried on swigging shots. I've always quite fancied Jamie (we've always

had a flirty thing but never kissed) so I wasn't really thinking about going there with Alex . . .

After Alex finished his DJ set he joined us for drinks and we were all mingling with loads of big important people. They seemed important anyway (I didn't actually know any of their names). I remember meeting one after another of these really high-up men and women who were clearly really rich because they were telling all these rich-people stories. The whole thing was just crazy – I couldn't believe where I was! I felt like I was in this place with all these uber-talented folk and there was me looking like a weirdo and dancing like a drunken idiot. I looked across at all the *Made In Chelsea* girls and they were standing there all cool and chic, compared to me who had my shoes off, dancing around, downing Jägerbombs. At one point I fell asleep on the side of the boat. Some security fella had to wake me up and said, 'If you don't get up now we're going to have to remove you from the yacht.'

Anyway, considering the state I was in, I really don't know how the next part happened . . . Somehow we all went back to Alex's friend's villa. It was this stunning apartment over two floors and it overlooked the marina. Jamie had disappeared somewhere else so it was just me and Alex . . .

Alex and I spent the whole night at the villa there, together. The next day we were stranded sat in the road in blistering heat waiting for his friend to come and pick me up. We had such a laugh though, it was as if we'd known each other for ages. We were talking about *everything*. We were in such deep conversations it was as if we were in some sort of therapy session! We were just being really honest with each other; at no point were we trying to impress each other because we knew where we stood. It was just one night and we both understood that. It was quite liberating actually! He asked if I wanted to go out for food later that afternoon and I said, 'Nah, I want to chill out, I'm so hungover,' so we arranged to go out in the evening instead.

* * *

Getting ready to go out again I felt all excited, like I'd been having this holiday romance. We met again that night on the yacht and stayed out until the sun rose. The filming days on *Made In Chelsea* are so much more relaxed than ours on *Geordie Shore*! They seem to have about two days filming and then four days off!

We got really pissed again and we ended up having a silly fight that somehow turned into game of 'tig'. We were running along the marina drunk and laughing at each other. Alex's friends, who were French, were trying to get a car for us but it took them about an hour to get us into the vehicle because we were rolling around on the floor so much. I was running about in bare feet and they kept telling me to put my shoes on because I'd stand on something and hurt myself. I told them I would be OK because Jesus never wore shoes and he turned out pretty alright. Then we went back to their villa again. All we did all morning was talk and laugh about stuff we were scrolling on Instagram while we ate Subway sandwiches with one of his French friends.

I was meant to get a flight home the next day at 6 a.m. but was still with Alex so I missed it. Instead I rocked up at Adam and Jamie's villa where they were shooting Binky for her In The Style range. I was still pissed when I arrived and I only had one shoe on and a manky toe (I must've stood on something after all because its gone pus-y and its killing me!). I decided to strip naked and jump in the pool in front of everyone. Then at one point I dragged Adam in the pool with me while he was trying to direct the shoot!

* * *

So I ended up staying longer but I'm back now. I feel so hungover but I had the most amazing time. Wish I could say the same for my toe. It's throbbing.

Monday 27th

@charlottegshore
I'm bored of waiting for my house to be finished . . . hurry up I wanna have sleepovers and pillow fights.

I've seen a mirror I want and it's going to change my life. Mam says I can't have it because it's too expensive but it's incredible. It will take over a whole wall, it's ceiling to floor. Imagine the selfies in that!

Mam is also going on about my toe. She says it's infected and I need to go to hospital to get the toenail taken off. No way. I'll be fine. It's full of blood and swollen and the nail is black, but I'm not going to hospital! It's not like I have a bad illness, it's a toenail, it'll grow off. She keeps saying, 'It's infected and it will only get worse.' She needs to chill out.

Had my second date with Le Garçon Kev tonight and in the flesh he seemed all weird and French and not remotely flirty again! We didn't even kiss this time so I don't think it's going anywhere. I just can't work it out because he was messaging me beforehand like he was really into it! I fancy him, but I don't think it's worth it. I'm not that bothered that I'm going to make a fool of myself. It might also have some-

172

thing to do with the fact I had to wear Birkenstocks to the date. I couldn't put any heels on because my toe was too painful to squeeze into anything remotely sexy.

Tuesday 28th

Went to see Beyoncé in Sunderland tonight and Melissa STOOD ON MY TOE and it LITERALLY EXPLODED! I am in so much pain! I hope this memory doesn't affect my love of Beyoncé. I might only ever think of her as someone whose songs I lost my toe to. I feel like the whole thing is going to fall off. Mam is still banging on about the fact she thinks I need to go to hospital.

* * *

I keep Googling the mirror. I have to have it. Mam says it's ridiculous and I can't justify spending that much on a mirror. But I don't care. It's got lights all round it! It's huge! And it's amazing.

Wednesday 29th

Woke up and my toenail looks like Sloth from *The Goonies*. It's so disgusting. Mam keeps coming into the room saying, 'You need to go to hospital,' but I'm not going. I'll just try and sleep it off.

* * *

Been in bed all day and the pain is getting worse. My toe has its own heartbeat and stinging sensation! I started crying and mam said she'd had enough. So she's taken me to the private hospital down the road.

* * *

The doctor said he had to remove THE WHOLE TOENAIL. He gave me three injections and then took it off, I just looked away. I can't believe I was so brave about it to be honest but it was hurting me that much I think I knew it couldn't get any worse. He had to scrape loads of stuff out too and Mam nearly fainted. The nurse had to put a fan in front of her face! After he'd done it the doctor looked at it and said, 'There's an infection under here.' Mam was nearly jumping up and down with excitement, 'I told you it was an infection!' OK, calm down. It's not like you need to get a wide-on about it.

@charlottegshore
People I love most my mama, my dad and my little brother.

Thursday 30th

I've rung the shop with the mirror and told them I want it.

Mam told me to ring them back and tell them I've changed my mind.

July 2016

Snogs I've had with an amazing man who I want to marry (and am now obsessed with): One (and his hair is LONG)

Emojis showing my annoyance that I seem to have signed my love life away to a dating show: 😠😠😠😠😠

Friday 1st

The gang are back from filming *Geordie Shore* and apparently Gary has been telling Sophie that he wants to make amends and be with me! Obviously though he said it all on camera so I didn't believe a word of it. This came at the end of the show, after he'd had his fun out there shagging loads of girls. I can't help thinking it's just very convenient to say all that about me at the end of the show!

* * *

Got a text from Gary saying he missed me and that the show wasn't the same without me. I replied that I didn't believe

175

him. The worst thing is that I still have feelings for him. I can't handle this again. I can't do it to myself.

As long as I don't see him in person then that will make things easier.

Saturday 2nd

At least not having been in *Geordie Shore* means I've kept my fitness up. I always used to put so much weight on in that house but I've slowly been able to start exercising again since the operation which is making me feel a bit better about myself. David's been with me because we're doing another DVD in November so we've got a lot of work to do! I love hanging out with him though, he feels like he's one of my family. I can tell him anything and he's really good at boy advice.

I've been messaging a boy called Ellis Lacy. He was on *The X Factor* a while ago and he's a good singer and is really cute. He's tall with tattoos everywhere! Everyone was talking about him on the internet in May because he did a Snapchat faceswap with Harry Styles and people thought it was Harry with a new haircut. I just thought he was fit and started following him on Twitter. And now he's asked me out! Tomorrow!

* * *

Had a check-up at the St John and St Elizabeth. The doctors there are so incredible. They said I was healing really well since the operation and were so lovely about it. It's hard to remember how hideous my first experience there was because they are just so amazing. It's a really wonderful place.

Sunday 3rd

Ellis was a totally different vibe to French Kev. He was really touchy-feely and it felt natural and nice. I'm going on a second date with him next week.

The mirror's in the sale! Mam can't moan now! The shop called to tell me and asked if I want it. OF *course* I WANT IT!

Monday 4th

Gary has been messaging saying he wants to meet up. We haven't seen each other since everything's happened. Oh God. I feel like I need to get that closure but I'm so so scared. The girls have been telling me there's no way I can meet him.

I need to have a proper argument with Gary face to face and tell him how I feel. He keeps saying he wants to see me and that he misses me and wants to get back together. Can't he understand what that does to me?

Wednesday 6th

Was booked onto a quiz show called *The Tipping Point* with Jimmy Carr and David Haye today. Charlotte's carer and all-round employee – Mam – was obviously booked in for driving duties and Sophie came along for the ride.

We needed to be in London by 11 a.m. so we set off at 5 a.m.. Me and Sophie brought blankets and pillows and were asleep before the car reached Durham services! But Mam was soooo slow that when I woke up at 9 a.m. we were way behind schedule. I told my number-one employee that this would need to be discussed at the next board meeting.

We were getting later and later, and the TV company messages at 10 a.m. to say they're going to have to replace me with Sinitta! Of all people! I told me mam to put her foot down.

Charlotte: Bloody hell, they are giving the job to Sinitta now. Get your foot down!
Mam: I can't go any faster, it's the traffic. I've been up since 4 a.m. I need a coffee, can we stop?
Charlotte: No way. They are giving the job to Sinitta, we need to get there for 11 a.m.
Mam: I'm really tired!!
Charlotte: Here, take these! [I gave her a pack of Pro Plus.]

Mam wasn't sure but Sophie and I persuaded her and she took them in the end. Suddenly the traffic cleared up and, before we knew it, we were at the studio gate for 11 a.m . . . Mam moaned afterwards that I flew out of the car and didn't even say thank you.

Thursday 7th

I've found a bed I want and it's massive. Everything in this house is going to be oversized and overstated! Mam says it's a stupid size and that I'm not a giant so I don't need a bed that fits about eight people. I think she just doesn't want to have to find new sheets that are big enough to go on it!

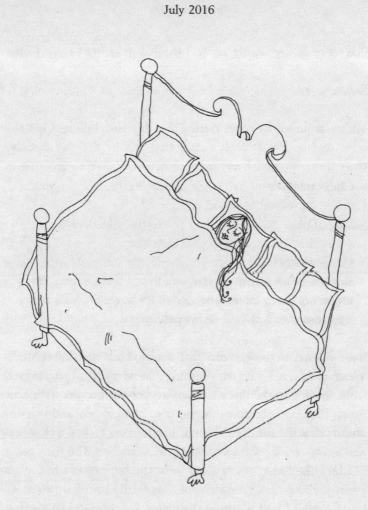

Friday 8th

Went out for some food with Ellis. He stayed over in my hotel but nothing happened. We only kissed (he was a good kisser!). I feel a bit scared to sleep with him for some reason. I don't think I'm ready.

Gary's been messaging again. I think I'm going to meet him.

Saturday 9th

We've arranged to meet during the day just before I get the train to London. It feels better that it's in the day because then there won't be any alcohol involved. We're meeting in a hotel restaurant.

Sunday 10th

> @charlottegshore
> Don't look back and wonder why things went wrong. Don't regret not doing more. It happened for a reason. Your better days are ahead of you. @sayingsforgirls

Saw this quote tonight and all I could think was 'WHEN???!' When are these better days coming and why can't I stop myself from looking back? I'm struggling to come to terms with how much hurt one person can cause me. I feel lonely and worried about what the future will bring. I'm longing to feel a closeness and a connection with someone again. Someone who truly cares.

I feel like I'm a far cry away from the happiness I felt when I was making that sandwich for Gary. I had no worries at all but whether I had buttered the bread appropriately. How fast things change.

Tuesday 12th

I'm meeting Gary in two days. I can't tell the girls. They'll kill me!! I can't tell anyone. But it's something I just have to do.

What is happening to Nathaniel!? Mam was watching something on TV and there was a couple having sex in bed in one of the scenes so she told me to turn over because it was too rude in front of Nathaniel and he just piped up, 'I've seen much ruder things than that.'

Thursday 14th

Well, that was all very weird. Not sure how I feel. I went for lunch with Gary. It's the first time I have seen him since he went away to Thailand four months ago, and the first time our relationship hasn't been part of a TV show.

I didn't bother getting dressed up. I looked like a tramp in fact. I just had my comfy onesie on and a jacket. No make-up and my hair tied up.

I felt really nervous before I was going to meet him, but when I saw him he just looked the same as he's always looks. He never looks any different: skinny, a bit haggard in the face and very orange. He'd gone too far with the suntan in Magaluf as usual and come back looking like a leather glove. I don't know why I fancy him – he looks all frail, like an old man.

When he arrived he just started asking normal questions as if nothing had happened. I wanted to scream and shout at him! But it wasn't the right environment to start smashing plates about. It was quite posh. I instantly realised a hotel wasn't the right place for this type of meeting. It was so quiet, there was no way we could have the argument I needed to have. The whole thing was just a bit of a let-down. Gary just talked about himself – what he was doing and what he has planned. The new car he's getting . . . as if NOTHING IS WRONG.

I tried to talk about what had gone on and he just kept brushing it away saying, 'You know I'm sorry, Charlotte. I'm sorry it happened.'

We were together for about an hour then I had to get my train.

Does this mean I need to see him again?? How can he actually think we can go back to normal after all he has done to me? What the actual fuck? This was a bad idea. Nothing can ever be salvaged.

Can it?

I need to get Gary out of my head. I actually can't wait for *Celebs Go Dating* to start filming.

Wednesday 15th

@charlottegshore
@realdonaldtrump hiya follow me please.

I'm so interested in Donald Trump and what the hell is going on over in America! When he said he was running for president I thought it was a joke. He's a reality TV star, isn't he? I wonder if he will follow me back?

Went to look at the house again and Mam took me into the bathroom. She and dad had ordered a brass bath behind my back to try and take my mind of the £20,000 one! She was showing it to me really proudly, saying how nice it looked in the space and I just turned to her and said, 'It's got to be removed.' That wasn't her mission. It's totally different to the one I wanted and it's the ugliest bath I have ever seen in my life. It looks like it's been left outside for so long it's gone rusty. I am not sitting in that bath. I will turn into the Tin Man.

She has now had to promise she will try to find me one like the £20,000 one but a fraction of the price. I don't think she will, but Letitia's competitive like me and she knows how to rise to a challenge.

Tuesday 19th

DONALD TRUMP is an official candidate for the Republican party. So he could actually be president! Isn't that so weird?! He will never beat Hillary Clinton though. She seems like she has balls of steel.

Wednesday 20th

Argh!! Decisions have to be made on the dining room and I'm sick of it. I can't be bothered. How bad can a dining room be? No one's ever going to sit in there so I told Mam just to keep it simple.

Friday 22nd

Filming started on *Celebs Go Dating* today. It's based around a celebrity dating agency in London with agents called Nadia and Eden and an amazingly camp receptionist called Tom. They're meant to find dates for the celebrities with normal non-celeb people. The idea is that they properly match us up according to personality type and things we're interested in.

The other celebs doing the show are Joey Essex, Stephanie Pratt from *Made In Chelsea*, Tyger Drew-Honey from *Outnumbered*, Paisley Billings who was a receptionist in a show called *Tattoo Fixers* and a YouTuber called Jack Jones. I love

Joey so much; he really makes me laugh, but I bet I won't get to see him much because the show is all about celebs finding love with normal people not each other.

We all had to go in one at a time to meet the producers and got read the rules. I'm not allowed to date anyone who isn't on this show! There was a long list of things that we can and can't do. I AM UNDER LOCK AND KEY! KATE HAS SIGNED AWAY MY LOVE LIFE FOR TWO MONTHS!!! WHAT THE HELL HAVE I DONE?

Nadia and Eden have been through loads of applicants to work out who would match best with who. They've had to go through DBS checks and everything to make sure they're not criminals and won't murder us on a date.

I had to do a big interview with them about the sort of man I wanted. It was a bit like a therapy session. I told them I want to date someone who wasn't going to finish with me if I accidentally wet the bed. And someone who has pubes, because I like pubes.

Then they asked me about past relationships and I obviously broke down in tears. I couldn't help it. The Gary stuff still feels so raw when I have to talk about it. I told them, 'My last relationship was so shit. I don't want to get upset again because all I do is cry about it. It was awful.'

I still don't quite understand how this is going to work though. I hope it doesn't do my head in.

Saturday 23rd

It's Laura's birthday and we're in Manchester for the weekend. Before we went out I tweeted that I was off to Neighbourhood (it always helps if you do that because then they give you free drinks!). We were in the VIP area when Melissa saw that Ash Harrison from *Big Brother* had tweeted me back to say he was going out in Manchester tonight too and that I should come and say 'hi'. Mel then proceeded to wet herself with excitement because he walked through the door and started coming over. I've bumped into him a few times before when I've been on *Big Brother's Bit on the Side* and we've sent each other a few flirty tweets. I always thought he was good-looking but a bit too grown-up and sophisticated for me. I thought he was out of my league.

But OH MY GOD, WHEN HE CAME OVER HE WAS SO FIT IN THE FLESH!

He was wearing a white shirt and had his hair tied back and once we started talking we didn't stop ALL NIGHT. I looked a mess and I had make-up caked on my face because Melissa turned up late and I'd had to do it myself. But he didn't seem to care. There was a lot of drunken chat, I can't remember most of what we said but he was gorgeous. I fell in love with him straight away.

* * *

We snogged and then he came back to our hotel . . .

Sunday 24th

I am in love. I know it. I can't stop talking about him and I can't stop thinking about him.

I think I've turned into a crazy bunny boiler because I've been messaging Ash all day saying things like, 'My phone's going to run out of battery but I'm devastated because all I want to do is text you.' He was saying really nice things back too. It feels like it's full-on already and it's amazing.

He's twenty-eight, he's older than me and I like that. He's very manly which is extremely attractive. He's got his own swimwear company too – and is a model.

* * *

ARGH. There was a pap taking pictures of us outside the club last night and now it's all over the *Sun*. Shit.

> Hot new couple? Charlotte Crosby was pictured leaving Manchester club Neighbourhood with male model Ash Harrison. Although there's no evidence to suggest they're more than just friends, Charlotte's easy-on-the-eye companion placed a protective hand on her shoulder as they left the venue.

What am I going to say to the show? I'm literally not allowed to be with anyone else. Nadia and Eden might as well just have a lock around my knickers.

Monday 25th

I told Kate to tell Nadia and Eden he's nothing more than just some guy I met in a club.

I can't stop thinking about him.

Tuesday 26th

Snuck back to see Ash in Manchester. I know I shouldn't be seeing him so I can't let anyone spot us this time. What's that saying about forbidden fruit tasting sweeter? Mmmm. I want to eat Ash.

Wednesday 27th

I LOVE ASH SO MUCH.

Invited him to the launch of Mark Hill's Pick N Mix Wand at Ice Tank in London. Everyone was there including Sophie and Chloe so they got to meet him. They all said they thought he was lovely. Sophie said she doesn't find him attractive though because she doesn't like long hair. I don't care, she only ever goes for charvas anyway. He has amazing hair. How can you not want to stroke it constantly?!

Later on we went to Libertine for drinks and afterwards Ash and I snuck off.

Friday 29th

Filming again for *Celebs Go Dating* and we had to go to a thing called 'the mixer', which is a room you walk into full of all the potential boys for your dates! I guess it's called the mixer because you have to mix with them – unless it just means you're allowed to drink loads of booze and need some serious mixers! It was so weird because they were just all circling me, Stephanie and Paisley like vultures.

When I agreed to go on the show I had high hopes that I might actually meet someone, but as soon as I got in the mixer and they were all surrounding us it felt so desperate. And that's not what you want to see in a man! I walked in and four blokes pounced on me and didn't even give me a chance to breathe. When you're in a normal situation in a bar boys don't behave like that! In the end I got pissed and started asking them all about the size of their willies to see how they would react. I just had to act stupid to get through it.

There wasn't anyone I fancied but we had to pick someone to go on a date with by the end of the night so I chose a guy called Danny.

Saturday 30th

Went on a date with Danny and got mortal then snogged him in the doorway of the bar.

That was the wrong thing to do.

What was I thinking?

I obviously wooed him with my chat about the fact I'd had anal bleaching. He didn't know what it was so I had to explain that, 'It's where you turn your bum hole white instead of brown.'

He did admit that he'd weed in his shoes while drunk though, which made me like him a bit. When I told him I'd accidentally wet the bed a couple of times he seemed weirdly turned on and said he would 'do backflips' if that actually happened.

Snogging him afterwards just seemed like a good idea. I kept thinking I had to do something otherwise it would be weird and wouldn't make good TV. I couldn't go on a date and not even kiss someone, could I?! Come on! That's going to be a bit boring to watch.

Sunday 31st

One of the good things about being on this show is that I've got to hang out with the other celebs more than I expected because we've been doing some bits of filming together. Obviously I love Joey because I know him the best. Every time we're together we have such a laugh. We're like brother and sister. He has a weird dress sense but I think that makes him unique.

I'm blown away by how lovely and kind and generous Steph is. I didn't really know what to expect of her but she has so much time for everyone and always seems to be in a good mood. I envy her for that because I can be so moody.

Paisley seems like fun. She's close with Steph though, so I haven't had chance to form a strong bond.

Tyger is so sweet, he's only young but he's such a gentleman. He's so lovely.

Jack is nice but irritating. He's meant to be funny but I just think he tries too hard.

When I meet new people I'm the best Charlotte I can be but when I'm around people I know I'm awful! Here's my rating of who I'm worst behaved in front of:

Adam and Jamie from In The Style: I'm always moaning with them. The best way to deal with me when I'm moody is DON'T BE POSITIVE – life isn't always good. You have to be realistic about things. Don't give me compliments either.
Kate: She always gets the brunt of my moods.
Me mam: But then I do phone her up sometimes out of the blue and tell her I love her so I think that makes up for it.
Melissa: We argue so much but we're like sisters so the love runs deep and we always forgive each other.

August 2016

Amount of time I've spent stroking Ash's lovely long hair: Approximately twenty hours (if you add up all the minutes)

One word to describe how Joey Essex makes me feel whenever I see him: Happy

Best food I've eaten all month: Gravy

Emojis to describe how in love with Ash I am right now: ♥♥♥♥♥♥

Monday 1st

The papers won't let go of the story about me and Ash, the *Sun* said:

> Charlotte Crosby has become 'inseparable' from hunky male model Ash Harrison after the pair first stepped out together in Manchester on Saturday 23 July.

Since then the hot new couple have partied together in London, and were pictured cosying up in a hotel room after they were spotted sneaking out of a nightclub together . . .

Wednesday 3rd

Oh my God, he's so fit. I can't stop looking at pictures of him. His hair is really nice. I'm so buzzing that I have a boyfriend with long hair. I am so uncool because I just keep messaging him and telling him how much I fancy him.

* * *

The papers are full of photos of Orlando Bloom and Katy Perry on holiday. He's totally naked on a paddleboard while she's just sat there in front of him casually drinking a beer.

My mate sent me the uncensored picture where you can properly see his willy (they pixelated it out in the papers). Why did he actually do that? His willy is a weird one, it's not even like a grower, it's very long and thin. I feel like he should get a circumcision. It looks like one of those very tall, skinny mushrooms that grow on the side of trees, or sometimes in the garden. I can't remember what they're called. Like a fungus. Like a magic mushroom! I hope it is magic for Katy's sake. Orlando was my first celebrity crush and now he definitely isn't any more.

Thursday 4th

The *Celebs Go Dating* agents Nadia and Eden are doing my head in. They have matched me with this guy called Jeavon who gives me the creeps. He's a butler in the buff and has really long flicky hair.

Friday 5th

The house is so massive that it's taking ages!! When is it going to be finished?? Dad called me today and asked me about tiles for the pool and I ended up shouting, 'I'm sick of fucking tiles! There's tiles everywhere!' Mam got the phone and started shouting back at me, 'You wanted it! Stop moaning and learn to be a grown-up!'

I had to get pissed before I met Jeavon, just to get through the date. But actually it wasn't that bad! He looked quite nice in fact. He had his hair up (obviously he was nowhere near as hot as Ash but I could pretend through my blurry drunken eyes . . .).

BUT . . . I don't know what was going on in my brain . . . I snogged him at the end of the night!

What is wrong with me?!

I wish I hadn't because I love Ash.

As Daniel Bedingfield once said – I've just gotta get through this.

* * *

Ferne McCann's had her nose job! She didn't tell anyone but she's just sent me a sneaky Snapchat of her with the cast on. I'm so pleased for her. I can't wait to see what it looks like. I sent her a message back saying, 'Oh my God, you got it done! What the hell!'

Saturday 6th

Came back home for the night in between filming. Went to the new house and there's a fucking bus shelter in the middle of the garden. What has the gardener done? Mam said, 'Paul the gardener will be so offended if he knows you've said that. He's worked his arse off for the last month!' But it looks so weird. I don't remember asking for a bus stop!

* * *

I got the most incredible email today. It was sent to Kate but addressed to me.

Hello Charlotte
  I really hope you get to see this.
  Firstly, I am a huge fan of yours and I think you are a fantastic woman!
  Secondly I'd like to share my story with you.
  I am 21 years old and five months ago I gave birth to my beautiful son. Happiest moment of my life. Since then everything was normal until earlier this week, I finally came on my period. I was late and had taken pregnancy tests to be sure but they came up negative so when I started bleeding and was in a lot of pain I thought it was normal after having my first child. However, the pain was bad and only on one side. With having a baby I just got on with it not wanting to call for help thinking I would be called silly for crying over period pains. The pain continued over the days and the blood wouldn't stop. I prayed it would go but it didn't. Finally I woke this morning in agony on my right side and I was going to try and ignore it again but

then my brain just switched to thinking about you and your experience and I knew I had to call for help. An ambulance arrived and I was taken to hospital. At the hospital the pain got worse, I went to do a urine sample and afterwards collapsed. After testing they discovered I was experiencing an ectopic pregnancy, my Fallopian tube had burst and I had severe internal bleeding. I was rushed to theatre to have my Fallopian tube removed etc. I was all alone; unfortunately my partner had to stay with our baby until someone could get him so all I kept thinking was how brave you were and how you was alone and so I said to myself 'if Charlotte Crosby can do it so can I'.

The surgery was a success. I am back to full health but still recovering.

I just wanted to say you are such a brave woman to have gone through what you went through alone with Gary away, at least I had my partner's support but also thank you.

Thank you for being brave enough to speak out after such a scary experience, if it wasn't for that I don't think I would have thought about you and gotten the help when I did. It wasn't just the surgical team that worked to save me, you had a part to play too. Now I can go home be with my fiancé and love and care for my child. If I hadn't thought of you and gotten the help I don't know if I would be able to say that.

So again thank you, I can't tell you how sorry I am for what happened to you, I can say from first-hand experience you are just wow! Well done for still being such a funny inspirational person even after your ordeal.

Sorry for writing such a long essay!

To think that my experience has actually helped save some-one's life? It really shook me up. It almost makes the whole thing worthwhile. When I wrote my bucket list for *Me Me Me* one of the things on it was to save someone's life; if sharing my experience means I've helped save someone's life then that's such a good feeling. I hope to really raise awareness of the condition and save lots of lives in the future too!

Sunday 7th

Everyone who's met him says they like Ash but they don't think he's marriage material. Which is stupid because he clearly is. Sophie thinks he's a bit too sensible for me. And I had an argument with Melissa tonight because she said there's no spark between us and that I'm not the same around him as I am with other boyfriends. She was really pissed and kept going on about it. I snapped at her in the end.

* * *

I've been scrolling through my messages and everything I send to Ash is so over the top I'm amazed it hasn't put him off me. I keep saying things like, 'I fancy you so much, I've never fancied anyone like this before . . .'

Talk about playing hard to get.

He just keeps saying, 'I bet you say this to everyone . . .' Like he doesn't believe me or something. How much more do I need to do to convince him? Have his beautiful head (and hair) tattooed on my fanny?

195

Monday 8th

Nadia and Eden quizzed me about Jeavon and because I said he wasn't as bad as I'd thought he would be they have told me to go on another date with him in case he's a 'match'. So we're going on a picnic. How bad can that be?

* * *

The picnic in the park went very sour. Firstly I didn't fancy him AT ALL when he arrived. I stayed sober the whole date this time and I could not bear him. I can't even bear to write his name now. The long hair. Everything. I can't stand him.

Then, just to pass the time I asked him about how many girls he'd been with in the past.

I said I didn't want an exact number but asked him to say 'higher' or 'lower' depending on the number I gave him. When I got to fifty he told me to stop and said he'd probably slept with that many girls 'in eleven years'. Which was fine, that didn't bother me. But what DID bother me was when he decided to turn the tables on me and I told him I'd shagged around twenty lads and he looked at me with the worst disapproving face EVER.

EH?

I said, 'What's the issue? Is that bad for a girl?' and he replied, 'That is bad. For a lad it's not that bad.'

Is he for real? 'For a lad it's not that bad?' Talk about double standards!

I said to him, 'I've had about eight or nine boyfriends,' and he had the cheek to say 'That's bad. That's bad for a girl!' I was fuming by this point. What a hypocrite! I told him, 'Apart from my boyfriends, that's like having sex with one person a year. That is not bad!'

I told him the picnic had been a let-down. 'You brought a shit picnic and you said I'm a slag. There was a threat of rain earlier and now I wish it had rained and I wouldn't have had to sit through this.'

Tuesday 9th

Ash is unbelievably fit. We've been messaging each other all day. I am counting the days until I see him next. I'm in London loads for filming but we've said we're going to try and sneak dates in as much as possible. We're going to go to this amazing restaurant called Panoramic 34 in Liverpool that Kate has recommended. It's got the most amazing views of the city. I can't believe I'm dating a model! And he's really trendy! I feel like the daft one and he's the laid-back, chilled one. He says he thinks I'm crazy and funny and he's always laughing at me. I think the girls he usually goes for are really pretty but a bit straight which is maybe why he likes me. I don't really laugh at him much but because he laughs at me and I laugh at myself there's still A LOT of laughter!

* * *

All the celebs from the show were filmed in a pub chatting together about how our dates were going and I was trying to give Tyger some advice on how to behave with girls because he's been a bit rubbish. I said he needed to get nasty and have some attitude. His chat is still a bag of shite though.

Joey had one date where a girl couldn't stop burping and eating lemons! Joey has had some seriously weird encounters but there's a blonde model girl called Becky he seems to like. He was on a date with her and called me from the loo to give me an update. I asked if he'd kissed her and he said he had but no tongues, which I said meant he hadn't *really* kissed her. He reckons she's 'a sort' and tried to show me her on FaceTime but all I could see was a shelf of wine glasses.

No one else has kissed on any of their dates apart from me.

Wednesday 10th

It was the mixer again tonight which meant I had to face Danny and Jeavon in the same place! Luckily there were a few new guys in there because there is no way on earth I can face going out on another date with either of them.

* * *

Just got distracted . . . I've found a really nice photo of myself in my phone pictures.

* * *

Danny and Jeavon both started circling me asking if I wanted a drink. I felt really anxious because they were staring at me and I don't fancy either of them! Jeavon dragged me to the bar at one point and I just wanted a sambuca to calm my nerves. I said, 'Let's talk about that awful picnic!' and all he could reply was, 'It didn't go as well as I wanted but if I got another chance I'd definitely make it work.'

ANOTHER CHANCE!? WELL THAT'S A RIDICULOUS JOKE!

I just want ASH.

I gave Steph one too many shots to so we all ended up really pissed (it's the only way to get through it). I was getting bored so I amused myself by asking a group of guys if any of them had chlamydia. Then I asked if they'd ever had an STI check. And then if anyone had a big round bellend?!

Steph walked off and said, 'For God's sake, Charlotte!'

I thought it was funny.

After what felt like a million years I eventually started chatting to a guy called Brad from Grimsby. He had a lovely face and seemed fun.

But when I went to the bar Danny collared me and asked what was going on and I said, 'No . . . er . . . I don't know.'

He said, 'What's your problem then?'

I wanted the ground to swallow me up and then, to make matters even worse, Jeavon came over! Oh my God, it was so cringe. I had Danny in one ear and Jeavon in the other and they were both trying to outdo each other. Jeavon asked Danny what our date was out of ten and he said, 'A strong nine and a half.'

Then Jeavon asked what I would say it was. I said, 'I don't want to be put in that position!' and walked away. I went and sat on the stairs outside and Brad came out to chat to me. He asked me what the matter was and was being quite entertaining. I asked him how old he was and he got really evasive. He asked how old I thought he was and I replied, 'I hope you're not twenty-two.' Then he said, 'You'll find out if you take me on a date!' I knew he wasn't telling me because he knows he's younger than my age guideline which is twenty-five. He tried to convince me he was thirty which was clearly a lie. I reckon he is twenty-two. But he will have to do for my next date anyway because he's the best of a very bad bunch.

He is fit and he smells good.
Thank God for Brad.

Thursday 11th

Mam called and says she's found the perfect bath for me and saved me £19,000! Nice one, Mam. She has found a place that can make the bath like the one I wanted but for £1,000! Mission accomplished. She'd better not ask for a bonus. She will have to do A LOT more than find me a bath for that. She keeps saying she has such a hard job looking after me and the dogs but I've told her she has it so easy! She gets paid £10 an hour to be my driver when she's hardly driving me anywhere! She basically just sits and strokes the dogs on her lap all day and she calls that work?!

Charlotte's Guide To: Employing Your Family

This is always bit tricky because work environments are stressful and inviting your family member into it can often make you want to punch their heads in.

No matter what, they always think that they can get away with a lot more 'cos they're YOUR MAM. My mam thinks she can get away with murder, but little does she know that if she carries on not picking up her phone or trying to tell me what to do in MY OWN HOUSE she's getting sacked! Hahahahaha. Only kidding. Even if we ever were to fall out it wouldn't be for long because she's my mam at the end of the day. It's some genetic thing we are born with where people with our blood are just too hard to stay mad with for long.

Ferne popped by
to visit me at my
Mark Hill stand.

Our tent at V Festival was too hot.

The bigger the better.

Hard Rock Hotel with Sophie.

Love my little Nana.

We always do Halloween best.

I love Jamie!

Crazy road trip with
my best friend Anna.

Having a pool is so handy… and a gym!

Dildo hair tong.

At the Burberry fundraiser for the Ectopic Pregnancy Trust.

Love him!

Our holiday in paradise.

Fun helicopter ride.

At my book signing.

The Brits: the night I got the
worst dressed award and people
said I looked pregnant.

Really missing Ash. Wish I could see him all the time. *Celebs Go Dating* is getting harder and harder. The more time goes on, the stronger my feelings for Ash are getting. WHAT THE HELL AM I GOING TO DO? I could get sacked for this. It's against all the rules. DAMN.

All the most amazing things come at the wrong times . . .

Friday 12th

I want a baby with Ash. I'm so broody.

If it's boy I want to call it Hudson Harrison or Moses Harrison. For a girl I quite like MeMe but that's a bit like the title of my first book. Imagine if I write a baby book and call it *Me Me Me and MeMe*!

I keep talking to Ash about babies. I think at first he thought I was joking but tonight he sat down and said, really seriously, that he didn't think it was a good idea.

I just can't help it. All I want is a baby!

I must be getting broody because of the operation but I think it's also because everywhere I look people are pregnant! Sam Faiers has had a baby, Billy Faiers has had a baby. It seems like a fun thing to do! My friends keep saying, 'Are you stupid? You've only been with him for a couple of weeks!'

Sophie is so angry but I said I don't care . . . I just want the baby.

Saturday 13th

Feel a bit fat today. I'm still trying to work out three to four times a week but since the operation I've been on a contraceptive injection and now the doctor has told me that it's an appetite accelerant. So that's why I've constantly been thinking about hot dogs lately! I told me mam and she said that she was about to ask me why I was constantly shovelling in carrots and hummus every second of the day. Hummus is OK but only in moderation – not when you're inhaling the stuff!

Nadia and Eden have been asking what I expect from my date with Brad. They think I will have a ball of a time with him. They said he really likes me and is excited. But they always say that.

I'm not looking forward to it.

I've now decided I think Brad is twenty-four which is a year too young for me. I tried to check Facebook to see how old he was but couldn't get anything. I'm just going to have to get drunk.

I said on camera that even though he seems young he does seem like he has a big willy. Sometimes you can just tell.

Sunday 14th

I've been telling Ash I love him ever since we met but I do actually mean it now. I've fallen for him big time. He is so amazing. He has such nice eyes. He looks like Jesus and you know how I've always wanted to have Jesus as a boyfriend! Me and Jesus. Finally together.

Monday 15th

Went to the In The Style summer party last night with Ash and got stupidly pissed and started messing about with his

Snapchat afterwards. I recorded a video on his phone at about 4 a.m. and wrote a caption over my mouth saying, 'This is where my penis goes,' and now it's been picked up online! I didn't think it was a big deal but now loads of people are messaging me saying it's the worst thing ever to happen and that Ash is revolting. Oh SHIT. I can't tell anyone it's me because of *Celebs Go Dating*! I feel bad for Ash because now everyone thinks he's an idiot.

* * *

I'm not looking forward to this date with Brad tonight. None of the others have been any good and I'm so over this whole dating thing. At least he's coming to Newcastle so I don't have to go far. We are going to the Chicken Coop and I'm taking a Tupperware box of gravy with me because they don't have a gravy side dish. I hope he doesn't get excited and think I have too many wifely characteristics because of my culinary skills – I'm not ready for him to ask me to marry him.

* * *

Brad loved the fact that I brought gravy! He said I got a hundred brownie points and that my gravy was up there with one of the best gravies he's ever tasted. I made him play a game of hot sauce roulette. When you ate something really hot you had to drink milk to try to stop your mouth burning. I was having such a good time I didn't feel like I needed to have any booze – what was wrong with me?

His age was still bugging me. I said, 'You are a handsome, attractive man . . . how old are you?'

He kept answering the same thing: 'Why are you bothered? Age is just a number!'

There's something fishy. Why won't he tell me?

I asked what he did for a living and he said he works in a fish factory. I wonder what he smells like at the end of a shift. (Clue: it rhymes with angina.). I asked if he had ever come across a mermaid and he said he had then started telling me this story about when he saw one once with a long tail. I fell for it until he said she revealed her face, said, 'Hiya!' and waved!

We had a good night and I know if I wasn't with Ash – and OBSESSED WITH HIM – then I would probably want to give things with Brad a go. We do have a lot of chemistry and he's got a good personality. He also paid for the food which was a nice touch. I said on camera that his hot-sauce face looks like the same as his man-sauce face. But people expect me to say stuff like that. I hope Ash doesn't get annoyed when he watches it back. I can't stop thinking about how I'm coming across on camera with other men. I don't want to do anything that embarrasses him.

There was a pap outside and he started saying, 'Who's your new lad, Charlotte?'

Great.

Tuesday 16th

Ferne revealed her new nose on *This Morning* and it looks incredible. I'm so pleased for her. I messaged her afterwards saying how pretty she looked.

She chatted to Ruth and Eamonn about it and they were all so lovely. I couldn't help thinking that if Ferne was to go on *Loose Women* I bet they wouldn't have had a go at her for

August 2016

it like they did with me. My whole body was shaking before
I went on that show because I knew I was going to get picked
on, and I did. Just because I had a nose job!

When I look back at old pictures of myself now I can't
stand it. I think I look so ugly. I just can't believe that
people can look at me and say, 'She was so much better
before.' That's a big lie! Why would people say that? I
looked like Vicky Pollard. My old face was so fat it looked
like it was swallowing my facial features. It was ridiculous.
I looked so rank!

Wednesday 17th

Back in London today for a double date with Joey and the
blonde model girl Becky, who he's now calling his 'posh salty
potato' Becky. As I've been friends with Joey for years I've
told him I want him to give Brad a once-over to see what he
thinks of him.

We were filming in the taxi on the way to the bar in
Camden and I said, 'Why are me and you wasting our time
with Brad and Rebecca?' and Joey joked, 'Well, if you want
to go on a date with me and you then I'm up for it . . .' At
least I think he was joking. He said I can do better than most
of the guys I've been with. But then he hasn't met Ash . . .

We were having shots before the others arrived and Joey
asked if Brad was fit. I typed his name into Google to show
him on my phone and HE WAS ALL OVER THE INTERNET!
Not only that but there was an 'exclusive interview' with the
Mirror about our date at Coop!

OH MY GOD!

When I read that I was fuming. I couldn't believe he'd sold a story on me!

Joey's date Becky arrived before Brad, she's a proper lady and gorgeous. Brad rocked up late and when Joey asked him what he did for a job and he told him he'd got the sack from the fish factory because of the show. I looked at him and said, 'Brad, I have a question to ask you. There was a story in a newspaper. Did you sell a story?' He looked like he didn't think he had done anything wrong and just shrugged. 'A newspaper called me up and asked me a few questions, but it was all positive.'

I was in shock. 'If a newspaper calls you, you don't DO that!'

Brad insisted they didn't offer him any money and he seemed genuine. I guess he's just naïve because he wasn't really to know, was he? In the end I laughed. 'I don't even think Joey would have done that and he's the thickest in all the world.' Joey didn't like that one very much!

Joey then asked Brad how old he was and he avoided the question again. Becky said she thought he was twenty-six and Joey said he thought he was twenty-eight. In the end he had to come clean . . .

HE IS TWENTY YEARS OLD!

I knew it!

Oh and he has a kid!

Friday 19th

The dating agency sent us all on a speed-dating night to see if there was anyone new we wanted to date.

I met one guy who looked about forty years old and he

decided to ask me some quick-fire questions to see how compatible we were: 'Lights on or off? Inside or outside? Dogs or cats?'

Then I asked him some of my own: 'Big or small? Have you ever pooed yourself?'

He paused which I took to mean he HAD pooed himself.

I would have had more luck speed dating a bottle of sambuca.

One fella looked like he was wearing blue contact lenses – they made him look like a weird alien. He asked if I would rather have a three-grand bracelet or something someone had made themselves. Before I had a chance to answer, he presented me with some peculiar, disgusting piece of metal that he'd clearly made himself in the garage. He then asked if he could take me on a date and I said I didn't want to be rude but . . . absolutely no chance, mate. He wouldn't give up though and said, 'Have a think about it and look at the bracelet,' and then had the cheek to tell me he might not choose me anyway because he might opt for Steph or Paisley instead!

There was no one who gave me any fanny flutters. But then guess who turned up . . .

BRAD.

And this time I was SO happy to see him.

I told Brad I had thought about it and I wasn't bothered about the child thing but it was just the fact he'd lied about his age. He said he hadn't told me the truth because he knew I wouldn't go on a date with him and he knew we would get on so he wanted to make sure I gave him a chance. And he does have a point. I have got on better with him than anyone else. We all need a date for the 'final dinner' party, so I told him we could go out again. I just hope Ash doesn't get jealous when he watches it.

Brad is fit and everything but he's still not Ash.

The best thing about this whole show is Tom the receptionist at the dating agency. He's so funny and cute. He's like something out of a Disney film. He's just so delicate and dainty and leaps about all the time like he's a cartoon. He doesn't seem like a real person because he's so sweet and perfect. He could almost be a little fairy.

Sunday 21st

Spent the most amazing weekend at the V Festival with Mark Hill to promote some of his products. I was on a stand doing meet-and-greets, putting people's hair up and giving them glitter roots while shouting on a megaphone. I was like an extra-loud glittery hairdresser! I was feeling very energetic on the first day but then I started drinking with Anna and Melissa all evening (Justin Bieber was a bit shit but Anne Marie was amazing). We were staying in a bell tent and were just sweating everywhere all night. The next day I was SOOO hungover and I had to do loads of filming of hair tutorials. I never want to watch those back again. I don't usually get hangovers but this was BAD.

Saw Mark Wright in the VIP tent on the Sunday and he looked a bit moody. I found out it's because he had a massive great fight with Danny Dyer yesterday! Or at least his mates did. Something kicked off by the toilets anyway. I'd be on Danny Dyer's side. I reckon we'd really get on if we hung out. He's really naughty and cheeky.

Monday 22nd

I was filming in Oxford Street in London and had a massive nervous-breakdown crazy-arse meltdown in the middle of the road. I just couldn't do it anymore. I miss Ash too much. I told the producers I really like someone on the outside. I was screaming and crying. They sat me down and I told them all about Ash and how much I loved him and how I couldn't cheat on him and that this was just really bad timing. They were really nice and suggested Ash comes to the agency and I have a date with him but I know there's no way he would want to do it.

209

I called him and he said exactly what I thought he would say. He doesn't want our relationship on screen. He's seen what's happened to all my other relationships and he doesn't want to be in the public eye anymore. He has his swimwear business and modelling and that's all he's interested in.

It feels like I've been on this show for a lifetime! I've been with Ash a month now and I've only seen him a couple of times.

Tuesday 23rd

Brad took me to the dog races – he did absolutely nothing wrong but I'm just not in the mood any more. I'm finding it really hard to enjoy myself when really all I want to do is tell everyone I'm with Ash. And I feel bad for leading Brad on. At one point he put his arm round me and I know he wanted to kiss me, and probably felt like he should, but I couldn't turn my head towards him. The woman behind the bar started asking on-camera what the date was like and how it was all going and I admitted we hadn't snogged even though we'd been on three dates. Brad asked her if she thought it was weird that we hadn't kissed and in the end I had to give him a peck on the lips.

Wednesday 24th

As soon as the adverts were out of me doing *Celebs Go Dating* Gary has decided he will write a column about trying to find Gaz a girlfriend! I can't believe I ever dated him, or loved him, or cared about him at all. He makes me feel sick. He's just a vile human being. I can switch off every feeling I ever had now because I know that we were never ever EVER meant to be. It was all just a thing that materialised from us both being together on a TV show. There were never true, genuine feelings there. It was just in the bubble of *Geordie Shore* and now I'm away from that I can see it so much clearer. I'd be really happy never to have to see him ever again in my whole entire life.

Me and Brad had to go to the agency today for a 'compatibility test' with the body-language expert Judi James. It was like being in the headteacher's office! She asked Brad loads of questions like whether he was a fan of mine and he said 'used to be'. He told her he liked me because I wasn't putting on an act and that I was the same in real life as I was on camera. But then he also said he thought I had a guard up. Then she started asking me how Brad compared to other people I've dated (WELL HE'S NOT ASH!!) and in the end she decided that we have the same sense of humour and good body language and gave us 70 per cent.

I don't want Ash to see this when it goes out on TV. I don't want him to think I am better suited to Brad than him!! I haven't spoken to him much about any of the dates and I don't think he wants to know. He just wants me to get on with it, get it over with and out of the way so we can be together.

I HATE THIS!

* * *

Oh, and in other brilliantly timed news, Kate has also signed me up to be the face of a new dating app called ShowReal. This means I am now committed to being 'single' for ANOTHER two months after *Celebs Go Dating* finishes. GGGGGRRRREEEAT. Kate might as well just cut all my hair off and give me a nun's outfit.

211

Thursday 25th

Did some filming and photos for ShowReal today. It launches in November but there's loads to get sorted before then. It's basically like Tinder but much better because instead of pictures of people you see videos they've uploaded talking about a few things different things – you film some five-second clips of yourself answering different questions. It's clever because you get to find out a bit more about what the person you are interested in is all about and you actually see what people really look and sound like because it's a video instead of just a photo.

I also met with Alex Peace-Gadsby and Munira Oza who run the Ectopic Pregnancy Trust. They came to the studio where I was shooting (Kate had arranged it, they didn't just rock up uninvited). They told me they had had loads of phone calls just from people reading my story in *heat*. People who had thought, 'Shit that's happening to me!' Some of them rang in and said they knew they had the same symptoms as I was describing in the article and said they'd been turned away from their doctors because the doctor just said it was normal pains from pregnancy and that it would be fine until the first scan. One girl was having the pains really badly and had been rushed to hospital. She was reading my interview while she was in the bed. Her husband was away for work so he couldn't be by her side but she said that reading what I'd gone through and seeing that Gary hadn't been there for me meant she felt better knowing she was lucky because her husband was coming back to support her and she wasn't alone. I couldn't believe it. When I look back on everything that's happened to me this year I never could have imagined that something so horrible could end up helping so many people.

I'd had emails and messages saying how much I'd helped other women but until I met the people from the Trust I didn't realise how much ignorance there is around ectopic pregnancy

The Trust has been supporting a woman for the last three years whose daughter died from having an ectopic pregnancy. Her daughter didn't even know she was pregnant. She was on a night out with her friends and had to call an ambulance because she was in that much pain. The first thing the para-medics said to her was, 'Are you drunk? Have you been taking drugs?' They just thought she was a stupid girl and was on the street. They left it so long before they tested her for pregnancy that she collapsed on the floor and had a seizure and died.

I was in shock.

People need to know the signs and the symptoms. Everyone knows the signs for a heart attack or a stroke but no one knows what it is for an ectopic pregnancy. The trust also said they had something like a 600 per cent increase in traffic to their website after my interview. They asked me to be a patron of the Trust. I'm so honoured! They said that I have opened the door to younger women who they need to target because they are more at risk of it happening to them. And hopefully I've made more men aware of the symptoms too.

I told them I was over the moon to be asked and felt very grateful. It's mad when you think out of something so dreadful you can get something important that really makes a difference.

Charlotte's Advice on: Signs of Ectopic Pregnancy

1. An ectopic pregnancy is when a fertilised egg implants outside the womb, usually in the fallopian tube, which was what happened to me.

2. The important signs to look out for are abdominal pain and vaginal bleeding – don't ignore these like I did, get medical advice straight away.

3. There's no obvious cause, but my consultant told me the risk factors include taking the morning-after pill (like me), previous pelvic inflammatory disease, having a coil, taking the mini pill, having had pelvic surgery or some infertility treatments.

4. There's only a 1 per cent chance of having an ectopic, but when you've had one the chance increases to 10 per cent. Once you've had an ectopic you should make sure you see a doctor early in any future pregnancies.

5. I was told I could have died – in the UK about five women die from complications as a result of an ectopic pregnancy every year.

Friday 26th

I have a new job lined up as a TV presenter! I'm going to be hosting a new show on MTV called *Just Tattoo of Us*. I had my first meeting with the people from the production company Gobstopper TV today and I'm so excited about it – it sounds amazing. It's centred around couples designing tattoos for each other that they then have to get done without knowing what it is. So obviously that means there will be fireworks! The only downside is, I'm not doing it on my own, I have a co-host and it's Stephen Bear who's just won *Celebrity Big Brother*. I've known him since he was on *Shipwrecked* and he's literally the WORST PERSON I could be paired with.

Saturday 27th

Weekend with Ash! Went to Panoramic 34 and it was incredible – there was such an amazing view and we had about eight thousand courses. I'm not even kidding. Got really pissed and then went back to the hotel. I can't remember much after that. I probably passed out naked as usual.

Sunday 28th

I love being holed up in a hotel room with Ash. In a weird way I think the fact that we can't tell anyone makes everything more exciting. We've chatted about what we're going to do when *Celebs Go Dating* finishes. I've said we should go to Ibiza for a few days and I think he's going to book it. Will be so nice to get away from everyone else!

* * *

Joey and Steph have started dating! They're not meant to get with each other but they've been sneaking off behind the producers' backs and prefer each other to the dates they've been on. Fair play to them. I think they make a cute couple but I do think he's more into her than she is into him. I hope he doesn't get his heart broken.

Monday 29th

The first episode of *Celebs Go Dating* aired on TV tonight. From what people were saying on Twitter they really like it, which is good.

I was with Ash when it went out and it was really odd watching it with him there! I forgot that I'd been interviewed at the start of the show about past relationships, so was embarrassed when I appeared on camera blubbing about Gary again! It's hard talking about it in front of people because I know everyone knows all about my life, and I know what they're all thinking, so it puts me under pressure. I think crying is an instant reaction and a bit of a safety blanket because I don't know how else to express myself.

* * *

I've been asked to do loads of dating shows before like *First Dates* and *Dinner Dates* but I've said no to all of them because I always thought, 'I can't imagine anything worse than being on a date with someone you don't like but you've got to go along with it!' And I was right! I'm the type of person who gets feelings so fast that if I am into someone then I can't pretend I have any interest in anyone else.

I can't wait for the show to be over so me and Ash can be official.

September 2016

How I felt getting papped looking half asleep in Ibiza: Pissed OFF

Arguments I had with a certain someone because of there being a pap in Ibiza: Several

New fancy job title: Ambassador of the Ectopic Pregnancy Trust

Thursday 1st

@TheMimmyWoman1
I cannot wait to place an order for a motor home instead of sitting in the house with the dogs, the hubby and the boy. Off we go!

Me mam and dad have bought themselves a camper van so they can go on road trips. They went to the Motor Show in Birmingham and have to sign for it somewhere in Barnsley. It won't arrive until next June but Mam keeps going on about it: 'It's top of the range!' They're going to be like something out of *Meet The Fockers*. They want it so they can go on holiday and take the dogs. Melissa isn't trusted to dogsit any more because Baby started eating her own poo last time she was on Mel's watch. Mam says that now they have to look after the dogs and the house they are 'basically like prisoners' and can't go abroad so they have to have a holiday home on wheels. We've gone thirdsies on it – I'm paying a third, Mam is paying a third and Dad's paying the other third. They've told me this means they have majority share and can overrule me on matters such as who drives in it and where it goes. I'll get my licence back in no time and then let's see who takes charge of the Crosby camper!

* * *

Gary was a guest on *This Morning* today and it was a really odd interview. It was WEIRD. I don't even know what he was on there for and he looked so uncomfortable. For the whole morning it was advertised as if it was a thing about me! The headline came up as 'Later! Gaz on *This Morning*: "Gaz and Charlotte: what's next?"'

Then he was suddenly on the sofa with Ruth and Eamonn (who I LOVE). They gave him a really hard time. It was strange though because at one point they asked him to speak through the TV directly to me because they thought I would be watching! He looked straight at the camera and said: 'I hope we can be friends and look back on everything. There will always be a place for her in my life. I do hope she meets someone.'

Then Eamonn asked him what his gift was for attracting women, and Gary said, 'Don't be a knob. And be honest. Don't be cocky.'

GARY SWORE! STUPID IDIOT!

After it finished I wanted to climb through the television screen and give Ruth the biggest high-five going! She gave him such a grilling . . . at one point she said, 'You did hurt her, Gary,' and he looked like he was squirming. I know when Gary is uncomfortable and he was definitely hating it.

Ruth, you are a legend!

* * *

Fourth date on camera with Brad and this time we went fishing. I figured this would be a good place, which wouldn't put anyone in a romantic mood, and so it would be easy not to have to kiss him. I had a rod and a massive box of maggots – if that's not going to quash any sort of sexy mood I don't know what is!

It ended up being quite a funny date and we did have a laugh. I caught a fish and decided to call him Simon. I said on camera that I thought fishing was better than sex because when you go fishing and catch something it's a good thing! Thought that was quite a funny joke actually . . . Maybe I should be a comedian.

I felt bad for Brad because he was trying really hard. It's just circumstance and bad timing for me. He was asking me if I thought we were compatible because we get on so well. He keeps saying he likes me but he wants to know if I feel the same because he can't work out what's going on in my head. He's really genuine and I feel really bad. I told him, 'Of course I like you,' but I don't think it sounded very convincing. He said he feels like I have a massive guard up. I couldn't tell him the truth but I tried in a coded way. I said, 'I'm just scared to like you because of the other factors.'

But I did ask him to come to the final dinner at the end of the show.

Can't wait to get it out of the way!

Friday 2nd

It was the last day of filming for *Celebs Go Dating* today and my last visit to the dating agency – HURRAH! We had our final dinner and it was actually quite emotional because we've all spent so much time together.

I told Nadia and Eden that the show had definitely helped me get over Gary, which is not what I thought would happen. Eden was really sweet to me and said that he thought I needed to discover who the real Charlotte Crosby was and that I didn't need to play up to the cameras and be silly all the time. I told him I didn't know whether the real Charlotte Crosby was ready to come out yet. Then Eden said, 'The real Charlotte Crosby is a beautiful human being,' which made me cry. Again. Well I might as well have finished the show as I started!

Brad came as my guest to the dinner. I don't know if it was because I knew I had to tell him it wasn't going to work, or whether he was just winding me up regardless, but the way he was eating his salmon at the table really made me cringe. I took Eden to one side and said I wasn't feeling it with Brad. I said I was starting to question things and was picking holes in things he said and that I didn't like that he'd spat his salmon out on the plate. I felt so nervous because I genuinely didn't know how I was going to break it to Brad. He must have sussed something's up but I still feel bad on him.

Everyone was starting to argue at the dinner table. Jack and his date Sherin got really tetchy and Brad started trying to join in! I think we'd all just had too much to drink. And Joey and Steph kept snogging at the table like we were at school.

In the end I had to take Brad outside. I was so scared of how he might react and my lip starting wobbling as soon as I began talking. I said, 'You know how I have a lovely time with you and get on with you so well. But you do show signs of immaturity sometimes . . . doing this experience has made me find myself and I need to focus on the real me . . .' Then I started crying.

Then Brad came out with it. 'Can I just ask one thing? I've seen in the papers that you have a fella.'

OH DEAR.

I couldn't exactly say, 'Yeah you're right!' so I said, 'I do not have a boyfriend in the slightest, I just don't feel I can go back in the room and pretend . . .'

He was amazingly gracious about it. 'OK, I'll get myself off and you get in there and have a good night with the rest of them.'

I felt so bad.

As soon as he left I burst into even more tears. I felt so embarrassed facing everyone inside afterwards. I just needed to get drunk. So I sat back at the table and started grilling Joey and Steph about whether they'd had sex instead. They were denying it but it's obvious they have.

At least someone's found love on this show.

Saturday 3rd

The episode of my picnic with Jeavon aired last night and everyone's been on my side after him basically calling me a slag. I do love my fans.

The house is all going wrong. Mam has ordered the wrong colour table for the dining room. I told her it needs to go back.

@TheMimmyWoman1
Today has been highs and lows! I have learnt how to work the coffee machine @charlottegshore! Took delivery of the wrong colour furniture #disaster

I'm coming off this contraception injection. I have put on so much weight – nearly a stone! I can't stop eating. I've had this uncontrollable appetite, it's horrendous. The doctor says I can go on the pill instead. I can't believe he only told me it was an appetite accelerant after he'd given it to me. On top of that, I couldn't do any exercise for twelve weeks after the operation so it's fair to say I'm not feeling massively body confident at the minute.

Did a poll on my Twitter today to see if boys preferred girls' boobs or bums. Bums got 71 per cent.

Sunday 4th

Been having a good scroll today. My regular scrolling obsessions are:

Boys
Ash: Because I want to know what he's doing.
Gary: I need to know what he's doing to check he's not doing better than me.
Mitch: But not on my phone because he's blocked me. It's annoying that I can't directly scroll Mitch so I have to do it on someone else's phone like Sophie's or Melissa's.

Girls
Vicky: I always stalk her. I want to see what she's up to and what's she's been doing. Her Instagram can get a bit boring though!
Perrie Edwards: I am a massive stalker of hers because I think she is absolutely beautiful.
Sahara Ray: She is my absolute favourite person to follow. She's just stunning. She's from Australia but lives in America. She went out with Justin Bieber for a bit and doesn't wear clothes very often. Her figure is amazing and I am literally obsessed with her. I don't even know how I found her, I just started scrolling and came across her. I think she's a model or something. She looks like she has a good life and she's different and interesting.

Monday 5th

@charlottegshore
Tonight I am evenly spread across @celebsgodating on E4 and @channel_5TV narrating tattoo disasters UK. Make sure you set one to record!

I'm going to move into the house next month! I can't believe I am getting my own place. It feels such an achievement. Me dad – aka Gary the Project Manager – has been trying to keep me informed and involved throughout the whole build but sometimes I feel like he thinks I'm uninterested because I don't know what he's talking about. Today he said, 'What do you think about these door handles?' and I had to very kindly say, 'Don't bother asking me about stuff like that, just put anything on.'

Wednesday 7th

I'm trying my hardest to train for the next DVD. I'm doing an all-over body one, which is a bit like the first one I did. I actually like knowing I have a DVD scheduled ahead of me because it keeps me in shape. If I didn't have it booked in, Kate would plan my schedule every weekend and I wouldn't have time to do any exercise at all! My weight fluctuates so I need to do something. I don't think people believe that I still do my own DVDs at home. When I'm doing the workouts in the lounge I sometimes talk back to the telly because Richard is on the DVD saying things to me like 'Are you OK, Charlotte?' and I reply, 'Yeah!' thinking he's actually talking at me through the TV.

Thursday 8th

I had a bad night with Rhubarb. She is going through a stage of barking all through the night at nothing and then she pooed on my carpet. I woke up and it was all over the place so I had to scrub it off in the middle of the night. I thought, 'I can't even handle my dog so I'm not ready for a baby.' Ash will be relieved.

* * *

There are more and more reports of me and Ash being together. I can't wait for it to all be out in the open so we can be free and in an official relationship. The papers are saying that *Celebs Go Dating* are really pissed off with me too. We've booked a trip to Ibiza but we're going out there when the show's still on so I'll have to hide.

The papers are ridiculous sometimes anyway. There was even a story about me and Joey the other day because paps saw us having a drink together when we were filming the double date. The report said that Joey had asked me out on WhatsApp. I haven't a clue where that came from.

When I asked him about it he said, 'You did ask me out!' Which I didn't!

I said, 'No one asked anyone out!' and he laughed, 'I don't know . . . I've been getting it wrong then!'

I've never really fancied Joey, he looks too young for me. I can't imagine having a passionate kiss with him – it would be like kissing my little brother. I've got a soft spot for him but I think that's more in a friend way. He cares for me and I care for him and he always gives me advice and says he really wishes I would find the one.

* * *

Joey's really into Steph but she seems to be playing her cards close to her chest. She's like his ideal girl. I reckon she has her guard up and she doesn't give much away. From the outside looking in, Joey is head over heels. Steph is one of the nicest people I have ever, ever known. But I just don't see how those two are a couple. I think maybe for Steph it's something fun. It won't last though. I mean, she's not going to settle down and have kids with Joey Essex, is she?

Saturday 10th

Back in Newcastle and went to the house with Mam. She was really chuffed because she's finished the dining room.

The walls are like a mustard-gold colour. It's disgusting. I don't know what me mam was thinking. The table and lights are really nice but they don't match the walls at all. Mam keeps saying it looks gorgeous. But it's revolting. I told her I won't be able to physically sit in there because it will make me depressed. Mam is going to have to change it and I'm going to have to oversee every step.

Sunday 11th

Kate got an email from Alex at the Ectopic Pregnancy Trust.

> We wanted to share a bit of news with you and Charlotte as it shows all you have been doing is resonating with those who need to know and we want to say thank you again for it.
>
> Today Munira has taken a phone call from a teacher at Prestwick Academy. A group of school children won £1,000 prize money. They are distributing to three charities and have chosen to give the Ectopic Pregnancy Trust a third. The key point here is that young people who would probably never even have heard of such a condition a few months ago, yet alone have empathised with it, chose to put ectopic pregnancy on their agenda as important. They now know the condition exists which could save their or their friend's life or fallopian tube in the future! This is great news.

Getting this kind of feedback really gives me comfort and helps me when I feel down about the ectopic pregnancy.

Monday 12th

Me and Ash have been talking about all the stuff we're going to do together when we can go public. We're going to go skiing in March. I think I'd prefer to learn to ski than snowboard first because at least you're standing on two feet. I don't want to be professional or anything, I just want to get down the hill! Ash says he will start teaching me at the Chill Factore in Manchester so I don't plummet on my arse like a fool once we get there. He's also going to come with me to Australia when I next go out there for work. I've got a trip planned next April. He will look so good in the surf with his long flowing locks. Like Jesus. I reckon he'll be able to walk on water too if he puts his mind to it.

Mam has called and said the bathroom in the house is DONE and the new bath is IN. Am going to see it tomorrow!

Tuesday 15th

OK so the bath is amazing, but the tiles look rank. They have to come off. They're really small and square and they look horrible. They have to change.

Thursday 16th

Been having more chats with the producers of *Just Tattoo of Us* and the show sounds so amazing. I would definitely watch it if I wasn't me.

Melissa thinks I'm going to end up fancying Bear. Which is ridiculous because he's an idiot and he was so crazy and annoying on *Celebrity Big Brother.* I just think he will do my head in. But deep down I know she could also be right.

Me and Bear have known each other for five years and have a bit of a colourful history. We exchanged numbers in 2012 when he was on *Shipwrecked* – we both said we fancied each other and were going to go on a date! But when we saw each other on a night out he cracked on to another girl so nothing ended up happening. Then he started dating Vicky, which was weird because I always knew in the back of my mind that I'd texted him before. They were together for about six months after she left *Geordie Shore* but I wasn't very close to Vicky then so I never spoke to her about him. Then a while after that I saw him in a club with Lillie Lexie, who was obviously Gary's ex, and I tweeted about it. He denied he was with her, which was a lie, so we had a falling out over Twitter. So it's fair to say we have had drama already. He was on *Ex on the Beach* with Gary and now he seems to be dating HER. She's all over his Snapchat. He's denying they're boyfriend and girlfriend but they've just gone and got matching love-heart tattoos and they're wearing coordinated outfits.

What the hell is it going to be like when we have to be on camera together?

Friday 17th

Paul the gardener keeps asking me to come over so he can show me new bits he's done in the garden. Mam is constantly worried I'm going to say something about the bus shelter and offend him. He's really brilliant at what he does. I just think it's going to take me a while to get used to it. I managed not to make any jokes about waiting for a bus (and them all coming at once). Just.

Counting down the hours. Ibiza tomorrow!

Saturday 18th

Off to Ibiza with Ash! So excited!

I spent the whole time at the airport trying to hide behind plants in the hope that no one would recognise us. Surely everyone in Ibiza is too wasted to care who else is there and whether they're having an illicit affair behind the backs of the producers of a dating show anyway?

Sunday 19th

Our apartment is lovely and it feels so nice to be away from everyone and just hang out by ourselves. We've been drinking cocktails by the pool and snogging everywhere. Off to a club tonight.

Monday 20th

Eww. Why did I drink so much last night? Can't remember a thing. At least I didn't wee the bed.

Tuesday 21st

Sunbathed and snogged all day. Now off to a meal in STK Ibiza – it's really fancy in there and we're going to make eyes at each other across our steaks so everyone will look on with envy at what a happy long-haired couple we are.

Wednesday 22nd

> @charlottegshore
> Had a beautiful meal in @STKibiza last night and the company
> was a bit alright too 😏🖤👫

Last night was such a laugh but today something feels different somehow. I don't know what it is . . .

I've been panicking because I know there's a pap outside the apartment. Ash has been annoying me a bit because he keeps saying, 'They haven't got anything!' as if I'm being stupid and paranoid. But I know what I know and I wish he would be a bit more understanding. He has been doing my head in telling me to be positive and have positive vibes and it's just not like that. How can you always be positive when you've got a photographer outside trying to take a picture of you looking shit?? Not everything in life is positive. Stop being so stupid and deluded.

Flying back to London tonight. Wish the flights from Ibiza weren't so LLLLLLLATE.

Thursday 23rd

SO OF COURSE THERE WERE PAP PICS OF ME AND ASH.

They're all over the internet. He's got his top off (admittedly he does look very hot) and I'm slouched next to him on the balcony looking like I've just crawled out of a bush. I'm now in trouble with *Celebs Go Dating* and EVERYONE.

My giant mirror has been delivered. Mam said 'It's so massive it took about seven people to carry it in. You had better not change your mind about this one, Charlotte!' Going to see it on Sunday.

HOT

September

tepid

Friday 24th

Decided to throw an Ann Summers party – the rep is my friend Christina's mam so we know her really well. We played so many games and quizzes and got really drunk. She brought loads of sexy outfits over and we were all trying them on and playing with the dildos. I was hitting myself in the face with one on Snapchat and it was picked up by the *Daily Mail*!

@charlottegshore
Tonight @Annsummers party with the girls, loads of wine, loads of sexy things, what more could you ask for?

Saturday 25th

My In The Style range was nominated for a *Fabulous* magazine fashion award today! Just call me Victoria Beckham!

Sunday 26th

The mirror is BEYOND all of my dreams! It's perfect. I love it! Mam said she and the builders wanted to hide behind their hands when I went into the room to look at it in case I changed my mind. Don't think they could bear having to try and get it out of the house again! Mam told me she'd said to them, 'If she doesn't like it she can take it back,' and they'd replied, 'You are joking, aren't you??'

It's honestly so big that no one is ever going to be able to move it ever. It's even too tall for the walls in the house and has to be put on a tilt.

Monday 27th

I'm feeling really fat at the moment. I can't wait for the effects of the contraceptive injection to wear off. Maybe I shouldn't have decided to get the biggest mirror in the world!

Tuesday 28th

Very very proud tonight. My girls have managed to piss on the mats for once. ABOUT F* * *ING time!

Both Rhubarb and Baby have weed on the matt! Mam says Rhu is much harder to train than Baby was because she does between fifteen and twenty wees a day, all round the house.

Every time they wee you have to put them outside so they get used to it. It's the same principle with the mat – you leave the wee on it so they can smell it and they know to go back there to wee again. I probably need a bit of that training.

Friday 29th

The house is ready for me to move into! There are still going to be loads of bits being done while I'm there but it's basically finished. I am going to spend the night there on Monday and I'm sooooo excited!

Saturday 30th

Posted a selfie and loads of people were tweeting me saying, 'Leave your face alone!' Every time I pull even the smallest pout people go mad and think I've had my lips done again and then the papers start picking up on it saying, 'Fans go wild and warn Charlotte to lay off the surgery!'

Sometimes I Instagram a picture that really makes them look massive just to wind people up.

I purposely post the pictures where my lips look the biggest they possibly can and I say to my mates, 'Give it five minutes and there'll be loads of comments. I'm trolling people and they don't even know it!'

October 2016

What I look like with a rash on my face: A speckled toad

Celebrity I opened my big mouth about during a Facebook Live: Her name rhymes with Methane Welly

Emojis to describe how happy I am to finally be in my new house: 😀😊🍸🍺📿

Saturday 1st

I am finally in my new house and it's beyond all my wildest dreams. I did a tour for people on Snapchat and everyone's been so nice about it. One of the papers said that whatever people think about me I have had the last laugh because my house is so big I can't even get up the stairs! It was just a shell when I bought it and now it's my dream home. I even have my own walk-in wardrobe and a gym! This is probably the only time in my life that I've felt a proper sense of pride. When I walk into the house I can see all my hard work right in front of me. Obviously I was pleased when my DVD went to number one but this is real and I can see it. Work's not going to last for ever so I am trying to spend my money wisely.

Whenever anyone asks me to describe it I tell them it reminds me of a secret kingdom. In the kingdom there are lots of different types of rooms and every room has its own theme. There's the African room: this is filled with pictures of elephants, a cowhide rug, an antler light and giraffe wallpaper (not actual giraffe skin, just giraffe print). Then we have the pink room which is one of the bedrooms – it's so girly, you walk in there and you feel like a Barbie doll. Then we have the poker room which I like to call the Las Vegas room. It's all black from the ceiling to the floor and has a big black corner settee and a huge 70-inch telly. On the walls are big playing cards – it's very cool and feels a bit like a casino. I don't even know where I got my ideas for all the rooms, they've just evolved as I've seen things in the shops. I'll be looking for paint one day and then I'll find some wallpaper I want and that's how it all comes together. The mirror in my bedroom was one of the most expensive things I bought for it. I'm quite chuffed that I did it all myself and didn't have an interior designer or anything.

My favourite room of all is the pool room with the swimming pool in it (obviously, it would be a bit odd if it didn't have one with a name like 'pool room'). The bathroom is another favourite room because I love sitting in the bath for hours. It has tiles everywhere and feels like the jungle because there are loads of plants. Baths are seriously underrated.

It has five bedrooms (because the office also has a mezzanine floor with a bed in it) and in the whole house there are sixteen rooms. Mam cleans the place. It keeps her busy and keeps her in a good job as Charlotte's carer and key employee.

It's so big though! I'm going to fill it with different friends every night. Apart from when Ash comes over. Then it's going to be our gigantic love pad. He's going to come up as soon as I get a few days here but I've got to go back to work in London on Monday so there's no point.

Sunday 2nd

I keep walking round the house and I can't believe its all mine! Lauren stayed last night and we decided we should christen every room by having a drink in all of them. Even the toilet and the cupboards. I quite like the cupboards . . . they make me feel cosy. The rooms are massive and it's like my voice is echoing around them!

I've decided I'm going to keep my house really tidy. I am not going to be the messy Charlotte from the past. Me mam always tells everyone that I can obliterate a room in under ten minutes (it takes about thirty seconds) but this time she is going to be shocked because I am going to become a woman and treat my new home in the manner it should be treated. Like a princess.

Monday 3rd

Kim Kardashian has been robbed at gunpoint in Paris. It's been all over the news and it's so shocking! I feel so sorry for her. What the actual hell would you do if men with guns came into your room? You would be so petrified.

Me and Lauren got really scared the first night in this house. I've got one of those intercom systems where you press the buzzer and the camera pops up so you can see who's at the door. It was midnight and we were lying in bed and Lauren said, 'What would you do if the intercom went off now and you saw someone standing there?' I shrieked, 'Oh my God, don't say that!' We freaked ourselves out so much that we started planning our escape route in case it actually happened. But that's nothing compared to being tied up at gunpoint in the bath!

* * *

I did a Facebook Live chat for In The Style this afternoon and said something I shouldn't about Lorraine Kelly. Now the whole world has gone mad. Someone asked me if there was any celebrity that I hate. I couldn't think of anyone, I don't hate anyone, so I tried to remember someone who'd been nasty to me. I said: 'Lorraine Kelly. She was so horrible to us when I went on her morning show. She didn't even just be horrible in one answer, that would have been enough. She continued and continued. She had it in for us.'

It's now been picked up by the papers as if I was being really nasty. I didn't mean it to be nasty. I had a smile on my face when I was saying it, it was only meant as a joke!

Oops.

Kate isn't happy. But I don't regret what I said. It was back when I went on her show to promote my last book and she gave me a real grilling asking if I was embarrassed about wetting myself on television. I just remember her telling me she didn't think it was normal. I know that! But it's funny and it's not like I'm doing it on purpose, it's accidental. I just felt like she had it in for me. Lorraine had then asked if I'd thought about getting help. Which was basically what Janet Street-Porter had been saying to me on *Loose Women* too.

As long as my friends and family still love me and accept me for who I am, that's all that I care about.

Tuesday 4th

@Lorraine_Kelly
Baffled by this. I did ask last year whether she was embarrassed about wetting herself in public. She said no. Rather odd to bring it up now.

Wednesday 5th

@charlottegshore
I would like to thank the CAKE GOD himself @jordanG9728x for saving my life for my lil brothers bday.

The new pill is so much better than the injection. My appetite has gone totally back to normal now and I'm not wanting to eat everything in sight. I managed to resist eating Nathaniel's birthday cake which was a result.

Thursday 6th

@charlottegshore
So I joined the @mydadwroteaporno team and it was a BALL! Never laughed so hard! Make sure you check out the podcast it's out today.

My guest appearance on the podcast *My Dad Wrote a Porno* went out today. The guy behind it is Jamie Morton. He worked with me on creating my YouTube channel and we're really close mates now. Jamie came up with the idea when his dad asked him to read the first chapter of a book he had written. Jamie was so shocked when he read it, he decided to make a podcast of him reading it out. Now it's so successful I don't think he needs to do anything else!

It was a really fun chat. I was introduced as an 'entrepreneur' and a 'proper businesswoman' which I quite liked. I guess I am a businesswoman really: I have my DVDs, my books, my clothing range and my make-up. They said I was like the real life Belinda, who is the main character in the porno, and we all decided she could have her own fitness DVD but it would be called *Sexercise*. I told them that I couldn't understand how sex burns calories because I just lie there while I'm doing it. I said, 'You're meant to burn a KitKat but I'm lucky if I burn a Smartie!' and they were cracking up. It was so much fun.

We had such a laugh talking about the mile-high club and whether it's illegal to have sex on a plane. I told them I thought they would turn the plane round if they caught you at it because it would be classed as 'disorderly behaviour'. They didn't agree but had to change their mind when I told them the story about someone having a shit in a toilet and the plane turning round. Imagine doing a shit so bad that the plane had to land! I said, 'If a plane turned round for a turd then they will turn round for someone coming all over the sheets!'

They asked if I'd ever indulged in a bit of lesbian action, like Belinda. And I told them about playing naked Twister with Chloe on the show once. They asked what my weirdest sexual encounter was and I admitted that one of my boyfriends liked his nipples to be licked but it gave me flashbacks of getting milk from me mam's breast. They said that I should have a crack at doing my own erotic book. Wonder what I'd call it? *Letitia's Love Nest*? *Charlotte's Web of Wonderful Willies*?

Friday 7th

My DVD shoot is looming and I don't feel anywhere near fit enough yet. I need to prepare every day and I'm going to Mexico tomorrow with David for some hard-core PT sessions. There's so much pressure when you're filming a DVD because everyone analyses every ounce of you. It makes me feel so anxious and self-conscious and I put so much stress on myself.

Sophie is coming too because it means she's got a good excuse to get fit and we can both tan and scroll together in between workouts. Also, she's a good guinea pig to test it on. If she can handle the routines then most people can! I'm going to miss Ash though. Considering I've been with him since the end of July we've hardly spent any time together. We basically have a WhatsApp relationship. Full of loads of heart emojis. He's definitely coming to stay when I'm back from Mexico though. Then we can romp about all over my new massive bed, watch ourselves in my ridiculously huge mirror and bathe in my gigantic bath.

I should be chuffed that I've kept most of the weight off for three years since my first DVD. I do feel like this should be the size I will be for the rest of my life. I still get tagged in pictures from when I was massive in *Geordie Shore* – Series

3 to Series 7 are the WORST! I'm constantly having to relive those moments on Instagram. I feel like I'm a different person now, I'm a better and happier person. I look at those pictures and I feel like it was a sad time. I wasn't confident and I was always sluggish because my diet was so awful. I was constantly eating badly, every single minute of the day. I thought that was a normal feeling until I got fit and healthy. It's not just about the way you look – obviously you feel better because you lose weight – but it's your mind and your general health that changes massively. Before I couldn't walk up a flight of stairs without getting out of breath! After I'd started exercising I could actually run to the car without feeling like I was going to die.

Saturday 8th

Grandad Tommy – me mam's dad – came round to see the new house today and he was all over the place! He was walking from the hall and fell down one of the steps and shot right out the back door! I just heard him mumbling, 'This house is bloody massive, why does she need so many split levels?'

I love Tommy. I also like the fact that he and my nana still get on even though they're not together any more. He always takes the piss out of her saying things like, 'She was such a violent woman when we were married.' He really makes me laugh.

Have bought a Fitbit and am taking it to Mexico. I'm in a group with my mates Anna, Laura and Christina from home and we're going to do challenges against each other. They will never beat me though – I'm so competitive. (The only reason I've suggested we get one now is because I'm going to basically be exercising all day every day while they are stuck in their office jobs.) Sophie's got one too but I don't need to worry about her. She's so lazy and never even bothers to try and win!

Sunday 9th

Spent all day working out and making sure I my Fitbit score was WAAAAY ahead of everyone else's. Anna has been trying to walk up and down the road at home and Christina has been doing sprints while watching TV. BUT I WILL LEAVE THEM FOR DUST.

Monday 10th

Still winning. They might as well just give up now.

Wednesday 12th

I love David so much, he's literally like a relative. We talk about anything and everything. We go into such depth about things. He likes to know a lot of girly things and how we think. He looked at me this afternoon and said really seriously, 'You know when you get your period, what does it feel like?' I replied, 'It feels great, I like having a period. It's like the best time in my whole life. I like having a good old bleed. It feels like you get it all out. Its good when you have a period when you're feeling fat because it always makes you feel more skinny.'

Thursday 13th

No more cheat days for me at the moment. I am on a super-strict diet – poached eggs on toast or porridge for breakfast, soup for lunch and chicken and veg for dinner.

I don't usually weigh myself because I'd rather go by how my clothes fit. But when I'm doing a DVD I'm more conscious of my weight. And it's so hard. I remember when I used to buy a size 16 dress and I was constantly trying to hide my shape all the time because I felt so embarrassed about how I looked. But I still feel like that inside. I still think I'm that person. I don't feel happy with how I look. I've talked to David about how I've been feeling about my body and I think he feels bad because on the one hand he's there to help me prepare for the DVD but he also knows I shouldn't give myself too much pressure.

Here's what I think of my body TOP TO TOE:

Forehead: Bad, it's bigger than Ant and Dec's. It's so big I have a fringe to cover it up sometimes.

Eyes: They're OK. I don't mind having brown eyes. They could be blue though – I like wearing blue contacts sometimes. Blue's a nice colour.

Nose: I really like my nose. It's neat and lovely. It hurts sometimes though from the scar tissue and I have to have steroid injections, which I don't like.

Cheeks: They're fine. Nice cheeks. Nothing much to say about them.

Lips: I love my lips – even though loads of people criticise them and say they are too big. I only have them done about once a year but people are obsessed with thinking I have them done all the time. I think I look like Pete Burns sometimes.

243

Neck: It's a nice length neck. Not too short, not too long.
Shoulders: A bit round and I have a wide back like me mam.
I feel like a swimmer and I can't even do a proper dive so I
don't know where that's come from. But I'm fine with that.
I can get over it. I never really wear backless dresses anyway.
Boobs: I'd rather not have any. Me mam hates her boobs
too. I don't usually wear a bra but when I do it's a 34D
and I'd rather my boobs were smaller. I also have a 'uniboob',
which is something called symmastia and I've had it since
I was born. It didn't bother me until I tweeted a picture
of me in a low-cut dress and loads of people started saying,
'EW, what has she done to her boobs? They are weird!' So
I got a bit of a complex and now I can't ever wear V-necks.
Belly: It's always the area I'm most conscious about. It's
obviously not anywhere near how it was before and I feel
so much more confident about that area now, but I can't
lie, the ectopic pregnancy really knocked me back and I
think when you've been bigger you always still get worried
about the things you used to worry about so even though
you're not so big any more it's instilled in you. I'll probably
never be happy with it. I think it's what I will always see
and the main cause of my body issues. I have always felt
like I don't look good enough and that I'm too big.
Bum: Like my bum, it's a nice one. Little and cute.
Legs: I love them. I'm over the moon with my legs, always
have been. I love my legs so much. I praise them every day.

Friday 14th

Every celebrity who's done a DVD knows the pressure there
is on you. It's like the whole world around you is waiting for

you to slip up and it does stress me out. You know someone could easily get a picture of you from a bad angle and, no matter what you really look like, that's what will be shown.

A girl I follow on Instagram, who has the best figure you'd ever seen, posted a brilliant example of how a bad shot can make you look ten times bigger. She put one picture of her standing up looking all confident and slim, and the other one of her sitting down when you could see three rolls of fat. Everyone is the same. Different angles show a different picture altogether. I always worry about the one picture that might be at a bad angle because everyone will jump on it – they're waiting for me to slip up again. When I was in Australia after filming the first DVD, a pap was hiding in the bushes of the hotel and he got some pics of me looking puffy. I'd just come off a twenty-four-hour flight, was jetlagged and due on my period; of course I looked puffy! I looked great two days later but by that time word had gone out and we heard that paps were being offered BIG money for a 'fat' pic.

Nice.

But then I think I've been a bit too skinny at times before. I have this one jumpsuit that I wore in *Geordie Shore* when I first lost all the weight and it's so thin and tight that it was a killer even to get on then. I don't dare try it on again because I know I'd split it down the seams.

Saturday 15th

We're doing rehearsals for the DVD – we have to make sure we get all the moves right because we don't have loads of time to shoot it and everything needs to be perfect. You don't want me falling over mid lunge during one of the workouts!

I have to make sure it's all there in my head. I only have to learn the lines for the start of the exercises, the rest of the time I ad lib and try my hardest not to laugh.

Me and David having been working to create the routines for months. We obviously have to make new ones that are going to keep people interested otherwise they'll get bored. This is the third DVD after all!

We're rehearsing between four and five hours a day which is why it's better being somewhere sunny. Am killing it on Fitbit. Everyone's getting pissed off with me because they're saying I have an unfair advantage.

Sunday 16th

Little Mix have released an amazing song called 'Shout Out to My Ex'. I loved Little Mix when they were first on *The X Factor* and they've just got better and better over the years. I've never discussed it with her but I like to think the song is Perrie's way of saying that Zayn was shit in bed.

THAT WOULD BE A BRILLIANT WAY OF GETTING REVENGE!

It's always good to write a revenge song. I wish I'd been able to write a revenge song about Gary. This is how it would have gone . . .

Gary, your hair looks like bird poo
And shagging you is like going to the loo
I wish we'd never got so tangled
Because my heart got truly mangled
I'm much better off without you about
You make me want to scream and shout

You're not all you're cracked up to be
I'd rather have sex with a big oak tree

Monday 17th

Even though I've been exercising loads I still feel paranoid and keep looking at myself in the mirror thinking I look fat. Maybe I do look fat? I keep worrying what the magazines are going to start saying about me and its niggling at me constantly, like I have a person on my shoulder saying, 'You're still a fatty, you will always be a fatty.'

I was crying at breakfast and I couldn't eat. In the end Sophie went to the restaurant and came back with two Nutella waffles and said, 'Fuck it, Charlotte, I can't be arsed with it all. I don't know how you do this!'

Thanks for the support, Sophie!

A horrible rash has come up all over my body. I don't know what it is. I've just Snapchatted about it to see if anyone knows what it could be. 'Starting to get really worried about me face!' I said. It's awful. I look like I have measles or something. Everyone said they thought it could be heat rash but I don't know.

My face really stings. And I still feel fat and shit.

Went to see a doctor and he said it was connected to the sea water and that other guests had had it. Kate told me that as soon as I mentioned it on Snapchat someone got in touch with her and said that her dad had the same rash while he was on holiday here and when he'd got home he'd been told it was a secondary viral infection! Kate's panicking because she said he was so ill he had a fit and lost his memory for fifteen minutes. But I told Kate the doctor told me not to worry and it will go.

@charlottegshore
So everyone thinks the rash might be a heat rash? Is it common to get one on your face?

Wednesday 19th

@charlottegshore
my face stings 😞

I feel so physically exhausted and down. I keep getting headaches. I can't eat. Spoke to Kate on the phone and she's worried about me. I can't stop crying. I want to go home.

Sunday 23rd

Back from Mexico and Kate's come to the hotel for a catch-up meeting. She's still worried about the rash and she knows I'm feeling under pressure. I keep breaking down. I just feel like I'm not good enough. I'm getting anxiety. I feel so down and awful in myself.

* * *

Kate took me to the St John and St Elizabeth and they've done loads of tests on me. I've been diagnosed with a urinary infection and signed off work for two weeks with exhaustion. We're going to have to cancel the DVD shoot. I feel disappointed in myself but I'm also relieved I don't have to go through it all.

Tuesday 25th

Kate's booked me to see a counsellor. I've been in such a state and she's worried. The St John and St Elizabeth have recommended a woman who is totally removed from everything I've done or am doing.

The counsellor was lovely and told me she thinks I'm suffering from anxiety and body dysmorphia. I told her how worried I've been feeling and how bad I feel about myself. I know all the pressure I've been putting myself under is unhealthy and that I should look in the mirror and see a pretty healthy girl, but I don't. I just feel like I'm not good enough.

Ash is coming to stay with me in the hotel for the night and says he wants me to show him my white bits. But I can't talk to him about how I'm feeling, it's something I need to deal with myself. Even I don't completely understand it. I just know I feel shit and everytime I look in the mirror I feel like crying again.

* * *

Ash is here. And he's making me feel so much better. I think it's the hair . . .

> @charlottegshore
> Don't want it to be morning cos I don't want you to goooooooo
> 🖤

Wednesday 26th

What even is body dysmorphia? Because it's a mind thing and not a physical thing I can't see how it exists.

> @charlottegshore
> when all your mates are at home and you're in a hotel in London eating a bowl of sprouts. I'm strange.

Thursday 27th

Body dysmorphia must be a thing. I've been reading about it and loads of other people have felt like this. I have got to the point where I hate looking at myself and I think I'm fat and I can't imagine not feeling like that ever again. I know I get compliments where people say I look great but at the same time, every day I get a hundred comments slagging me off saying I'm fat or I'm ugly or I have bad skin. I have so many horrible things said about me on a daily basis that it's only normal that they make me feel ugly and disgusting. You don't ever remember the nice things after a while. I know I try and tell myself it doesn't matter and I don't care. But it does. And I do.

> @charlottegshore
> I'm cream crackered. A month away from home and I'm ready for friends and family and little pups.

Friday 28th

It's soooo good to be back home!!

Ash is coming to stay for a few days tomorrow and we're throwing the party to rule all parties for Halloween! I can have a proper pool party! WHOOP!

> @charlottegshore
> Baby keeps trying to have sex with Rhubarb's head.

Saturday 29th

Ash loves my new house (especially the big massive bed that could sleep about eight people!). It's so nice to have him here. And guess what? The dining room has been transformed and I'm pleased to report it now looks amazing. It's got dark flooring and dark walls which perfectly match the dark table. I rang me mam and told her I now feel really satisfied with every room.

She came over and pretended she'd forgotten something but I know she just wanted to meet Ash. She gave me a wink to say she likes him. I'll have to find out what she thinks when he's gone.

Mam and Dad have rented their place out now and they're staying at me nana's while I'm here, but when I'm working in London they live in my house (Mam needs to be there to clean and look after the dogs!).

Nana is me mam's mam Jean and she's hilarious. I love her. She's small and round and can take a joke, which is why everyone adores her. Me dad thinks she's marvellous.

Jean always wants to move for some reason, she must have lived in about fifteen different houses and she still wants to move again! Mam says she's like a gypsy and has told her she needs to chill out because she's nearly eighty.

Mam says she's hating living at Jean's because they don't fit into the beds. Me dad is six foot four and his feet get crushed on the cast-iron bed frame so he has to have it to himself so he can sleep diagonally. So Mam has to sleep in the single bed and Nathaniel is on the floor!

Sunday 30th

It's handy Ash having such long locks. We can share bobbles and everything!

Mam doesn't think he's the one though. She has told me she can't see any chemistry or any connection between us.

I hate it when she thinks she knows everything.

@charlottegshore
Yep I'm going on @imacelebrity and I can't wait
So excited man.

@charlottegshore
That was a joke by the way.

Bloody hell, I didn't expect a stupid tweet to kick off that much! I said on Snapchat I was joking but now everyone's gone mad saying I've upset my fans because people thought I was genuinely going in there!

I only said it because everyone around me – even my friends and family – was saying they thought I was going in and I just wasn't telling them. So I thought I'd wind everyone up. But just for like two minutes. It was meant to be a bit of fun!

Monday 31st

Threw a massive party at mine for Halloween. Ash came dressed as a sexy pirate. I was a zombie schoolgirl. Ash said I looked hot but I couldn't see past my ugly image in the mirror. The only way to forget about it was to get mortal. We ordered a takeaway and when the buzzer went I didn't even bother looking at the camera on the control panel, I just opened the gate. But when I went down to get the food I'd accidentally let in a load of zombies. My drive was full of them! It was like a scene from 'Thriller'. One was crying, 'Charlotte, I can't believe it's you! I can't believe you let us in!' I didn't know what to do and they all started asking me for selfies. There were about ten of them and I ended up giving them the money I had to pay for the takeaway because I didn't have any sweets for trick or treat so I just said, 'Take this and share it out,' so they would leave. I went back in and everyone was annoyed with me because I'd come back empty-handed and given away all their money.

At least my mates are an understanding bunch . . .!

November 2016

Awkward encounters with Gary at a public event: One

Life-changing encounter: BIG ONE – with a boy whose surname rhymes with hair

Emojis to sum up my dramatic new encounter and love dilemma: 😏 😬 😊 😌 😄

Tuesday 1st

I am loving the new clean and tidy me. I have got so into it! When Mam tries to use the washing machine I can't stand it. I had to ring her today and say, 'Can you get your wet clothes out of my nice clean washing machine please? You need to leave my washing machine empty because all your wet huge Bridget Jones knickers are in there invading my space!'

Jamie Laing came up this afternoon for his E4 chat show *In Bed With Jamie* and he totally caught me off guard by asking about my night with Alex Mytton in Cannes! I didn't know what to say so I said, 'There was a spoon, I'm sure there was. We were in bed a long time.' He kept pushing me for more info and laughing but I insisted, 'There was a lot of spooning, because that's all that happened . . . We were definitely not naked.'

The show doesn't air till just before Christmas but it's all going to kick off then!!

I would have loved us to hang out in Newcastle so I could take him on a pub crawl but we both had to get the train back to London for different work things. Kate had booked our tickets ages ago on 'a really good deal' so we're in First Class. She told me she sent the same deal to Jamie's agent but I don't think they got it in time so they ended up in Standard Class. It seems weird that the Geordies are in First Class while the posho is slumming it!

Mind you, Jamie nearly didn't get the train. We had to leave him and the crew at my house because his director kept wanting him to redo his 'arrival'. So when you watch it he will be arriving at a house with no one in it!

Wednesday 2nd

Back in London. And I am now officially the face of the new dating app, *ShowReal*.

It was the launch today, and I had to do a few interviews. Obviously people kept asking about Ash so I had to shut them down. I just said I've been on a couple of dates with him, but we are both dating other people.

Me and Holly went to the ShowReal launch party in Dstrkt. Steph Pratt came with Olivia from *Made in Chelsea* (the one with stupidly tall legs who had a one-night stand with Alex too, he does get about that boy). Was so brilliant to see them and we had such a laugh. Steph and Joey have split up now

(I thought it would be her ending it with him but think it was actually the other way round) so she's young, free and single again and I told her the world needs to know! When we came out of the club there were loads of paps and fans following us about so me, Holly and Steph went into a shop to try and hide – and ended up buying some condoms. Then me and Steph had a kiss. I don't know why!

Thursday 3rd

So hungover. Stayed up all night partying in my hotel and now there are pictures of me and Steph are in the papers and I look like I'm half dead. They're making out we had full-on snogs too, which I find hilarious.

Friday 4th

Had to film *Drunk History* at 6 a.m. for Comedy Central. Should have been called *Hungover History*. Still feel like shit now. Don't think I was on form.

Got the train to Manchester to see Ash. It was so good to see him and we had such a fun night. Now I just want to eat pizza. Pizza has all the answers to everything when you're hungover.

Saturday 5th

Back home to Newcastle. I LOVE MY HOUSE! It's so good to get back to clean sheets and fresh flowers. Mam said I left it in such a mess after Halloween that it's taken her nearly a week to clean. Keeping on top of having a clean and tidy house is getting to be too much stress. I'm bored of it. I think I'll leave it to me mam again. After all, it's in her job description.

Ash is with me and we've turned the bedroom upside down again with all our suitcases (and rolling around!). Wish I could click my fingers like Mary Poppins and everything would just miraculously tidy up again.

We're hungover so I told Mam I'm staying in bed all day if she needs me (I'll be stroking Ash's head for comfort).

Sunday 6th

Found out this morning that me and In The Style won that award for best celebrity collaboration at the *Fabulous* magazine High Street Fashion Awards. Am so chuffed! Beyoncé was the runner-up!

It was the MTV Europe Music Awards in Rotterdam tonight. It's the first public event where me and Gary have been in the same place since I left *Geordie Shore*. I wondered if he'd pretend nothing had happened like he did when we met up on our own in August. At first it was dead awkward because I saw the cast and everyone ran over to speak to me because they haven't seen me for ages and he had to hang back on his own in the corner of the room. I don't know why but I did feel a bit sorry for him. No one would stand with him because they're all closer to me. When I got to the bar I thought, 'I'm just going to have to speak to him.' You wouldn't forgive your worst enemy for the things he has put me through but somehow I felt like I just had to. . .

We didn't talk about what had happened. I took him aside and said, 'Look, I don't want it to affect our night. I don't want it to be awkward.' And after that he just kept buying me drinks all night. Every time I looked round there was another drink.

Monday 7th

@charlottegshore
waking up to find I got a pic with Zara Larsson last night I
love her.

I don't even remember meeting her! Am chuffed I managed
to get a picture though. Result!

Tuesday 8th

Now magazine have run a piece they did with me for ShowReal
and they're making out my lips split during the interview because
I have had so much surgery! For fuck's sake – some people are
so ridiculous. Honest to God. They're a pair of fucking lips! It's
like obsessing over a freckle on your face. People need to get a
life. During the interview I was picking them – which I do all
the time because I have dry chapped lips from the cold – and
they happened to bleed. It's winter. I needed some lip balm! I
picked a bit of skin off and it was bleeding a bit. Now they're
saying my lips 'exploded' mid interview! I can't be bothered to
tweet about it because that will just make it worse. It's pathetic.
Whenever people see me in the flesh they're surprised and say,
'They're not even big!' It's only because I pout so much in pictures!
   It's so DRAINING! People are so obsessed with having a
go at people about their surgery.

@charlottegshore
So sick of travelling now! And dragging my suitcase round
with me! So glad to get some time at home!

It's Sophie's birthday today so we're out on the toon tonight. I'm so glad I met her all those five years ago. She makes me laugh. She makes me smile. She doesn't mind if I'm vile.

Wednesday 9th

I'm finally at home and looking forward to some relaxing time, lying in bed, not getting dressed, not having to talk to everyone constantly or be polite to people all the time. I just want to be in bed and not even speak to anyone.

259

But I've woken up and there are literally about fifteen gardeners here and they all want a cup of tea or coffee. I can see in their eyes they want biscuits! I can't even sit in the sitting room because they are outside and I end up awkwardly staring at them. I can see they are thinking 'COFFEE'. Then the gate starts going because there are new deliveries and someone's here to clean the windows. Then a bloke comes to get the measurements for the new table. WHAT TABLE?

I've had to ring me mam: 'Can you get out of bed and sort these gardeners out and make them coffee? I can't believe they are working in the winter – come over now, please. And what is this about a table?'

* * *

Ash sent me the most gorgeous bunch of flowers just to say he misses me. They're sunflowers and roses and are perfect.

Thursday 10th

I'm actually feeling a bit lonely in the house, it's so big! I love it and love all the rooms but, if I'm honest, most of them I hardly sit in. The front room – the African room – is so beautiful but I've only been in there about twice. I reckon I only use two rooms – the bedroom and the kitchen. And sometimes the pool.

Mam, Dad and Nathaniel are at Jean's at the moment. They have been educating her into the world of movie nights and curries. I called them tonight and they told me they couldn't speak because I was disturbing their marathon movie session.

They've been making her drink loads of wine too, so they can watch whatever they want!

Ash is coming to stay again tomorrow. We will definitely be using the bedroom. I'm going to put my Fitbit on and start burning serious calories.

Friday 11th

Had a lovely day just slobbing about with Ash. But something seems a bit different. I don't know what but I feel like I don't have so much to say to him. And his hair isn't as beautiful as I remembered.

Saturday 12th

What's going on in my brain? Can't shake this negative feeling about Ash. Maybe Mam is right and we don't have much in common. Now the more I think it, the more I notice it. He's going home tomorrow and this time I am actually glad. I don't think I can do another day of this.

How can things just change?

Tuesday 15th

Did a shoot for OK! magazine in my new house. I was so proud showing everyone round! Can't wait for it to come out. It was a bit like when me dad's mam Doreen came over. She just took photo after photo. She's obsessed with taking photos of everyone ALL the time – everyone ends up running away! That must be where I get my selfie obsession from. But she means no harm and she loves us all very much! Sometimes I'm glad she's taking pictures because I never have any nice ones of the family.

I have to start packing next week for a whole month in London. I've only just moved into my house and I have to leave again!

Wednesday 16th

Am doing a tour for ShowReal and I'm paying Anna to be my driver for the next four days. It's brilliant having her there! The only problem is she gets SO SO tired. If she was an animal she'd be a sloth. She wouldn't be able to do half the things I do because she has to sleep all the time or she will die.

Anna's ShowReal Tour Diary #1:
Crosby Household To Leeds

Drove 90 miles to the apartment in Leeds, and had to be at the club asap. So quick change and straight out. This is standard procedure in the life of Charlotte. Being on tour you miss the amazing suite you're in because you're in such a rush to drop your stuff off, get ready and straight back out.

Me and Charlotte didn't take our Fitbits off for the entire night. We are still in challenges with our friends back in Sunderland so we spent the first hour walking around the VIP section with our vodka fresh lime and sodas to get our steps up. Charlotte is the most-competitive girl I know. After so long walking round in circles I give up, but not Charlotte. If she's in a competition she is coming first in that competition.

Charlotte had to go up on stage to promote ShowReal. One of the event organisers insisted she played games on stage. She wasn't happy about this because after years of practice doing club appearances, she knows too well what works and what doesn't. Drunk club-goers want the music on and to be partying with Charlotte, not playing games. After all, it's not a nappy night. After ten minutes of 'who can eat the hottest spiciest pepper', the club started to get rowdy. People started flinging the peppers about and then people in the crowd start flinging drinks and ice cubes. One of them aimed at Char and hit a woman bouncer's head. After that it was game over and back to VIP we went.

After that it was photos. Standard procedure for a club appearance. Fans form a huge queue to get their picture with Charlotte. By this point me and Charlotte were tipsy and just want some hotdogs from the JustEat van promoting the event.

Thursday 17th

Down to London today and the weather was the worst EVER – it was pouring with rain and we had to drive at 40 mph down the M1. I drove Anna mad with my choice of music and my loud singing.

Charlotte's Guide To: The Best Music To Listen To On Car Journeys

I make it a point to only listen to songs with artists that sound like 'smelly' so any playlist like this is good for me:

1. Nelly Furtado – anything by her. She is a goddess. But my favourite's are 'Man-eater' and 'I'm Like a Bird'.
2. Nelly and Kelly (Rowland) – 'Dilemma'
3. Kelly Clarkson – 'Stronger'
4. R Kelly – 'I Believe I can Fly'

When we finally got to London we met up with our friend Luke in the evening and went for a steak. Obviously walked to the restaurant and back to get the steps up!

Friday 18th

So now we're in Manchester after another terrible journey.

Anna's ShowReal Tour Diary #2: London To Manchester

200 miles and SO much traffic works! This journey took over seven hours!!! We were stuck in the car and on the motorway.

As we were in the car for so long we kept stopping off at the services to get lots of snacks. Charlotte decided to turn my car into our house. The glove compartment was our kitchen. And that's where we would keep our snacks for the journey. Every time I asked for a Peperami Charlotte would let me know she was just going to the kitchen. We were sat in the sitting room you see. The back seats were the bedroom and the boot was our wardrobe (with all our suitcases in).

At Starbucks Drive Thru the girls from the window tried to get selfies with Charlotte. Not very easy getting a selfie in a Starbucks Drive Thru by the way, so they asked her for a couple of signed mugs instead. Things like this make the journey good and rewarding. Knowing how much people love her.

FINALLY when we got to Manchester we were so glad. Couldn't wait to just get to the Airbnb, get into bed and watch some television. When we arrived it was all new, we realised we must be the first guests at the house as all of the Ikea wrappers from the furniture and kitchen utensils were in the bin. After dragging all our cases in, I heard Charlotte kicking off in the sitting room. 'We are leaving. Right now! Put the stuff back in our wardrobe [the boot of the car].'

I rushed in to see what was happening – the TV didn't work. Nothing had been tuned in and I'm not sure there was even an aerial. No Wi-Fi either. Heard Charlotte's voice noting her mam and Kate explaining we had been travelling ALLLLL day and there is no TV!!! As if it was the end of the world! I persuaded her to stay. 'Let's just get a takeaway and go straight to sleep!' Sometimes you have to reason with Charlotte and let her know that driving around in the dark looking for a hotel isn't a good idea when we have been stuck in the car all day.

Saturday 19th

Today me and Anna got up and went to the Manchester Christmas markets. It was all lovely and festive. We drank hot chocolate and Baileys and wore our woolly hats and big coats.

Anna's Show Real Tour Diary #3: Day Out In Manchester

It was so packed at the market, we were all squished in like sardines and people started to notice it was Charlotte. This is when I begin to feel sorry for her. People sticking their phones in her face trying to get a photo and whispering as if she can't hear. Obviously, being a reality TV star, it's expected, but sometimes when there are so many people doing it it can become very intimidating for her. After all, she is only human. So we had cut the day short. Back to the Airbnb with no TV we go.

Ash came over to spend some time with us in the apartment. But he was just lying there on the sofa hardly saying anything and he was being so boring. He was doing my head in so much I ended up having a massive row and telling him to get out.

* * *

Ash came along to the ShowReal event but as I was working I didn't want him glued to my side, so I asked him to let me get on with what I needed to do while he hung out with his friends.

Anna can see how much I'm withdrawing from him. She says I can't be with him. I feel really bad. She's so right, I just need to get it over and done with.

Sunday 20th

Back home to Newcastle today.

Anna was counselling me all the way about Ash. She said I need to finish with him. 'This can't go on; he isn't for you. I've seen you in relationships and this is all wrong. He's not your type of boyfriend.' How did I fancy him so, so, so much before and now I don't fancy him at all?!

Anna loves Letitia's Sunday dinners! On the way home we laugh and joke about how there will be the smallest spoonful of mash and one Yorkshire pudding each. We are greedy girls and want man-portion sizes after our long journey! Got home, ate our mini portions and went straight to bed with Baby and Rhubarb. Me dad came in and took a photo of us and started taunting us, saying, 'It's the two foreheads!' We have matching foreheads, you see.

@charlottegshore
The dogs are settled and no barking from Rhubarb. This is an early Christmas miracle!

Monday 21st

@charlottegshore
Awful weather and all I wanna do is stay home and have one
more night here . . . but gotta get my packing done for LDN
for a month.

Mam, Dad and Nathaniel are staying. I told them it makes
more sense for them to be here when I don't:
a) have mates over or
b) have a boy in my bed or
c) have serious life admin to do*

I hate being at home on my own. It's so boring. Everyone tells
you that the first time you get a house is going to be so
amazing being there on your own but I couldn't be more
disappointed, it's the worst thing I've ever done in life! I'm
not scared being there, it's just a lonely life to lead. Normally
in that situation it would be that you've grown old and your
partner has died, you're wandering around with no company
apart from perhaps a couple of cats and you're pondering the
end of life as you know it. Well I feel like that and I'm 26
years old. I feel like a widow! I don't recommend it. I would
tell anyone 'don't ever get your first house alone, always move
in with your friends or your boyfriend.'

I keep asking my mates to come and stay with me but I

---

* re point C: That's probably a lie and actually a time when I do
want Mam here. I need her to facilitate the life admin. Today is
the perfect example because she has to help me pack my cases.
I threw a load of outfits at her and some essentials.

think they're a bit sick of me, to be honest, they all have their own lives and their own boyfriends and they have jobs to go to so they can't have sleepovers with me all the time. They're happy with seeing me about once or twice a month and I think that's enough for them. So I end up just asking me mam and dad and Nathaniel to stay there instead!

She then looked at me and said, 'Is a vibrator really an essential?'

Well, yes it is, Mam! I'm away for the best part of a month!

A Few Words From Anna Robinson About: Being Friends With Charlotte Crosby And Looking Back On Her First Few Months In Her New House

Charlotte's new house is absolutely amazing. We are all so proud of what she's built. Well, she didn't do all the brick-work personally but it is like one huge trophy to say: 'This is what I have accomplished.' Well done, Char! Her mam and dad managed the build and made sure everything went smoothly and I did my bit to chip in. Me and her mam painted the huge fence that surrounds her house. I got £100 for doing it   it took that long, that no way was I doing it for free!!

We are all so close to Charlotte's mam, Letitia. She is literally like a second mam. You can talk to her about anything and she would never think badly of you and is always there for good advice. She's much more like a friend than your mate's mam.

We all go round to Charlotte's and either have 'healthy food nights' or if we're not on a health kick then it's a 'bad takeaway night'! Usually a few bottles of wine go along nicely as well. The kitchen is all open plan so we can all chat and cook at the same time. The house is so big there's always something to do whether that's playing pool or watching a movie in the cinema room. Sometimes when we get drunk we sit in a small cupboard under the floorboards and all squeeze in! We like to call it the chamber of secrets! Her dad laughs at us and he's like, 'Of all the rooms in the house, you girls choose to sit under the floor in a cupboard!'

When we're trying to get our bikini bodies we either do *Charlotte's 3-minute Belly Blitz* or *Charlotte's 3-minute Bum Blitz* DVD in the cinema room. Or we all go in the gym room and Charlotte takes the lead as our instructor. There will be one of us on the treadmill, one on the stepper, one skipping and one on the floor doing some sort of ab exercises and then we rotate. Working out with your friends makes it so much funnier than alone!

Charlotte has a swimming pool which is amazing! Her mam Letitia gets worried when we go in there after having a drink because she's convinced a Michael Barrymore scene is going to happen! But the only things that happen are dance routines and attempted synchronised swimming! We put the speakers on full blast and have such a laugh. Sometimes it ends up as a naked pool party! Running around literally with not a stitch on. Then we all wake up in the morning with the worst anxiety and delete our Snapchat story hoping and praying no one has seen it when in fact so many people have already written all over Facebook, 'Good night? When's the next naked pool party?' And all our Snapchat followers have seen our boobs and bums! EMBARRASSING! Our group motto is Letitia's too: 'You've only got one life . . . LIVE IT!'

Whenever we go over to Charlotte's house we usually don't move for a night or three. Plenty of pampering and face masks! Sleepovers are fun at Charlotte's. It's so good that at our age we still make time for each other. I think that even when you get older it's important to stay close and have your friends. Through life you will always need your girls and we all have such a strong bond.

Tuesday 22nd

My OK! shoot is out and the house looks even more amazing in glossy paper format! I wish I could frame every picture and put them on my wall. Although that would be a bit weird because then I would have pictures of the rooms I am sitting in on the walls of the rooms I am sitting in. . . trippy!

This Fitbit is starting to drive me insane. I can't stop checking how everyone else is doing on theirs and I'm so competitive I need to beat them!

* * *

Went for a check-up about my nose. The doctor says it's all doing fine but I just need to keep having the steroid injections. I asked him about the symmastia too and whether there's anything you can do about it. He says its uncommon and usually people only get it from a boob job gone a bit wrong, but I have had it since birth. He says it is possible to fix, but it needs a specialist. I'd like to get it done. But I want him to do it because he's amazing! How different can boobs and noses be?

WHAT AM I GOING TO DO ABOUT ASH?

As the months have worn on it feels like everything I thought was so cool about him has turned into utter boringness. How does that even happen?

I've never just gone off someone like this. Maybe me and Ash was just a thing, and wasn't meant to be a relationship. Maybe it just accidentally turned into one.

I feel like such a bitch though. I've been really horrible to him lately and he hasn't taken the hint. If anything he's just been loads nicer to me!

Wednesday 23rd

Did a shoot for *heat* to promote Hartley's 10 Cal Jelly Pots – they've signed me up as the face of them and its uncanny because I genuinely love them! I've been eating them for a sweet snack ever since I started losing weight. I had to wear exercise gear for the shoot and the tops were really tight so I felt a bit self conscious about my body. Everyone was telling me I looked great but I just felt like shit and started getting those anxious feelings again. I was asked about my body and fitness tips (the piece is going out in January) and on paper I should feel good because I've managed to keep the weight off for so long since I began, but because I'm not doing the DVD I don't feel so trim and I still feel like that fat girl inside. I was also asked about Ash and I had to say, 'Honestly, don't get too excited!' If I was genuinely in love with him I would want everyone to know and would be shouting it from the rooftops but I'm not. I know it's not right. I need to man up and do something about it . . .

* * *

Went to a charity event for the Ectopic Pregnancy Trust at the Burberry store in Regent Street this evening. It was so amazing and posh in there – they had the store open just for us. I was going to do a speech to open the event but I felt too nervous in the end. Alex from the Trust didn't mind though, she said she was glad I could be there. Burberry gave everyone who was there a big discount and a percentage of what we spent went to the charity. That was obviously all the excuse me and Mam needed and I ended up buying myself a bag and somehow Mam managed to persuade me to buy her one too!

Thursday 24th

Filming starts on *Just Tattoo Of Us* tomorrow. What the hell is it going to be like? I'm really worried about what's going to happen with Bear. I'm either going to absolutely hate him or really fancy him.

Ash said he wants to come and support me on the show. I'm here for nearly a month so I've got an apartment to stay in while we're filming, but the days are going to be so long I told him there's not really much point. He sent me some nice flowers to say good luck, which was sweet.

What is going to happen with Bear? When we see each other tomorrow I know that he knows that I know that once upon a time we used to fancy each other. There's going to be something weird in the air.

Shit, what if I really do start fancying Bear?

Friday 25th

I LOVE BEING A PRESENTER!

Bear looked really fit. We actually argued most of the day about when I tweeted about him and Lillie Lexie, and he was still denying he was with her in the club. But it was funny banter and at the end of filming I went up to him and said, 'I think I can be friends with you tomorrow.'

When I got home Ash was sitting in the apartment waiting for me. I should have been happy about it, but all I kept thinking was, 'Is he going to be like this every night?'

The hours we're filming are ridiculous. It's already nearly midnight because we've been in the studio so long. So Ash is just wasting his time being here. He should be off somewhere doing his own thing, not waiting for me.

Saturday 26th

Oh my God it was such a good day! Bear (or Stephen as everyone calls him) is really trying to do something to my brain. He's being SO charming and nice. I don't know what he's up to.

The show is such a good show too! I reckon it's going to do really well. Me and Stephen each have to hang out with one person in the couple. We have to be there with them for the whole journey and help calm them down when they find out their other half has given them a shit tattoo!

We had such a funny time and get on so well. We were Snapchatting a weird thing about tampons today and everyone said they thought it was really funny and we were crazy.

Ash was at the apartment again when I got home.

Sunday 27th

Stephen bought me a bear. He is being so incredibly nice to me all the time and keeps trying to kiss me when no one's looking! He doesn't seem to care that I have a boyfriend. He said, 'So are you single at the minute?' and I told him about Ash and that it's not really working out. I explained the whole story about how I feel and that I'm in an awkward position. He just shrugged and carried on. It's like he knows he has nothing to worry about.

Everyone on set is saying they can see what Stephen's doing. He's trying to win me over. And it's working. He's winning me over in the worst way because I'm really starting to fancy him.

Monday 28th

Stephen is making it so obvious that he fancies me and even though I know he behaves like that to every girl, it's so hard not to fall for it. He goes and gets me dinner every day. If I'm cold he gives me his coat. He makes me cups of tea and coffee every second, he's always asking if I want something! Kate has been here and she says she can see how easy he is and how charming. She knows I'm falling for him too. I need to do something about Ash.

Tuesday 29th

We had a day off so Stephen and I went Christmas tree shopping because we said we wanted our dressing room to look nice. It felt just like a date. Whenever we're left in the dressing room he tries to kiss me.

Ash isn't at the apartment any more . . .

Wednesday 30th

I have officially cheated on Ash.

I kissed Stephen last night and it was so nice and exciting.

I asked him to stay at mine and when we got to the apartment I had to turn my phone off. It's the first time I've ever done anything like that! I felt so bad.

We didn't shag, we didn't even take our clothes off. We just snogged and snogged all night. He left early this morning so no one from production would guess what was happening. I don't think Craig from MTV would be very happy if he knew.

Craig really makes me laugh though. I've known him for such a long time. He always tells stories about me, like about when I first met him after he took over from the big boss Steve at MTV. Steve was introducing him but I didn't listen to what he said and was convinced Craig was a runner so I started barking orders at him trying to get him to bring me a sandwich and a juice! Another story he always tells – which I totally don't remember – was about me calling him and waking him up at 3 a.m. to have a go at him about something that had happened in Geordie Shore. I was ranting down the phone saying, 'Good luck in your next job!' and then he heard a pause, then me saying to someone, 'Oh . . . double cheeseburger and fries please.' I was having a full-blown argument in the middle of a 24-hour McDonalds!

After what had happened with Stephen, I texted Ash straight away saying, 'I can't be with you any more.' I couldn't carry on after something had happened with Stephen. He replied as if he was expecting it and was really understanding.

I have never got on as well with anyone as I do with Stephen. I thought Mitch was the closest I would ever get to a boy because we were on the same wavelength but Stephen is on another level. He is totally mad, just like me, and we have so many stupid jokes together. We can't leave each other's side. This must be what having a soulmate is like.

I am so happy.

December 2016

Nights I've spent with Stephen: Too many but not enough

Names I call Stephen: Morewhall, Noodle Head, Pea Head (any small head ones because his head is tiny), Baby, Stephen, Bear, Radgie Pancake

Names he calls me: Coconut Head

Emojis to describe my feelings for him:
😊🖤😚😼😂😙

Thursday 1st

I don't know what's going to happen with us, I don't think he does either.

We talk about the stupidest stuff all day. We've decided we're going to build businesses together and live in a massive castle with a big drive. It's ridiculous how we talk. We're the weirdest two people you can put together in the world. He's just as crazy as me. It's so stupid. And I am obsessed with him.

Friday 2nd

My make-up range with Easilocks is out today, it's called Fliqué. I am so excited about it and Stephen has been so cute tweeting and Snapchatting about how good it is and telling everyone to buy it. He's so lovely and charming. I think people who watched him on *Celebrity Big Brother* would be shocked. It's like he's a totally different person. But I know there's a Hyde to the Jekyll hidden somewhere.

* * *

Stephen has slept at my apartment every single night. We haven't shagged yet though.

The other night we got drunk and still didn't do anything.

I don't know what's going on and I don't know whether to trust him. I feel weird because I had a boyfriend four days ago and now I'm on a show with someone I used to flirt with and then fell out with and we're spending every single second of every day together. I'm confused. I don't want to sleep with him yet because it isn't one of those things where it's just going to be a shag. I know it's so much deeper than that. And he does too, which is why he's not pushing it.

Saturday 3rd

People are starting to get wind of the fact that we're growing so close and there's speculation in the papers. He's not been making any secret of his feelings on set either and I'm sure the crew know even though they don't say anything.

We're so similar that I know we're good together. We've

decided we're going to start a business and have it registered it with Companies House. It's called His 'n' Hers and will sell loads of cool merchandise like phone cases, key rings, cups and sweatshirts. We came up with it all in the dressing room and we're going to make it happen!

Sunday 4th

We've snogged. And snogged. Over clothes. It's made it so much more intense.

We know it's stupid to flirt at work but it's just getting so much more than that.

He scares me because I know he has another side to him. Look at all the things he's done. Look at how he was with Lillie in *Celebrity Big Brother*. When she confronted him he just shrugged! He seems like he's got another side to him and that really petrifies me. I've never been scared by a boy like I am by him.

He keeps saying he'd never hurt me and that he hasn't felt this way before. He says none of the others were his proper girlfriend. But I bet he's said that to all of them.

* * *

Melissa is here staying in the apartment with us now because she's swapped with Lyndsey who was doing my make-up all last week. I think she feels a bit awkward being here with Stephen. She doesn't like meeting new people, she gets shy.

Monday 5th

There's a Snapchat that Lyndsey took of Stephen with his hand up my jumper last week that's been picked up somehow by the *Sun* because a fan got hold of it. Now everyone is speculating that we're together.

> Last week, Bear was seen mucking about with the surgery-loving northerner, and appeared to be dry-humping her with his hands up her jumper.

Surgery-loving northerner? That's a new one!

People have been on Twitter going nuts. They're hating on Stephen saying things like, 'Don't go anywhere near him, he's worse than Gary!'

* * *

I nearly caused a riot at The Clothes Show today! I was there for In The Style because we have a stand there. But the Mark Hill team were also there so I wanted to go and visit them at their stand because I do loads of work for them and thought it would be good.

Turns out it wasn't good.

I was Snapchatting while I was there and suddenly everyone got wind of it and hundreds of girls started following me and Melissa. Mel nearly got trampled on and all these girls were diving on us like we were in the middle of a football pitch. Security were getting really mad and freaking out because there were so many people crowding round. Kate got into trouble from the security guy for having an unplanned stand visit.

* * *

Tuesday 6th

We've FINALLY shagged. Wow. I made him wait so long and it was really worth it. It was soooo good (I hope Mel didn't hear us from the room next door!). He has a gorgeous body. He's like a little Action Man. And he has loads of abs, I don't know how many he has, but he definitely has more than a six-pack.

Charlotte's Guide To: The Perils Of Falling For A Work Colleague

This is something I seem to fall into quite easily. It's not only really annoying but makes things very hard at work when you end up hating their guts afterwards. And another thing, why are the work colleagues always arseholes? Someone very intelligent once said, 'Don't mix pleasure with work.' (Or was that 'business with pleasure'?) In other words, don't kiss your co-worker ON OR OFF CAMERA! Well, it turns out I'm not that intelligent and didn't listen to that person. So, if you have made the same mistake as me . . .

You're fucked! I literally have no advice. I ended leaving my last job because I fell for the last prick on that show. Let's just hope this one is different . . . (but I'll try not to get my hopes up . . .)

Wednesday 7th

Now for the bad news . . .
Stephen is on the next series of *Celebs Go Dating*. And he

starts filming in about six days. This means we definitely aren't allowed to be officially boyfriend and girlfriend. It's karma for what I did to Ash.

* * *

Geordie Shore was on tonight. It's the series they filmed without me in the summer and tonight's episode was the one when Gary has an 'epiphany' about me, which Sophie told me about back in July. He tells Aaron he doesn't want to go on the pull because, 'I realised that I actually miss Charlotte a lot more than I thought I did.'

Then he tells Sophie that he's beginning to miss me too: 'I'm starting to think, "What is actually more important . . . pulling? Or rescuing things with Charlotte?"'

He then proceeds to tell Holly, 'I'm going to go to Charlotte, "Look I haven't pulled in Napa. I realised in my head what I'm doing. Grow some balls, drop the ego. I actually like you. I want to be with you." I've finally realised that I do want to be with Charlotte. I might have fucked things up in the past but I've got to give it another go. If that means not pulling for the rest of the time I'm away, that's what I'll have to do.'

Holly is brilliant though and she says, 'It's great that Gary has finally realised his true feelings for Charlotte but for me . . . he's too late.'

ER, TOO LATE? Slight understatement.

It was filmed so long ago that he knows there is NO WAY I would get back with him now. Anyone would be a better boyfriend than Gary Beadle.

Thursday 8th

If there was a camera set up in our dressing room at *Just Tattoo Of Us*, there would be a whole different show from the one that's going to air on MTV. Me and Stephen can't keep our hands off each other and when we get in the dressing room and no one's looking we're just all over each other. It's so exciting and so full-on.

> @charlottegshore
> Sometimes everything just . . . changes.

Friday 9th

Here's the sort of thing me and Stephen do together:

1. We have one type of kissing called the 'tongue tornado' – this is where you don't touch lips but you swirl your tongues around each other.
2. And we have another called the 'postage stamp' – this is where the two tongues press onto each other flat, like they're stamping down.
3. We do them all the time while we're filming and everyone gets really annoyed. All the crew say things like, 'Stop it now, it's making us feel sick.'

Saturday 10th

Last day filming tomorrow. Need to sleep for a week when I get home.

Sunday 11th

It was the final day of filming today and Bear and I have had a MASSIVE ARGUMENT. I went for him on camera and we had a huge row. It's a proper explosive episode.

The series culminated in us having to do what the couples had been doing in the show all along: we had to choose tattoos for each other. I didn't have any good ideas for his tattoo so I just got the tattooist to do a portrait of me with a finger pointing out saying 'You're fired!' like Alan Sugar on *The Apprentice*. We've got a running joke that I'm more famous than him where he replies, 'But I'm the people's champion! I won *Big Brother*!' I knew nothing I got would bother him anyway so it didn't really matter.

I didn't have a clue what mine was going to be, but I told him he could only do it in the middle of my back where no one could possibly see it. I found a place that sits below your shoulder blades on the left-hand side so even if you have a Bardot off-the-shoulder top on no one would know. I knew he would do something random.

I didn't know it would be evil.

It is SO BAD. I am still in shock. I have been crying all day.

The tattoo he had done is an animal that's half bear and half cheetah and when it was revealed on camera he basically said it was because I had cheated on Ash with him! He said it ON NATIONAL TV! It was so awful. I ran off in tears and he didn't even come to comfort me to see if I was OK.

Melissa is so angry with him. She said she was expecting him to come out of character as soon as the cameras stopped rolling but he didn't. She says he's worse than Gary. At least if I was upset or hurt Gary would come after me to see if I was OK. It feels like I've been stabbed in the heart. He said it was my fault for overreacting and that I acted like a baby. He should say sorry! It's not nice for him to let me be that upset.

* * *

I texted Kate. I am fuming! She told me I didn't really 'cheat', so I should just call him an idiot, just brush it off and love the beautiful tattoo. She told me all about its symbolism.

She's already researched online the symbolism of the animals, a cheetah exudes the essence of the 'warrior goddess' and represents beauty, elegance and grace and a bear represents grounding forces and strength.

Secretly I know she's right. The tattoo is beautiful and I can live with being a warrior goddess.

Stephen still hasn't apologised. He hasn't said anything. I don't know what to do or think.

I messaged one of the crew and asked them what they thought, they've seen how affectionate he's been with me and how close we are. They told me they thought I'd been played and now they hate him too.

What have I done? I'm so confused.

Monday 12th

Stephen didn't sleep at mine last night. He went back to his house and it's the first night we've spent apart. I woke up really panicking that these last two weeks have been a joke on his behalf.

* * *

We've made friends. He says he didn't mean it and that he still feels everything he said about me and wants me to be his girlfriend once he's finished on *Celebs Go Dating*. Having thought about it in the cold light of day I think maybe I did overreact a bit. Yes he was nasty to me by not apologising but he didn't even do anything that bad . . . it's not like he cheated on me. He got me a tattoo. And now I look at it, it's actually quite a nice one. If he hurt me that much over this what will it be like if he actually does anything bad to me? What on earth am I going to be like if we ever do get together?

Mel says she can't forgive him. I don't know if they will ever be friends now. It's really awkward that she has fallen out with him.

MTV have said they are making our tattooing scenes into their own episode. The series was meant to be seven shows but they're adding another because so much happened when we did the tattoos for each other. Oh shit.

Tuesday 13th

After months of refusing to take anything for her menopause, Mam has finally given in to the doctor's advice. She rang me today to tell me it was the best decision she's ever made and she feels like she's on an ecstacy tablet all the time. I'm going to get back and find her with glow sticks dancing around my living room.

Wednesday 14th

> @charlottegshore
> walking in the wind is possibly the hardest thing in life.

Thursday 15th

Now Donald Trump has been elected president I keep thinking WTF is happening in the world?

Friday 16th

I am very hungover after going for what was meant to be 'a few drinks' with Adam and Jamie and ending up gatecrashing a party in their hotel that turned out to be people who worked in Thomas Cook. Everyone was asking me for selfies and following me around but I didn't care I was so pissed and was jumping up and down on the dancefloor. Then we left and I got into the lift, fell over and wet myself and refused to get up and Adam had to drag me along the corridor in the hotel and put me to bed.

Stephen's hating doing *Celebs Go Dating* and keeps saying he doesn't want to do it any more. I've told him not to worry about me and that he's allowed to kiss a couple of people like I did otherwise it's going to look weird. I said I understand and that I know it's just a show.

Saturday 17th

Stephen came to Newcastle for the weekend and met the family. And they love him. Especially me mam. I think she loves him more than me. She is OBSESSED WITH HIM!

He was really funny with Nathaniel too. I told him about Nathaniel's autism and explained that he's not very good at socialising so when he met him he just said, 'NATHANIEL! OH MY GOD!' and was really over the top. It was such a brilliant thing to do. I could see Nathaniel trying to hold his laugh in but he couldn't help himself. It's the first time I've seen him like that.

Sunday 18th

Stephen's been telling me he loves me from the day we first met but now when he says it I know it means something. I say it back to him too. And he calls me his 'very-soon-to-be girlfriend'. It feels so different to anything I've ever had before. I want to be with him for the rest of my life. I don't have any doubts. We're on the same level. We have no worries about one of us not understanding the other one because we are both basically the same person! We have so many silly things we do; we are always laughing from the minute we wake up. He does a stupid thing where he pretends to turn into a gorilla – a really angry one – and he grabs me and throws me about. He says, 'The gorilla's about to come out!' and I say, 'No, not the gorilla!' because it hurts when he tickles me. I prefer it when he pretends to be the 'baby monkey' and gets all cute instead. We have so many silly things we do.

Monday 19th

I hate my Fitbit. I hate it. It's ruining my life. Found out one of our mates has beaten my steps and got 60,000 in one week. It's not fair because she has horses. I have been stuck in a studio most of the time so how can I compete? I am in such a mood.

Tuesday 20th

It's Stephen's birthday in January. I am going to treat him so much. He's the best boyfriend I have ever had. He is always treating me and always buys me flowers. Stephen puts me first in everything and pays me so much attention.

Wednesday 21st

Watched an old episode of *Geordie Shore* tonight and I couldn't help but tweet about how me and Gary had actually visited a love lock bridge and put a padlock on.

> @charlottegshore
> An interesting fact about this EP that's being played now on @MTVUK me and @GazGShore actually went to love lock bridge and did our own.

> @charlottegshore
> but it never got shown on the actual show. It's still there somewhere on the bridge. can't quite remember what it said.

I knew people would be intrigued by it. I just wanted to wind people up.

Thursday 22nd

HA HA. I do love social media sometimes!

I put up a picture of me with curly hair to show how you can use a set of Mark Hill curling tongs. But all my fans were convinced the tongs were a sex toy!

Thought they were anal beads.

Definite sex toy. That's our girl, Charlotte.

Totally thought you were holding something naughty to start with #dirtymind.

Yes I love products that don't just have one function . . . by day a hair curler, by night . . . anal beads.

Oops.

* * *

I'm back in London and am staying with Stephen and his family. They're all so amazing and just like him. I love them all already. His dad's called Stephen too and is really funny. His brother Rob lives at home and is such a fun and genuine person. He kissed me on the cheek and made me feel really welcome. Stephen also has a brother Danny who is older with two kids who's a really successful businessman (not exactly sure what he does but it's got something to do with a bakery and bread) and a sister called Hayley.

* * *

It's so weird thinking that things have only been going on between me and Stephen for three weeks. We've got so close. I went to the doctor's today for another steroid injection in my nose. Stephen said he wanted to wait for me and went shopping while I was in there. When I met back up with him, he handed me this massive Selfridges bag. 'What the hell's this?' I shrieked. 'It's your Christmas present!' he smirked.

WHHHAAAAT!!?

He can't get me a Christmas present! We've only known each other three weeks. WHAT THE HELL? I felt awful because I hadn't got him anything.

I looked in the bag and there was a Creed bag so I knew it was a Creed perfume, which is basically the most expensive perfume you can buy! There's a men's aftershave and they've started doing girls now. There was another bag beside it and it had a really posh word on it that I couldn't pronounce: 'Bulgari'. I didn't know what it was but I knew it wasn't cheap.

I refused to open it in front of him because I was too shy. Opening presents in front of someone is always so awkward. If you don't like it you have to pretend to like it but you can't actually tell them that you don't like it, it's embarrassing! It's even worse when you really like that person and you've only known them for THREE WEEKS.

So I decided I wasn't going to open it. I told him I wouldn't open it until Christmas.

Friday 23rd

It really pisses me off that Stephen has dated every girl that I don't get on with! I get so angry about it! I keep Googling him and all these photos come up of him with all his exes!

FUCK THIS!

I now know what it's like when a boy says that they don't want a girlfriend who has been with everyone they know! I hate thinking about the other girls he's been with. He doesn't like it when I say that to him though, he says it hurts him and he gets really sad about it. He's always really nice about his exes too which is annoying. And I'm sure he loved Vicky because Marnie says he used to talk about her a lot in the *Big Brother* house.

Saturday 24th

I was on the train back to Newcastle and the present Stephen gave me was in my face shouting, 'OPEN ME!' I tried to have some willpower but it lasted about thirty seconds before I caved in and opened it. I opened the small one that I couldn't pronounce first. And inside was the most amazing tiny, delicate diamanté bracelet – a thin chain with a little pendulum at the end and one chain shorter than the other. It is so sparkly and beautiful. I was like, 'What the hell?!!' I knew it was seriously expensive. The Creed perfume is so gorgeous too. It's £250 a bottle! It smells amazing.

I messaged Stephen straight away and said, 'Oh my God, I can't believe it. I love it!'

I don't understand how he got it so right! How did he know what I would like? It was dead on and he doesn't even know me that well. I thought he must have asked someone but he told me he hadn't. This is proof we are soul mates. He can see inside my brain.

I already knew I liked him so much but now I like him even more.

* * *

Mam couldn't believe it when I showed her the presents. She is so happy because I've never had anyone who looks after me financially. It's always been me paying for stuff.

I've never been with someone who's on the same level as me and is earning good money and wants to spend it on me. I've never been treated the way he treats me.

You'd think I would have been looked after by Gary but I honestly cannot remember a time that me and Gary went for food and it was just us. Virtually everything we did was on the show which meant it was all paid for by the show. I haven't even been to Gary's house. I've never even met his mam! I vaguely remember once going somewhere and I didn't have my purse and I asked, 'Gary, do you mind getting me a ham sandwich?' and that was about it.

Stephen doesn't let me pay for anything. Even if I offer he literally shouts at me. If I need to get a taxi somewhere he will insist on booking the Uber. It's like we're fighting to get to the phone first.

Stephen's a total different person to the one who was on *Celebrity Big Brother*. I think the bad guy is his character who he puts on for the camera. I told him I think he plays up to the camera even though he denies it.

* * *

Out with the girls tonight. It's tradition to have a Christmas Eve pub crawl around Sunderland . . . Can't wait for everyone to smell me coming (my new Creed perfume that is, not my vagina).

Sunday 25th

Oh my God. What a night.

So, we went out for our traditional pub crawl and obviously I took it too far. Me mam and dad were sleeping at mine because it was the first time I could be host and have the family round for Christmas dinner. The problem was I took everyone back home with me after the night out and decided to have a pool party.

So at 7a.m. on Christmas morning me mam came downstairs to find random people collapsed around the pool. And one couple were HAVING SEX over the office table! I don't even know who they were! I think we met them at the kebab shop and brought them back with us!

Me mam said to them, 'You're going to have to leave NOW. It's Christmas Day. My son Nathaniel is awake and wants to open his presents and you're shagging in his dad's office.'

Then she walked into the pool room to find me collapsed asleep in a towel on a sun lounger. She said, 'Charlotte, you're going to have to go to bed and get some sleep before you get up for Christmas dinner.' Then me mam went back in the room to see if the couple had gone and the girl was sucking the boy off! She dragged them both out and kicked them out of the house!

Shit.

I am in so much trouble.

* * *

Luckily Mam and Dad saw the funny side so when I woke up and came down to dinner, everyone was laughing about it. Who even were those people??

Dad bought me a vintage sign from eBay that says 'Bus Stop' to go in the garden. I couldn't stop laughing.

Monday 26th

Mam is obsessed with Stephen! He tells jokes all the time and she always laughs at them and then afterwards starts repeating them! We were in the car today and Mam said, 'Remember when we drove past that graveyard and Stephen said, 'Oh, people are dying to get in there!'

Er, yeah, Mam, it was over a week ago, it's time you got over it.

She's already bought him a mug for his birthday in January which says 'Mr Perfect'!

Went out for Boxing Day night with Sophie to Revolution. I tripped and went flying in the street. Obviously there was a pap there to record the moment.

Merry Christmas, everyone!

* * *

Really missing Stephen. He's going to come up and stay in a few days but I NEED to see him before then so I'm going to go and hang with him while he does some PAs. We're meant to be staying away from each other until he's finished *Celebs Go Dating*. But I love him!

Tuesday 27th

Went with Stephen and his cousin Ray to one of his PAs in Exeter. Kyle was on the same one so it didn't matter so much when someone tweeted that they spotted us because I could pretend I was with him instead. Me, Stephen and Ray are like the three musketeers. We had such a laugh. Stephen is hilarious and doesn't like anyone on the phone when they're with him because he says it's really antisocial. So the whole entire journey I wasn't allowed to scroll AT ALL. He gets so angry if he sees me on the phone!

Stephen is actually quite old fashioned when I think about

it. Mam says he's chivalrous. He pays for the lady and doesn't like people being on their phone all the time. That's a proper gent!

* * *

Wednesday 28th

We've been spotted out together and it's in the *Sun*, with a supposed source from the club in Exeter saying:

> Charlotte was keen to take a back seat while Bear was meeting and greeting fans as if she didn't want to be spotted by too many people. When he'd finished his work commitments they kept themselves to the VIP area and seemed very cosy. They left together and seemed more than just friends.

Shit. *Celebs Go Dating* will go mad with him if they think we're together. Karma sucks.

Thursday 29th

Mam has bought a Fitbit and joined the WhatsApp group so I had to get mine out again. I can't have her on it without me, it will wind me up.

Friday 30th

Mam is already being so annoying. I was out and she texted me the most patronising text ever: 'If you get yourself to the gym and do another couple of thousand steps you'll be in the lead.'

I replied, 'First of all, I'm already in the lead, I just haven't updated my Fitbit and, secondly, I have been on the Fitbit much longer than you and don't need your advice.'

After that I just kept sending her abuse: 'You are thick and you are the loser so I am in the lead! I have done so many more steps from you.'

Got home and updated it. Turns out she won. She's been walking the dogs – that's why!

Saturday 31st

Stephen invited me to Brighton for New Year's Eve but I decided to stay home with my mates and have a pool party. Marnie and Chloe came and we filmed loads of it on Snapchat. It was fun but not as fun as if I'd been with him . . .

I've written a poem about him:

Bear is cute
he plays the flute
he has nice hair
he likes to share
his things with me I think he really cares
I like his nose
he has really long toes
I think it's best we keep this secret so that no one knows

I miss him . . .

January 2017

Number of balloons I bought for Stephen's birthday:
I couldn't count them all but let's just say I cleaned out Clinton Cards

Emojis to describe how I feel about Stephen: 🖤👰👶

Sunday 1st

Ouch. Head hurts. Was a fun night but wish I'd seen Stephen after all. Miss him and need a cuddle.

Monday 2nd

I have had a brainwave. I am going to put the Fitbit on Baby. She does a lot of steps and is constantly walking around! She's running all over the place. Surely this way I will win every Fitbit challenge!

Tuesday 3rd

It turns out the Fitbit needs to be touching human skin. So it hasn't worked and I've now lost loads of challenges as a result.

RAGING!

Me and Stephen get on so well and it's been making me think back to when I was with Gary and realise how wrong we were for each other. Gary would look at me so weirdly if I did some of the things I do with Stephen. He never wanted me, but I couldn't see that we just weren't right. We would never make it in the real world!

And we're much closer than me and Mitch EVER were even though we've only known each other a month and a half. But I am so, so scared of being hurt. I always have that nagging feeling in the back of my head. I'd like to think he would be different with me than he's been with every other girl but doesn't everyone think like that? I don't want to be made a mug of again.

We do such random things every day. In the morning he will always give each other silly cuddles and he acts like he's a big baby. We even have a stupid voice we do for each other! And we call each other 'Morewhall' because my favourite whale is the narwhal but he can't pronounce the word properly so it's turned into Morewhall for some reason. So I always say to him 'How's my little Morewhall?' How pathetic does that sound?!

People hate being with us because we're too full-on and can't stop touching or kissing each other. We are together every single night.

Wednesday 4th

Posted a pouty picture on Instagram (standard behaviour for me) and once again there's been a ridiculous amount of comments telling me I've 'gone too far'! I have to laugh sometimes. It's obviously a slow news day for the *Daily Mail* too because they've put it online: 'Charlotte Crosby suffers social media backlash'!

Uhh your lips are disgusting! They look swollen! [Too] much injection.

Char you lips look ugly. . .stop pleaseeee you are so beautiful.

You're ruining your looks. You're naturally pretty.

IF YOU SAW ME IN THE FLESH YOU'D KNOW I'M JUST POUTING, YOU FOOLS!

If I ever stop being famous and want to get back into the limelight I'm just going to have LOADS of plastic surgery so people talk about me all the time – people are obsessed!

* * *

I've done something to my back. Feel like an old woman. I'm in agony.

Ouch!

Thursday 5th

I'm back down at Stephen's for a week. His mam Linda is so sweet, she's helped us so much with the His 'n' Hers stuff. As soon as we set the company up we ordered some merchandise and got it all sent to their house. His mam helped us do all the packaging and taught us how to fold up jumpers up in a nice way. She's helped out so much with it all and it's clogged up her whole sitting room. I've ordered her a bunch of flowers to say thanks.

Friday 6th

Went to see a massage therapist about my back but it's still killing me. What have I done?

Have been trying to get Ray to help me with a present for Stephen's birthday. I remember he said he wanted a Louis Vuitton bag when we were in the car going to one of his PAs but I can't remember which one! I don't have Ray's number so I had to grab Stephen's phone when I was with him today and make out I needed to speak to Ray about something. Stephen kept asking why so I said it was a secret. I think he has an inkling it's to do with his birthday but he doesn't know what it is.

* * *

Ray has told me what bag it is. I'm definitely getting it.

Saturday 7th

I've booked us a holiday as part of his birthday present – I'm in a carefree, whirlwind I'm-in-love kind of mood! I am not going to worry about whether we're together by the time *Celebs Go Dating* ends – we are going on holiday in March and we are going to LOVE IT. I feel like I'm being swept away by the ocean. Well, I hope that's not actually the case because then there's definitely no future for me and Stephen. I'll have to marry a whale instead.

I've booked the Dominican Republic! I can't wait to see his face when he opens his presents! We've both talked loads about wanting to go away when he finishes *Celebs Go Dating* but he thinks he's going to be the one booking it. He has spoilt me so much so I want to make this the best birthday ever.

Sunday 8th

I have such a laugh with Stephen's family. Me, him, his dad and Rob sit and watch films together all the time. Linda works at a school in the day and often works in the evenings at the community centre so she's not there as much.

Today Linda made the best Sunday dinner I have ever tasted in my whole entire life. I wish I could be at Stephen's house on a Sunday for the rest of my life until I die. (Me mam on the other hand can never get it all right – something's always cold on the plate. Deep down she knows I'm not happy with her Sunday dinners.)

Monday 9th

Stephen's trying to woo me with cooking too! He's just mastered the art of making boiled eggs and he's very proud of himself. It used to be his dad who made the eggs but the duty has been passed down to Stephen. He's made me three boiled eggs so far – his dad hovers over me for the whole time I'm eating them and asks how they are.

Tuesday 10th

I still feel strange sometimes not knowing what's properly going on with us. He's still filming *Celebs Go Dating* and even though I am trying to be cool about it I can't stop thinking about what he's up to on there. Also I have to remind myself that I told him he should kiss people! I have told him I understand what the show is like and that he should never ever worry what I think. I'm not going to start kicking off at him when it airs. I just told him to get it over and done with so we can move on. He says he can't stand the show and has run away from a few dates!

Wednesday 11th

We've been papped wearing the same jumper, which makes it blatantly obvious that we've been sleeping in the same place. The *Daily Mail* has worked out that Stephen wore a jumper with some lips and the words Camden Town on it when we were filming together in November, and now they've caught me in the same one.

Thursday 12th

I love staying at Stephen's house. His family are so funny and lovely; you know when you just laugh the whole time? Normally when you go to someone's house and they live with their parents you both rush up to the bedroom so you can spend time on your own but we just want to hang out in the same room together. His brother Rob is brilliant too – he's dead funny but he's a bit more sensible than Stephen. They're very different!

Charlotte's Guide To: Having A Poo In Your Boyfriend's Family's House

1. Laden the toilet bowl with toilet roll! Put it right in the water and all around the bowl! Not all people

remember to have a toilet brush and if you make a stain up the side, not only will you be embarrassed but you will have to pass the blame on to a poor family member. The toilet roll also cushions the poo's fall avoiding the 'Big Splash'.

2. FLUSH IMMEDIATELY. As soon as the poo has dropped you must flush! This avoids the smell travelling from the bowl to the bathroom. It's a great trick; make sure to remember this one. I like to call it the SQUEEZE . . . DROP . . . FLUSH!

3. Open a window . . . Another chance to get rid of the smell if you forgot to follow #2.

4. Run the tap! This will mask the sound of any loud plops that the toilet roll cushion just can't withstand.

Friday 13th

Chloe is going into *Celebrity Big Brother* – she is going to be mental in there! She will cause so much fun and outrage! No one will know what to do with themselves!

I've had a couple of weeks off and I'm starting to get worried. I'm used to being so busy I can't breathe and now I'm the one waiting in a hotel while Stephen does a dating show.

Maybe I need to get pregnant and then I will get my own show!

I would 100 per cent keep the baby if I got pregnant with Stephen. He wants to have ten children, which I have said can't happen because I will just burst at the seams. He wants a boy first called Teddy Bear. The rest of his name choices are awful – he likes Rocky and Phoenix. I'm not having either of those names! I like Elle, India or Inka for girls.

Saturday 14th

Stephen has been asked to do *Ex on the Beach* but he says he won't do it because he's with me. Gary NEVER said that. Stephen's already passed so many tests!

It's his birthday tomorrow. I've decided to move to a hotel as I have such a massive surprise in store for him so he's going to come over after he's been to see his family.

Each night when he comes back from filming I keep asking questions because I want to know what's happened but he won't go into it. He just says, 'We don't talk about that.'

Sunday 15th

Stephen's birthday today!

Stephen had dinner with his family and then he came to see me in my hotel.

I went to Clinton Cards and bought every single balloon in the place and got them all filled with helium. I spent £200 on balloons! Don't know how I managed to get them through the door. I literally had every life situation covered – even 'Happy retirement!' and 'Congratulations it's a boy!' There was a 'Mr and Mrs' one with massive roses on, a Darth Vader one and all these other random balloons.

When he walked into the hotel room I said, 'Welcome to birthday balloon kingdom!'

He was gobsmacked, his jaw just dropped to the floor, he was so overwhelmed. He was like, 'What the hell?!' and said no one has ever done anything that special for him before or made that much of an effort for him. I walked him through the balloon kingdom and told him what he was allowed to open first – he tried to go for the card but that had the tickets in so I told him to open the bag. Then I let him open the tickets. He said, 'I can't accept this!' and kept saying that he thinks the man should pay – but I told him he has no choice. They are bought and booked!

I was sorry I hadn't opened the door in my underwear or anything but I've hurt my back. Which also meant we couldn't have sex . . . So I promised I would do it at Valentine's instead.

Monday 16th

My back is hurting so much. It's been over a week since we had sex and Stephen is feeling really down. I've told him it's a proper relationship where you can just be happy to hang out sometimes. I told him he will learn!

Tuesday 17th

Chloe has been amazing in *Celebrity Big Brother*. She's been jumping in the pool, getting naked, having fights with Jess from *The Apprentice*, trying to get into Calum Best . . . I do worry she's going a bit overboard though. One of us should have spoken to her and told her she needs to remember she's not in *Geordie Shore*. She's behaving like she does with us and it's a bit too full-on. The audience isn't ready for that. There are older people in the house and she shouldn't do it out of respect for them. She's a bit naïve like that. She can still be the fun, amazing Chloe she always has been . . . but she needs to tone it down. I think everyone can see she has a heart of gold, but she's wild! Kim Woodburn is the most hilarious person I have ever watched. She's so angry! She kicks off and then she gets in the diary room and says, 'Hello, lovely, I don't know what happened out there,' as if she hasn't a clue what she's like!

Wednesday 18th

Our WhatsApp group chat went into uproar tonight because Holly is in Thailand with Kyle and she posted a NAKED SNAPCHAT!

> Sophie: Holly? Are you there? You need to go on your snapchat!

> Me: Holly! You need to delete your snapchat!

> Marnie: She's not replying. It's been up for an hour! She's naked!

> Sophie: HOLLLLLLLYY!

Thursday 19th

Holly's nakedness is clogging up my social media timeline! It's everywhere!

Friday 20th

Watched Donald Trump's inauguration and I couldn't believe how different him and Obama were, just by their manners. Barack Obama was standing by his wife Michelle the whole time, holding her hand, making sure she was fine, looking out for her, putting her first . . . and Donald Trump just looked like he couldn't wait to walk off from his wife quick enough! Made me sad watching it because it's such a moment in history and Obama was such a good president who everyone loved.

Trump reminds me very much of a character who should be on Beavis and Butthead. He doesn't seem real – he looks like a cartoon! But I find it all fascinating. What's going to happen with America? Who knows? Donald could be really bad and crap but you never know he could also be good . . .?

* * *

My back is feeling much better so I told Stephen we could have sex tonight. We had the *Celebrity Big Brother* eviction on in the background. We'd just started to get going when suddenly I heard the voice-over man saying, 'Chloe! You have been evicted! Please leave the *Big Brother* house!'

We stopped mid-thrust.

I put my hand on my mouth and said, 'What the hell? Did you just hear what I thought I heard?'

'I think so,' said Stephen.

I had to push him off me so I could have a closer look at the telly and Chloe *had* been evicted! I never in a million years thought she was going to go. I was having sex while the eviction was on – that's how much I thought she was safe!

Stephen was very eager to get back to it . . . so we missed her interview at the end. But I'm gutted. She had so much more to give that house! Including more lap dances for Jedward!

Saturday 21st

Stephen is really struggling on *Celebs Go Dating*. I think it's got worse since his birthday because he knows how strong my feelings are for him and it feels a million times more serious between us now. I had to sit him down tonight and tell him he has to get on with it. 'You were on this show before we met so I have no say on the matter. I will just let you get on with it and be as supportive as possible.'

Eventually he said, 'OK, right, I'm going to put my head back into it.'

* * *

He called me during filming tonight and he definitely has put his head back into it because he went on a double date with Jonathan Cheban! I know I told him to but when I came off the phone I had this awful feeling in my stomach.

I need to have a word with myself. YOU were the one who told him to do it, Charlotte!

I am convinced he's already kissed some people but that's fine. As long as it's no more than two. I'm not going to watch the show anyway. I know it's going to be hard because it will be on every night but it's the only way I will stay sane.

Monday 23rd

I'm going back to Newcastle for a few days. It means I won't see Stephen for a week – I've been with him every night for the last twenty nights! It was really sad leaving him but I'm looking forward to seeing my dogs. I can't wait for a hairy cuddle with them in bed, I've missed them so much.

Tuesday 24th

I wish I'd taken a photo of my bedroom this morning. My room is a tip. I've been home one day and it looks like a refugee camp. I had to empty my suitcases because I needed to repack again and when I unpack I like to tip everything all over the floor. Not just in one spot either, I like to kick it around a bit so it's spread evenly.

Wednesday 25th

I haven't had anyone staying so Mam and Dad have been here with Nathaniel. He loves being at my house because I've given him his own room – he wants to be here all the time. He has a whiteboard, an Xbox and his own balcony. He doesn't like it when Mam says they have to leave and stay at her mam's. He says, 'It's OK, I'm her brother, I can stay. If she has people here I just won't come out of my bedroom and she'll never know I'm here.'

Thursday 26th

Went out with Chloe and Sophie to Bonbar and then Bijoux and it was so much fun. So good to have Chloe back and to see the girls again.

Monday 30th

Back in London. Stephen can't stop posting stuff on Snapchat and it's getting us into serious trouble. Fans keep spotting that we're together at his house – and even though we're deleting them afterwards they get picked up.

Stephen even replied and said, 'She's pregnant with my baby!'

He's such an idiot sometimes. (I love him though.)

He's done a load of interviews for the magazines and has been so sweet about me: '. . . Charlotte ticks a lot of my boxes – she's funny, witty, clever, she's got all the right attributes, but as I'm filming *Celebs Go Dating* . . . it's a case of right girl, wrong time. But who knows what will happen in the future.'

The *Sun* have got reports of us kissing on *Just Tattoo of Us*:

Bear and Charlotte have been snogging loads on set . . . and have hardly kept it a secret to the crew. It's clear they are besotted with each other.

Tuesday 31st

Stephen posted another Snapchat of us and everyone's gone nuts because we're in bed together! We were under a duvet and Stephen was laughing because he had toothpaste on his eyebrow. It was only up for about fifteen minutes before he deleted it but people screengrabbed it and it got shared everywhere.

@charlottegshore get that toothpaste off his eyebrow @stephen_bear.

My two favourite people in bed together! go on!! @stephen_bear @charlottegshore.

@charlottegshore and @stephen_bear in bed together? Okay these are legit SO bloody cute!'

Brilliant snap, deleted pretty quick. Not surprised to see @ charlottegshore in bed with @stephen_bear. We've all be wanting it to happen.

February 2017

Arguments I've had with Stephen: One (and I don't want any more)

Celebrities I've been star struck-over at the Brits: Little MIIIIIX!

Emojis to describe my current mood: 😠😃🖤 😔😮🖤

Thursday 2nd

I have surveillance cameras on the house and can check them whenever I'm not there, so I can see when Mam is there and spy on her. She's usually in the house doing nothing but stroking the dogs. (She says she's cleaning the house because it takes so long after I've been there and turned it into a bombsite but I don't buy it.). I tell her to go in the back garden so I can watch the dogs running around. Sometimes I'll just tune in without telling her and she's out there pretending she doesn't know the cameras are watching her. But I know she's doing things she's planned in case they make

315

me laugh. She's there talking to herself or walking in a funny way. She's nuts that woman. And I love her.

Friday 3rd

We posted a picture of us on Instagram walking Stephen's dog East. And we're wearing 'His . . .' and 'Hers . . .' jumpers from our company. I think we look good.

I captioned it: 'I'm his.'

I can't help myself.

Saturday 4th

Me and Stephen went to an MTV Brand New showcase at the Electric Ballroom in Camden and someone has told the papers they saw us snogging among the crowds. They even got a picture of us. We were both really pissed and didn't think anyone would notice . . .

OH DAMN.

Stephen is in loads of trouble with *Celebs Go Dating*. But I don't feel like he should have got told off for this. It was an MTV event so it was technically work. And surely you are allowed to kiss other people when you're on the show? We haven't said we are girlfriend and boyfriend and he's still on the show going on dates. Surely they can't sack him for that?

Oh God. This is bad.

Monday 6th

Stephen said I had a nice nunny on Snapchat today and once again it's been picked up all over the place! He said 'Breaking news . . . she hasn't shaved!' He does properly crack me up.

Tuesday 7th

Celebs Go Dating is on TV in a few days time and I am DREADING it. I have to keep telling myself that he filmed lots of it when we had only just met. It was back in December and I had only just ended things with Ash. So I don't really have a leg to stand on . . .

Wednesday 8th

I was in bed with Stephen when I saw the first picture of him on the show with another girl. It was an online article about it and I was tagged in it. Stephen was asleep so I was looking at it on my phone and trying to hide it from him. There's a shot of him with blue all over his face because he's just kissed a girl with blue lipstick . . . my heart dropped.

This is not a nice feeling.

It's like someone has got an industrial hoover, stuck it into my vagina and sucked all my insides out. I feel empty. I've never felt this bad before.

Stephen has always said we are going to be a couple and that after the show ends we have a proper future together. I've planned it in my head. That's what made it harder. Maybe I shouldn't have built it up so much.

I haven't said anything to him.

It's so hard though.

* * *

I can't say anything to him . . . can I?

I texted Melissa. She reminded me that I set the rules out for him and told him that he could kiss two to three people. So there's absolutely nothing I can do about this.

I'm being tagged in article after article about him on the show and in every one there's a picture that I don't want to see, of him with someone else.

I might have to unfollow everyone I know on social media. I can't look at this for the next month!

Thursday 9th

The next episode is much worse than the first one. More images and videos are coming out as promotion for the show and in every single article it's always 'poor Charlotte' and 'behind Charlotte's back'. The *Sun* had an article this morning that said:

Charlotte Crosby will get a shock when she sees our exclusive pictures of her new boyfriend Stephen Bear passionately snogging TWO other girls while filming *Celebs Go Dating*

. . . our incredible pictures show him getting intimate with two other women behind her back.

According to them he was even filmed on camera asking one: 'Do you fancy a shag?' He was all over this girl! I can't believe he was asking if she wanted a shag. I feel awful. He's done everything I said he could do but he's overstepped the line.

I read it and I got upset but I didn't cry. I held it in.

I'm on my way to see *Cirque du Soleil* in Newcastle with the girls.

* * *

As soon as I arrived, I said to Laura, 'Pour me a drink now.'

'Why?' she asked. I handed her my phone.

She looked at the article and said the same as Melissa, 'Charlotte, you weren't together when he was filming all this – you must try and remember that.'

'I know, but we were so, so close. We'd still spent every

night together doing *Just Tattoo of Us* and he was telling me he was crazy about me. I feel like a mug because I wouldn't ever have done anything like this to him.'

It makes me feel stupid. I knew it was going to happen so I don't know why I got so upset.

I couldn't stop myself. I sent Stephen a message on WhatsApp because he's in Ireland on a PA.

What the hell man
Arrggghh
Do you know the thing is I would have preferred to have been prepared for all this shit!
So did you sleep with her that night?
You kept me in the dark about it all
And have just left it to unfold in front of my eyes
Me getting dragged into these articles
It's not fair
If we were going to have tried to get through this together
you should have prepared me

Then I rang him and couldn't help kicking off. But he didn't react how I wanted him to, he went really weird. He doesn't pander to me and won't ever be pushed into a corner. Sometimes I think he winds me up on purpose. We had a screaming row and he didn't do anything to make it better. But his battery was low so the phone just went dead mid argument.

* * *

When I got home he'd sent me a nice message saying I had nothing to worry about and that he was only doing it to make it a good TV show and begged me never to take it to heart.

He said, 'I'm just saying silly things on camera. You have nothing to worry about LOL I'd never cheat on you.'

But he's a boy . . . don't they all say that??

I don't know what to believe.

ARGGGH

Friday 10th

Stephen's been sacked from *Celebs Go Dating* and it's all because of me.

I was in the taxi on the way home from an Easilocks shoot when he called, 'Charlotte, you're never going to guess what. . .'

He sounded weird. Almost anxious.

'What?'

'I've been fired . . .'

'What the hell?'

'I've been sacked . . .'

'No you haven't.'

'Yeah I have.'

He seemed really different, his voice was strange, like he was stressed and tense. There was a tone in his voice that I've never heard before. There aren't a lot of things that get to Stephen but this has got to him, I can tell.

All I kept thinking was, 'It's all my fault.'

I'm really worried.

I'm panicking.

Then, all of a sudden, my signal went off. I sat in the car and took a deep breath.

I've lost him a job. I feel so guilty. I tried to call him back but he wasn't answering. He was on the phone to his agent. When he called back I told him he should try and make amends on the show and start dating people again and throw himself back into it. But he said, 'I can't, they've sacked me because I wasn't interested at all.'

Got back to his and he seemed really quiet. Then he went to the kitchen to make a cup of tea and said, 'Will you be my girlfriend?'

It was such a nice moment. We gave each other a big hug. It's official. We're in a relationship!

But we're still not allowed to tell anyone until the show is over. It hasn't even started on TV yet!

GAH!

Sunday 12th

Stephen is up in Newcastle and we've had such a good night out with Holly, Kyle, Adam and Jamie. It was so much fun.

Stephen sent Mel a WhatsApp voice note on my phone asking if she would come out and said he wants to make friends with her again. I think Mel will agree to meet him next time he's up but she couldn't make it tonight. I know she doesn't like him but she's been pretty good at holding her tongue about him so far. She knows that if she talks about him too much it would drive a wedge between us.

Monday 13th

Celebs Go Dating aired on TV tonight but I didn't watch it.

It's been like living in a bubble since I've been with Stephen and I didn't anticipate how bad I was going to feel about one TV show. I know everyone is thinking he's been cheating behind my back but no one knows how long ago it was filmed.

Every time I'm tagged in an article I want to say something because it's really annoying and makes me look like a mug – so much has changed since then!

I don't know what else is to come, what else he might have done on there, all I know is that I need it to be over with. I just want it done. I've deleted the *Daily Mail* app and I've unfollowed loads of people and outlets on social media because it's getting to me. It shouldn't because we weren't together when he started it – but I have such strong feelings for him now.

Tuesday 14th

It's Valentine's but we're seeing each other in a few days so will do our special things then. Stephen treats me all the time so I don't feel like I need just one day to prove he cares about me. Valentine's is just for blokes who are crap and can't be arsed the rest of the year!

I've been invited to the Brits by heat Radio and I'm bringing Holly as my guest. I'm so excited! I've got my dress: it's sheer leopard print . . . it's really cool and rock 'n' roll.

Wednesday 15th

I'm trying not to talk to Stephen about *Celebs Go Dating* because it's a sore subject and I don't have a right to say anything. But I can't help how I feel. Having to watch him flirt and be into someone on telly isn't nice. There's still so much to go it's going to be dreadful. I have to try not to think about it. Just have to get through the day and avoid any sight of it.

Thursday 16th

I got to Stephen's tonight and his brother and his dad were in the sitting room. I arrived at 9.45 p.m. and they started saying, 'Oh the news is on at ten.' and looking at me really strangely. I kept thinking, 'What's everyone trying to get at?' Then they looked at Stephen and said, 'Do you want to watch the news, Stephen?' Then he started saying, 'Charlotte, I think me and you should go upstairs at ten when the news comes on.' Eventually it clicked in my head that they were talking about *Celebs Go Dating*! Obviously his brother and his dad wanted to watch it because they think he's so funny on the telly and find it hilarious because of the way he is.

So I said, 'Oh the *news*, of course, I'll definitely go upstairs and unpack my case when the *news* is on . . . I don't like the *news*.' We were all having this private joke about the news!

But when 10 p.m. came we were talking about something else and I still hadn't got the hint. So his dad said, 'The *news* is coming on, Charlotte, so you'd best leave the room.' I replied, 'Oh yes . . . the *news*, sorry.'

When we got upstairs Stephen turned the telly on and *Celebs Go Dating* was the channel that was on! AND IT FROZE SO HE COULDN'T CHANGE THE CHANNEL! I was screaming, 'Oh no!' and I ran out of the room. I was on the stairs but I couldn't go downstairs because it was on the telly in the lounge too, so I was stuck in limbo on the stairs whistling to myself so I couldn't hear what was going on.

Gave Stephen his Valentine's card. I wrote: 'I love your shaven bumhole, frog legs, spider toes, and not forgetting the WOTFY [which means smelly]!' I bought him some Jo Malone pomegranate hand wash and body wash. And I got him a selfie light for his phone.

* * *

He's taking me to Barcelona for the weekend! Can't wait! He said he wants us to get away from it all.

Friday 17th

Off to Barcelona! Got off the plane and checked our phones and there were loads of stories about us having split up. We've said it's to do with *Just Tattoo of Us* so no one asks questions.

We got to the W Hotel and Stephen upgraded our suite as a treat. It's amazing. We put the music on and started getting ready straight away. Went to the restaurant and had the best seat in the whole place, it was a booth overlooking the beach with a big rounded oval settee. We had piña coladas, some rum and coke and then shots. Then we decided to go to the club at the top of the hotel. He bought a table for just me and him. It was a bit of an extravagant thing to do . . . I made him promise to go halves because I didn't want him paying for everything.

Saturday 18th

Woke up, went to Zara and bought some jumpers because it's chilly on the beach as there's a bit of a cold breeze. We walked all the way along the beach. Everywhere you look you see something different. There were these men building a sand sculpture of a penis with water blowing out of it! Then there were these hippy men blowing the biggest balloons you've ever seen, people on motorised scooters, people playing tennis – it was like we'd walked into a mystical land. It took us a lot of time to get to the end and then we got some food.

* * *

In the evening we got all dressed up and went to this club called Carpe Diem Lounge Club that Sophie had told me about. There were beds in the middle of the restaurant and people getting massaged! It was the weirdest place. Then, at 11 p.m., some ancient house music and a DJ came on, so it turned into a club.

We got home and kept drinking more and then we went out on the balcony and made love on the chairs under the moon. It was beautiful. I had red lipstick on and I got it all over his face.

Then we went to bed and I had an accident in the night because I was so pissed. But he didn't even care that I wet the bed.

Sunday 19th

Woke up and went to the zoo and saw all the animals and had tapas.

Later on we were sitting on the bed and Stephen got a phone call from Luke Mills, Holly's agent. I put them in touch because I think Luke's great and I've been trying to help guide Stephen when it comes to getting some decent work opportunities. This phone call was Luke telling him he had a big deal for him with a clothing brand. Stephen was so chuffed and happy so we ordered some piña coladas to celebrate.

Afterwards he sat on the side of bed and looked at me with his big blue eyes. 'I'm having such an amazing time in Barcelona, it's the best time I've had in my whole entire life. I feel like you came into my life and you changed everything. Every single thing I think about now is better because you're in my life. I can't think of a time I had more fun. You do nothing but support me, you've been there for me. You knew I had to go on *Celebs Go Dating* and you never said anything bad about it and you didn't do anything apart from encourage me. I can't get over how amazing you are . . .' Then he turned away and put his head in the pillow.

'Why are you hiding?' I said and laughed.

As he turned back he had two tears running down his cheeks. 'Are you crying?'

'No, NO!' He started to wipe his face. I went a bit red because I felt embarrassed for him because I could see he was embarrassed.

This moment just confirmed for me that this is something different and special. I know in my heart he has never ever spoken to anyone like he's spoken to me.

Later in the night we went to Pacha – this was the big one. This is the first time I've been out with a boyfriend on our own and had amazing nights out. I don't feel like I need anyone else there. And obviously I'm not allowed to be on my phone while I'm there either. We got a table and started downing drinks and I blacked out! I know we had an amazing time though and were dancing around.

Vaguely remember waking in the night and Stephen asking me what I was doing on top of him because I was all over his side and he couldn't move.

'Why are you on top of me? I've got no room!' I told

327

him I'd wet the bed again and he said, 'Oh for God's sake, fine.'

I feel like I've been in a bubble. Barcelona has been the best time of my life. I don't want it to end.

Wednesday 22nd

The Brits were amazing!! Me and Holly were so excited! We stayed in the InterContinental hotel right next to the O2 and spent the afternoon getting ready. Then we were taken to the red carpet by the people from heat Radio. And guess who arrived just after us!? Little Mix! We tried to be cool when we saw them but I thought Holly might combust. Perrie told her she had been stalking her Instagram and I kept thinking, 'What about mine?' But then Perrie and Jessie both complimented my figure.

I felt so beautiful in my dress. I'm so glad I picked it.

We were on a table with some of the people from Kiss radio and Magic and my highlight was when Stormzy came on stage with Ed Sheeran. I love Stormzy! But then Robbie came on and he was singing but it wasn't coming through the speakers and he didn't know because obviously he had the music in his ears. It took about forty seconds before the music came on and it was really awkward and embarrassing. We were sat quite near the back so we couldn't see many famous people. We got lost on the way out and couldn't find the party, then ended up having to do selfies with loads of fans so by the time we were done we were knackered and went back to the hotel!

Thursday 23rd

My dress has been on one of the worst-dressed lists! But I don't care. At least I got on one list.

And some people have commented that they think I looked pregnant in it. I can sort of understand how because when you look at the pictures from a distance it looks like there's a round bulge but close up you can see it's flat. It's like an optical illusion – like that one where everyone was going crazy about the dress that looked blue and black or white and gold!

Friday 24th

OK, now this is getting silly. I posted a clip on Instagram of me getting ready for an In The Style photoshoot and had a jumper on. Everyone's commenting that I look pregnant *again* and I am confused. Actually starting to get a bit annoyed now. I don't look pregnant at all!

Adam from In The Style ended up writing a message because he was getting annoyed too! 'GIRLS!! We can confirm Charlotte is not pregnant – are you joking, look at her amazing figure!!! The ring light in the room causes a slight shadow on her stomach that is all!!'

I posted a video on Snapchat too: 'Just wanna clear one thing up, I'm not pregnant, it's starting to get really boring.'

It's this sort of thing that just makes me feel so shit and rubbish.

Whenever Stephen posts a photo of me he gets girls saying things like, 'She's so ugly, your last girlfriend was so much better-looking' which upsets me because it feels embarrassing. I don't mind so much on the ones I put up but it's the ones he puts up that affect me most. I don't want him to look at the comments where people are saying I'm fat or ugly and he can do better.

No normal person has to see themselves put down constantly like that.

Saturday 25th

Did some filming for *Just Tattoo of Us* and then went to Faces in Essex with Stephen. Never been there before and it was so fun. Met his sister Hayley for the first time too and she was lovely.

Sunday 26th

Didn't get back until 10 a.m. because we went back to a party at one of Stephen's mate's houses. I was so drunk!

Now I am hungover and feel hideous. I am co-hosting the breakfast show for Capital in Newcastle ALL NEXT WEEK! How stupid am I?

Had to get the train back home this afternoon and was feeling so rotten.

Monday 27th

My alarm went off at 5 a.m. and I wanted to cry. How do people get up and do this every day?

I was really nervous to start with but we had fun.

SOOOO tired though.

I called my friend Katie and she's just had a new baby. I said, 'It's so hard getting up at five in the morning!' and she said, 'Welcome to my world.'

I am not having a baby anytime soon!

* * *

After all that effort on my house, a bit of plaster fell down! Mam was messing about upstairs somewhere and I shouted, 'Something has just fell from the ceiling!'

She said 'It's like a little bit of plaster . . . it's from the door frame. Your house is still growing in the first year, it settles and cracks.'

What does that even mean? So it's basically growing? Like a baby! Mam's telling me the walls move, the plaster moves . . . You what??! My house is literally moving from around me. Next thing you know I'll be going up in a tornado like *The Wizard of Oz.*

Anna said to me the other night, 'Why are you never home? You've hardly been there since you got that house.' I told her, 'I don't feel like I can get attached because it's still moving and is going to run away from me!'

* * *

Tonight Kate showed me an advert that's running on MTV tomorrow about the new cast of *Geordie Shore.* MTV have sent it over so I can see it in advance. Kate doesn't like it. I looked at it and said I thought it was a bit weird but quite funny. It was Gary giving birth to new castmates.

Tuesday 28th

After I finished the radio show this morning I started getting tagged in a load of tweets about the MTV advert. And then the penny dropped as to why it was SO SO SO BAD! All my fans were saying, 'This is such poor taste because of everything Charlotte's been through!' I hadn't put those two things together when I saw it yesterday. I don't think I was paying proper attention. I thought she meant that because it was a 'new family' now I might be upset because I wasn't on the show any more. But that wasn't it at all. When it all sunk in I was so upset. How did nobody make the connection?

I kicked off in the Squad Goalz *Geordie Shore* group chat. They were all talking about it and sending pictures of pregnant Gary and saying how funny it was. And I had enough so I left. I am no longer in the group. There's no going back now. That is it!

Some of the girls messaged me privately after I left the group saying they were sorry and didn't want to upset me. I didn't hear anything from Gary whatsoever.

March 2017

Romantic stuff Stephen's done for me so far: boiled eggs, balloons in bed, lots of kisses, taxis, dinners, presents

Romantic stuff I've done for him: weeing on him in bed

Emojis to describe how excited I am about spending time alone on holiday with Stephen:
😬💜🍺💋

Wednesday 1st

I am pretty sure I know most things that have gone on with Stephen on *Celebs Go Dating* just by seeing stuff on the newsfeed. Even though I have unfollowed most people I am still not able to avoid the whole thing completely. I know he's snogged about three of the girls, I know he felt a girl's boobs and I know he walked out of one date and didn't turn up to another and spilt wine over one date. There's nothing I can do about any of them because we weren't properly together and we had an agreement. I was fully aware he was going on the show and I had to accept it. I'm sure most of the people

I know, like my friends, have watched it but no one talks about it because I said, 'I don't want to hear anything about it and I don't want it mentioned.' I'm so happy it's ending soon!

Stephen hasn't been watching it either which is so weird. It's like it doesn't exist for him.

I know people have watched him on the show and a lot of my fans don't like him. I do wish they could see the real him. But I think they will on *Just Tattoo Of Us* because it's a different side to him there. He winds people up on TV because that's how he is. But even if no one saw that side of him and everyone hated him I wouldn't care. It would just make me feel more special that I get to see that side of him. He treats me like I'm a princess and I've never been treated like that before.

Thursday 2nd

I'm happy *Celebs Go Dating* is over soon but it's actually surprised me that it's been much easier than I thought it would be. I was dreading it before but I've given myself advice that I would give to someone else and have been telling myself the facts: we weren't together; we didn't know each other that well so what's the point of getting angry about it. This is a new, mature me! Once upon a time I would have watched every single episode, cried at every single episode, had an argument about every single episode. This whole time we have only had one cross word or argument about it because I was upset.

* * *

The nurse from my doctor's surgery called today to let me know the results from when I got my fanny check the other week. I went for a check-up because I thought I might have BV (bacterial vaginosis, which is a vaginal infection – not sex related FYI).

I have such good relationship with my nurses and doctors in Newcastle. Most people would go in the surgery and say, 'I think I have some vaginal discharge' but I can just walk in there and say, 'My vagina stinks, what's the matter with it?' It's anything goes in there! All the nurses in the doctor's surgery are so lovely, they want to know how I am and what's going on. It's not like I'm going to the doctor's at all, it's more like I'm going to my mate's house!

When I was getting the swabs for BV I decided I might as well have an STI check-up while I was there, just to be safe. Then I had to make sure I did the rounds and knocked on all the nurses' doors to say hi before I left.

Ellen called me and said, 'So, Charlotte I've got your results.'
'Oh,' I replied, 'Do I need to sit down?'
'No,' she said, 'But you do need some antibiotics.'
'Oh, what have I got then?'
'Your STI results are fine but you've got BV.'
'Oh, so I haven't got chlamydia then?'
'No.'

Charlotte's Advice on: BV

1. If your vaginal discharge has a strong fishy smell, particularly after sex, is white or grey or is thin and watery – it's not usually itchy or sore – it could be BV.
2. You can either go to your GP or to a sexual health clinic, lots of them have walk-in services where you don't need an appointment.
3. They'll have a look and possibly take a swab.

4. It can be easily treated with antibiotic tablets or gel that they'll prescribe (there's no clear proof the stuff you can get over the counter works). If you keep getting it, you might need to take treatment for a longer period of time.

5. Keep an eye out for the symptoms coming back, it quite often does within the first three months.

6. If you keep getting it may be that something is triggering it like your period or sex.

Friday 3rd

Went to London to see Stephen. I got the train from Newcastle and was knackered because I'd done all week at the radio station. He rang me while I was still on the train.

'Right, I'm at Leon and I'll meet you there.'

'Why can't you wait in the car?'

'No, its Operation Bumble Bee.'

'What the hell are you on about?'

'I'll tell you when you get here.'

I stepped off the train and he was hidden behind a bin with a bunch of flowers – he jumped out at me and gave me a massive kiss. Then when we were in the car he rang his brother and said, 'Rob, bzzzzzz . . .' He was doing a buzzing sound. I heard Rob reply, 'Roger that.'

I was laughing: 'What is going on? This is so weird!'

When we got to his house he ushered me into his bedroom. He'd bought a candle called 'Ocean Breeze' to remind me of holiday and he'd filled his room with balloons (he'd copied off me). On the bed were five presents and a card. He said, 'You've worked so hard all week you need to be treated.'

How nice was that?!

He'd bought me Ty Beanies, because I've collected them since I was little, a key ring and two little teddies. The card was really nice and listed the things he liked about me which included: 'your morning breath', 'your kind heart' and 'your smile'.

Saturday 4th

I'm so happy at the moment and am so excited about the holiday! We are going to the Dominican Republic in two weeks' time. I can't remember the last time I went away with just a boy and we could chill. If it's anything like Barcelona, it's going to be soooo good. We're staying in the Hard Rock Hotel resort. It looks so plush! When I go away I am turning my phone off and not speaking to ANYONE.

THIS IS GOING TO BE BLISS.

Farewell, My Friends . . .

So that's where I'm at in my life so far. I wish I could have taken you with me on holiday but some things have to be kept private (even for me!). I am so excited about what's next for me and my journey. I still have so much of 2017 to look forward to and I can't wait for everything that's about to fling itself my way around the corner. We never quite know who or what is going to be coming into our lives but you can bet your life it will always have happened for a reason.

As me mam always says: 'YOU ONLY HAVE ONE LIFE SO LIVE IT!'

I want 2017 to be my best year ever. Here's my A–Z wish list for the rest of the year. Place your bets now as to which will come true.

And until we meet again – adios!

An A-Z of Things
I Want to Achieve in 2017

Achieve double-platinum sales on my fitness DVDs.

Buy a place in London.

Create the next big social media app.

Drive the Crosby Campervan with friends – when my licence is back!

Ectopic Pregnancy Trust: organise a fundraiser

Fliqué – launch my range in store in Ireland

Go on *Strictly Come Dancing*.

Holiday in America – if I'm finally allowed back in the country!

In The Style to become a global success.

Just Tattoo of Us to be shown in America.

Know how to work the heating in my house!

Learn to ride a horse.

Meet Stormzy and get a selfie.

New Crosby reality show to be commissioned.

Order a family of fish for my new pond at home.

Present *Love Island*.

Qualify as the ultimate Tetris champion.

Run a charity run.

Ski or snowboard – learn one of them and have an amazing snowy holiday.

Travel A LOT.

Undertake trampoline lessons.

Voyage on a private yacht to Ibiza for the closing parties.

Whale watching!

Xmas day – I do not want to spend it hungover in 2017.

Yes to an engagement (me not the phone).

Zoo – film with animals for a day.

Here's a poem to end on because I don't think you can ever have enough poems in life:

So there it all is,
Wasn't it the SHIZZ,
Told you it all,
Tried to make you all LOL,
But there were ups and were downs,
With those *Geordie Shore* clowns
With you I did share,
My growing soft spot for Bear,
So before you get bored,
Really horny or hard.
I'll say my farewell,
As I'm starting to smell!

Acknowledgements

I'm so grateful to be writing the acknowledgements for my second autobiography *Brand New Me*, for all the amazing opportunities that have come my way since *Me Me Me* and for the love and support of all my friends and family.

Mam, thanks for being the best carer, PA and driver a girl could wish for, Dad, thanks for being my business advisor, project manager and the family's rock, Nathaniel thanks for being the best brother and always making me laugh, I love you all so much.

My consultant Mr Emeka Okaro and the wonderful staff at St John and St Elizabeth, I am so grateful to be here to tell my tale after surviving an ectopic pregnancy. Alex and Munira at The Ectopic Pregnancy Trust, and the thousands of brave women who shared their stories and gave me so much comfort, thank you.

Lucie Cave, thanks so much for putting words to my voice again and thanks to Sarah, Emma, Grace, Georgina, Phoebe, and all at Headline, for bringing *Brand New Me* to print. Kate, Martin, Jade, Jackie, Joe and all the team at Bold HQ, thanks for all your hard work. Shane, Ben, Bree, Lisa and all the team at Stage Addiction, thanks for all things Oz. Adam and Jamie, thanks for the amazing fashion opportunities with In The Style. Shane at Easilocks, thanks for bringing my Miracle Makeover extensions and cosmetic range Fliqué to life. David and Richard, thanks for keeping me fit. Luke and all the team at Misfits, thanks for the social collabs. Kerry, Craig and Jake, leaders of my MTV family! Ross and Iestyn and all the team at Gobstopper, thanks for *Just Tattoo of Us*!! Millie, Julia and Catherine, the MTV PR dream team.

No acknowledgement would ever be complete without a massive shout-out to my amazing fans. Thanks to each and every one of you for supporting me every step of the way on this crazy journey called life.

The Bear family, thanks for welcoming me into your wonderful family. And last but definitely not least, Stephen Bear, thanks for being The One!